The BIG Bartender's Book

The BIG
Bartender's
Book

Jeff Masson & Greg Boehm

Mud Puddle Books
NEW YORK

The Big Bartender's Book
by Jeff Masson & Greg Boehm

© 2009 by Mud Puddle Books, Inc.

Published by
Mud Puddle Books, Inc.
54 W. 21st Street
Suite 601
New York, NY 10010
info@mudpuddlebooks.com

ISBN: 978-1-60311-186-7

Interior Design by Liz Trovato

For complete photographic credits, please see page 443

Printed in China

Contents

Introduction

by Jeff Masson

In compiling recipes for this book, it soon became apparent just how many different drinks there are out there and, more importantly, how awful a lot of them actually are. The purpose of this book, therefore, is not to list every drink in existence. Even if desired, this would not be possible as new drinks are being created every day and there are far more drinks out there not worth documenting than there are acceptable ones.

I have deliberately avoided drinks which call for "sweet and sour" as I feel this has no place in a cocktail and fresh lemon or lime and sugar can be used to much better effect. Similarly, I have tried to limit the drinks which call for odd, artificially flavored schnapps and syrups, confining the ingredients to those fairly easily found in your local liquor store.

My intent is to give clear, simple instructions on how to mix some of the finest classic drinks as well as some of the more modern inventions. Along the way, I have researched old drink manuals dating as far back as the 1800s and, where possible, I have mentioned the source where I found the drink.

The history of the cocktail is rather checkered and its origins are certainly not clear. The cocktail was first defined on May 13, 1806 in *The Balance, and Columbian Repository*, a Hudson, New York newspaper, as "...a stimulating liquor composed of spirits of any kind, sugar, water, and bitters — it is vulgarly called a bittered sling and is supposed to be an excellent electioneering potion inasmuch as it renders the heart stout and bold, at the same time that it fuddles the head. It is said also to be of great use to a democratic candidate: because a person, having swallowed a glass of it, is ready to swallow anything else."

The quality of cocktails has certainly varied through the past century or so. During American Prohibition (1920–1933), the sale of alcohol was illegal, but bootleg alcohol was still produced to a far inferior quality. Because of this, bartenders had to be a little more imaginative with their creations and often disguised the foul flavor of the hooch with sugar and juice.

Later, in the 1970s and 80s, the drinks were again quite poor in quality with blue colored drinks and plastic monkeys on glasses a common sight. Fortunately, in the 1990s, a cocktail resurgence came around with famous bartenders such as Dale DeGroff in New York and Dick Bradsell in London leading the way. They both realized that cocktails were not being properly made and researched old books for recipes that helped to change the way current bartenders made their drinks.

Today, the standard of cocktails seems to be very high, especially in larger cities such as New York, London, Barcelona and Paris. Bartenders are much more aware of how the quality of the ingredients used affects the cocktail and how important it is to use fresh produce. The demand for quality and finely made drinks is continuing to rise throughout the world.

I'd like to take a moment to thank those who submitted their recipes to me and I sincerely hope you enjoy making the drinks inside this book.

Cheers!

Mixology Basics

Bartending Techniques

When mixing a cocktail, there are many points to consider to ensure that you make the best possible drink. This section will explain the different terminology used in the book and offer advice on how best to prepare your drinks.

Shaking

This is the technique that most people associate with cocktails. The reasons for shaking are primarily to mix the ingredients together but also to chill the drink and add dilution from the ice. Dilution is a very important consideration when shaking a drink. Aim to have the shaker around two-thirds full of ice to avoid over dilution. Never use the same ice twice, even if it is for the same drink.

When shaking, always hold the shaker with both hands and shake like you mean it. You really need to mix the ingredients, so be sure to give the drink a firm shake for at least 10 seconds.

Unless you want to end up wearing the drink, never shake any fizzy ingredients! A drink which calls for soda, ginger ale, etc. should always have that ingredient added after shaking.

Stirring

To be used for ingredients which combine easily, i.e., gin and vermouth. Shaking works better for ingredients such as juices and liqueurs which combine less readily.

The advantage of stirring a drink is that it will be clear when served (ingredient dependent). A martini which is shaken will have an almost cloudy appearance when served due to air bubbles inside the liquid, but a stirred one will be perfectly clear.

To stir a drink, fill up a mixing glass with ice and add the ingredients. Slide a long handled barspoon or stir rod into the glass and stir for around 15 seconds. Again, this serves to mix the ingredients, chill and add dilution.

Building

This is the simplest of all drink making techniques. Simply take a glass, fill it with ice, then add the required ingredients. A quick stir before serving is beneficial to mix the ingredients together.

Blending

When blending a drink it is best to use crushed ice where possible. This lessens the wear on the blades. Start the blender on a slow speed and gradually increase until a smooth consistency is achieved.

Layer

This is usually used for pousse-café style drinks and involves pouring an ingredient into a glass so it floats on top of the previous one.

Generally, the liquid which should go on the bottom is the one with the lowest alcohol content and the highest sugar content as these are the heaviest. These are usually non-alcoholic syrups. Next in density would usually be liqueurs with their high sugar content, followed by spirits with a high alcohol content.

To layer, a teaspoon or barspoon can be used. Place the bowl of the spoon against the side of the glass and slowly pour the ingredient into the bowl.

Float

This is achieved in the same way as layering and involves pouring the last ingredient of a drink over a spoon so it sits on top of the cocktail.

Frosting

This is the term given to coating the rim of a glass with either sugar or salt. This can be done by taking a small saucer and pouring salt or sugar on it, moistening the outer rim of a glass with a lime wedge and then dipping it into the saucer.

When salting the rim of a glass, use a coarse salt and only salt half of the glass so the drinker has the option of whether or not to drink from the salted side.

Fine Straining

This is used for drinks which have ingredients such as herbs or fruit pulp which you do not want in the final drink. A tea strainer is placed over the glass and the drink poured through this.

Chilled Glass

This is of particular importance for martini-style drinks. As drinks served in a cocktail glass have no ice to keep them cold, it is very important that the glass is as cold as possible. Ideally, cocktail glasses should be kept in the freezer, but when this is not possible, fill the glasses with ice and soda water to chill and discard just before the drink is to be poured.

Basic Bar Equipment

With many different manufacturers offering a wide range of bar equipment, it is very important to choose the right one. Don't be fooled by fancy looks and design, it is often the simplest that is the best. Not all of the equipment detailed is essential. An "O" appears beside the optional items and an "E" beside the essentials. With the shakers, only one type is essential.

Boston Shaker (E)

Probably the first ever shaker used by bartenders in the nineteenth century and still used in most of the top bars today. Very simple in design and very effective. The Boston Shaker consists of two parts. One part is a smaller glass (sometimes metal) which fits into a larger diameter metal part. When a drink is shaken with ice, the metal contracts and makes a seal.

Cobbler Shaker (E)

This shaker is the one most commonly seen in stores today and dates to the late nineteenth century. It is sometimes called a three-piece shaker. It has the added advantage of having a strainer built into it.

Barspoon (E)

This type of spoon is essential if you are making stirred drinks. It is also very useful in layering ingredients and as a measuring tool as it holds the same quantity as a teaspoon. The best barspoons feature a flat disc on one end which is useful for muddling delicate ingredients such as mint.

Mixing Glass (O)

This glass is useful for making drinks to be served without ice. It should be a tall glass with a spout. A strainer is to be used with this glass when pouring the cocktail.

Hawthorne Strainer (E)

A piece of metal with a coiled spring round one edge. It is essential when using a Boston Shaker or a mixing glass to allow the liquid to come out, leaving the ice behind.

Julep Strainer (O)

A colander-like spoon used for straining out of the glass part of a Boston Shaker.

Tea Strainer/Fine Strainer (O)

Used to prevent small particles of ice and pieces of fruit/herbs from entering a drink after shaking.

Blender (O)

This is used for making frozen drinks.

Jigger (E)

A double-sided tool for measuring liquor. Sizes may vary but commonly one side holds 1½ ounces and is called a "jigger" and the other side holds 1 ounce or a "pony." In creating a properly balanced drink, it is advisable to use this device rather than estimating.

Pour Spout (O)

A device which fits into the top of a liquor bottle and allows for easier pouring.

Citrus Press (O)

These come in either electrical or manual forms. They are simply used for extracting the juice from citrus fruits. Take care not to press too hard as the white pith beneath the skin of the fruit can give the juice a very bitter flavor.

Muddler (O)

Usually made from wood, stainless steel or plastic and used to crush ingredients to bring out their flavors and aromas.

Tongs (O)

Used for picking up fruit or ice.

Ice Scoop (E)

Used to transfer ice from its container to a glass, shaker or blender.

Ice Bucket (E)

Used to store ice.

Paring Knife (E)

Used for slicing fruit. A larger kitchen knife can be used for larger fruits such as pineapples and watermelon.

Channel Knife (O)

Used to cut a thin strip of peel from a citrus fruit.

Peeler (O)

Used to get a large strip of citrus peel for a drink. A potato peeler will do the job.

Chopping Board (E)

Usually wooden or plastic and used as a surface for cutting fruit on.

Corkscrew (E)

Used for opening wine. Often comes with a crown top opener, too.

Grater (O)

Used for grating nutmeg or occasionally chocolate onto a drink.

Bottle Opener (E)

Used to open small mixer bottles such as tonic and ginger ale.

Glassware

When a delicious drink has been created, it is of the utmost importance that it is served in the correct type of glass. There are many glasses on the market now, but you have to beware: many are oversized. A 10 ounce cocktail/martini glass may look fantastic but is completely impractical. No one really wants to consume such a large drink and if you do manage to finish it, it will be far too warm by the time you're near the bottom of the glass.

Cocktail Glass

Often referred to as a martini glass. The ideal size should be around 6 ounces. Drinks are almost always served straight up in this glass. Many famous drinks including Dry Martinis, Manhattans and Cosmopolitans are served in this classic glass.

Wine Glass

This holds around 10 ounces and may be used for spritzers as well as wine.

Flute

This glass holds around 6 ounces and is perfect for serving champagne as well as Champagne cocktails.

Shot Glass

This holds between 1 and 2 ounces and is used for straight "shots" such as tequila, vodka, etc. as well as pousse-cafés.

Coupe

Can be used for serving champagne or for serving frozen drinks such as Frozen Daiquiris. It holds around 8 ounces.

Highball Glass

Named after the Highball drink which is usually served in this glass. It holds around 12 ounces.

Old Fashioned Glass

Sometimes called a rocks glass, it holds around 10 ounces. Perfect for short cocktails on ice and spirits on the rocks.

Toddy Glass

Intended for hot drinks, these should be made from heatproof glass, have a handle and hold around 8 ounces.

Collins Glass

A tall glass, commonly holding 8 to 12 ounces. Perfect for serving the Tom Collins cocktail.

Cordial Glass

Short, stemmed glass for serving liqueurs.

Delmonico Glass

Also known as a sour glass, this is similar to a short flute glass. Holds around 5 ounces.

Hurricane Glass

A slightly pear shaped glass commonly used for serving frozen and tropical drinks. Usually holds around 12 ounces.

Margarita Glass

Stemmed glass with a flared bowl, commonly used for serving frozen or straight up margaritas.

Garnishes

As the name suggests, garnishes are used as a decoration for a drink. However, they can also add an important aroma and flavor to the drink, too. They should be edible when possible (so leave out the plastic monkeys and umbrellas).

When fresh fruit is used, it should be washed and blemish free. When using olives, be sure to give them a rinse to remove the brine.

Citrus Twist

This is cut from the skin of the fruit. Using a potato peeler is the easiest way to make the cutting, but a knife can also be used. Aim to cut down the fruit lengthways, a strip around 1 inch wide. Avoid cutting into the bitter white pith of the fruit. Once cut, hold between the thumb and index finger, skin side facing the surface of the drink. Bring the fingers together quickly to release the oils onto the surface of the drink.

Lemon/Lime Wedges

Cut off the ends of the fruit and then cut in half, from pole to pole and lay flat on the chopping board. Cut the fruit lengthwise again, creating either three or four wedges, depending on fruit size. Repeat for the other half. These will keep fresh for a maximum of 24 hours.

Flamed Orange Twist

Select an orange with a firm skin. With a small knife, cut an oval shaped piece of peel around 1.5 inch by 1 inch with a small amount of pith. To flame the twist, hold a lighter or lit match in one hand and the twist in the other. The twist should be held between the thumb and index finger, with the skin side facing the flame. Position the twist so that when the oils are expelled, they will hit the surface of the drink. Snap the twist through the flame and it will ignite the oils.

Lemon Spiral

Hold the lemon in one hand and a channel knife in the other. Cut from the top of the fruit and rotate it while cutting. The spirals can be cut to the desired length and can be curled round a swizzle stick.

Lemon/Orange Slices

Cut off both ends of the fruit, then cut lengthways, pole to pole. Next cut slices of just over ¼ inch (not from pole to pole).

Mint Sprig

Ideal for juleps or mojitos. Choose a nice looking head from a piece of mint and place it in the drink. If serving with straws, place the sprig nearby so the aroma of the mint hits the nose as the drink is consumed.

Dust

Often nutmeg or chocolate powder are used for dusting. When nutmeg is used, always freshly grate it over the drink.

Terms and Definitions

Glossary

Abricotine Sweet apricot flavored liqueur.

Absinthe A distillate flavored with different herbs and botanicals including aniseed, fennel, coriander and wormwood. Recently reintroduced to America.

Advocaat Rich, thick Dutch liqueur made with egg yolk and brandy with a vanilla flavor.

Agave Succulent plant, a member of the lily family, from which mescal and tequila are distilled.

Aged The process of spirit storage in wooden barrels for a period of time to add certain flavors and remove others. Many different factors affect the process including type of wood used, size of barrel and previous use. It is common to char the inside of the barrel and to use oak as the wood.

Aguardiente Generic name in Spanish speaking countries and Portugal for brandy. Translates as fire water.

Amaretto Almond flavored liqueur made from apricot kernels and spirit. Commonly from Italy.

Amaro Italian herbal liqueur commonly drunk as a digestif. Translates as *bitter*.

Amer Picon French bitters flavored with orange and quinine among others. Commonly served as an apéritif.

Angostura Bitters Bitters originally from Venezuela, but now made in Trinidad using a secret formula. Classified as a food additive even though it has a high alcohol content. Very concentrated flavor, use sparingly.

Anise A clear liqueur made from anise seed. It may also include bitter almonds, coriander and other ingredients.

Anisette Aniseed flavored liqueur.

Apéritif A drink taken before a meal to stimulate the appetite. Examples include certain cocktails, champagne and wines.

Aperol Italian apéritif containing rhubarb, gentian, cinchona and bitter orange among its ingredients.

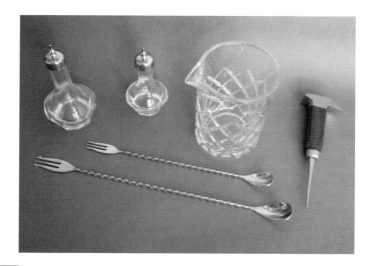

Applejack A dry spirit made from at least 51% apples. The American version of calvados.

Apricot Brandy Sweetened liqueur commonly based on neutral spirit and flavored with apricots.

Arak Unsweetened eastern Mediterranean aniseed spirit. Often diluted with water before consumption.

Arrack South Asian spirit usually distilled from palm sap, sugar or grain.

Armagnac French brandy distilled from grapes in southern France. Generally has a much stronger flavor than cognac.

Aquav Scandinavian spirit flavored with caraway, anise, coriander and citrus.

Aquavit Translates as water of life; from Latin term for spirits.

Bacardi Largest rum producer in the world. Originally produced in Cuba, now mostly distilled in Puerto Rico.

Baileys Irish Cream Irish liqueur made from Irish whiskey, cream and sugar.

Barspoon Long handled spoon for stirring drinks. The best have one end which is flat for muddling and a spiral handle. See *Basic Bar Equipment*.

Bénédictine French herbal liqueur which dates back to the sixteenth century. It was originally made by monks using a secret recipe. Reputedly, only three people know the recipe at any one time. The ingredients are believed to include nutmeg, cloves, cinnamon, peppermint, angelica root and cardamom in a brandy base.

Blend See *Basic Bar Equipment*.

Blender See *Basic Bar Equipment*.

Bottle Opener See *Basic Bar Equipment*.

Bourbon American whiskey made from a mash of between 51% and 79% corn. A little barley and either rye or wheat makes up the remainder. It must be aged in charred new oak barrels, commonly for at least two years.

Brandy Generic term for spirit distilled from fermented fruit.

Brut Dry style of champagne.

Building See *Basic Bartending Techniques*.

Byrrh French apéritif flavored with cinchona.

Cachaça Brazilian spirit made from sugar cane juice and usually not aged. Also known as pinga and aguardiente.

Calvados French brandy distilled in the Normandy region from a mash of apples.

Campari Bitter Italian apéritif created in the 1860s in Milan.

Canadian Whisky Usually multi-grain blends containing rye; lighter than most other whiskies.

Must be aged for at least three years. The most common example is Canadian Club.

Cassis See *crème de cassis*.

Chambord French raspberry liqueur which also contains honey.

Champagne French sparkling wine from the Champagne region of northeast France.

Channel Knife See *Basic Bar Equipment*.

Chartreuse French herbal liqueur, commonly in two styles: yellow (80 proof) and green (110 proof). Green is rumored to have 250 ingredients while the yellow has 187. These include spices, seeds and plants.

Cherry Brandy Sweet liqueur made from a variety of cherries and sometimes their stones. It can be based on brandy or neutral spirit.

Cherry Heering Danish cherry liqueur of excellent quality with a full flavor.

Chopping Block See *Basic Bar Equipment*.

Citrus Press See *Basic Bar Equipment*.

Citrus Twist See *Garnishes*.

Claret Red Bordeaux wine from France.

Club Soda Carbonated water.

Cobbler Drink based on wine or spirit which is

usually served over crushed ice and garnished with fresh fruit. A small amount of sugar is often added.

Cocktail Glass See *Glassware*.

Coffee Liqueur Often flavored with coffee beans, vanilla and sugar. Common examples are Kahlua and Tia Maria.

Cognac The most famous brandy. Made in the southwest of France in a strictly defined process. It is commonly distilled twice and aged for at least two years in French oak barrels.

Cointreau French sweet, colorless orange flavored liqueur. A premium triple sec of very good quality.

Collins Glass See *Glassware*.

Cordial Basically the same as liqueur. It means fruit squash in the UK.

Cordial glass See *Glassware*.

Corkscrew See *Basic Bar Equipment*.

Coupe See *Glassware*.

Cream of coconut A thick liquid usually made from shredded coconut and water.

Crème de bananes Banana flavored liqueur.

Crème de cacao Cocoa flavored liqueur. Available in clear and dark varieties.

Crème de fraise Strawberry flavored liqueur.

Crème de framboise Raspberry flavored liqueur.

Crème de Cassis Blackcurrant flavored liqueur.

Crème de Mûre Blackberry flavored liqueur.

Crème de menthe Mint flavored liqueur. Available in green and clear varieties.

Crème de noyaux Almond flavored liqueur.

Crème de violette French violet blossom liqueur.

Crème Yvette American violet blossom liqueur. Unavailable since the 1960s, there are plans to re-introduce Crème Yvette in the near future.

Crusta Drink served in a sugar rimmed glass with a long lemon spiral inside.

Cup Wine based drink, commonly flavored with liqueurs and fruits.

Curaçao Liqueur made of a sour or sweet orange peel, originally Dutch and named after one of the islands in the Dutch Antilles. It can be clear, orange or blue.

Cynar Bittersweet Italian apéritif made from artichoke hearts.

Dash Very small measurement roughly equaling 4 drops.

Delmonico glass See *Glassware*.

Drambuie Liqueur made with Scotch whisky, honey and many other herbs and spices. It has been produced since 1745.

Dubonnet French wine based apéritif, flavored with herbs. Available in white and red versions.

Dust See *Garnishes*.

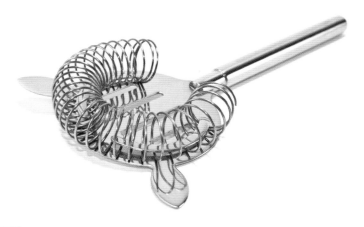

Eau-de-vie A fruit based distillate. Common examples include raspberry, plum and pear.

Elderflower cordial A non-alcoholic concentrate made from sugar, water, elderflowers and other ingredients.

Elderflower liqueur An alcoholic elderflower cordial.

Falernum A sweet syrup originally from the Caribbean made from almonds, ginger, limes, cloves and other herbs.

Fernet Branca Italian bitters with a grape spirit base. Branca Menta, a mint version, is also available.

Flamed Orange Twist See *Garnishes*.

Float The process of layering one ingredient on top of another in a drink. See *Bartending Techniques*.

Flute Tall, stemmed glass commonly used for serving champagne and sparkling wine. See *Glassware*.

Frangelico Italian hazelnut liqueur.

Frappé A drink served on crushed ice.

Frosted glass A glass which has the rim coated, usually with sugar or salt. See *Bartending Techniques*.

Galliano Sweet golden yellow Italian liqueur with an anise and vanilla flavor. Additional flavoring comes from up to 80 herbs, roots, flowers and spices.

Genever Dutch gin which is very pungent and often drunk neat. Available in Jonge (young) and Oude (old) versions. Also known as Jenever.

Gin Neutral spirit flavored with juniper and other botanicals.

Ginger ale A ginger flavored soft drink. Not to be confused with ginger beer.

Ginger beer Usually non-alcoholic ginger flavored drink which is more carbonated and spicy than ginger ale.

Glass, chilled See *Bartending Techniques*.

Goldwasser A clear liqueur that contains gold flakes and is flavored with herbs and spices.

Grand Marnier An orange flavored liqueur with a brandy base. Made in France.

Grappa Italian distillate from the leftovers of winemaking, including skins, seeds and stems. The French equivalent is Marc.

Grater See *Basic Bar Equipment*.

Grenadine A sweet red syrup flavored with pomegranate. Most grenadine today is just artificially flavored and colored sugar syrup, but if you look, real pomegranate grenadine is available.

Guinness Irish stout which is almost black in color.

Hawthorne strainer The most common cocktail strainer with a coiled spring around it to keep ice and fruit pulp from entering the drink. See *Basic Bar Equipment*.

Herbsaint Anise flavored liqueur commonly used as an absinthe substitute.

Highball One of the most common mixed drinks; consists of a spirit and a non-alcoholic mixer. Usually served over ice in a tall glass. Examples include whiskey and ginger ale, gin and tonic and brandy and soda.

Highball glass A tall, straight sided glass for serving mixed drinks. See *Glassware*.

Hurricane glass See *Glassware*.

Ice Bucket See *Basic Bar Equipment*.

Ice Scoop See *Basic Bar Equipment*.

Infused Often used in the production of liqueurs whereby fruits and herbs are steeped in alcohol to allow their flavors to pass over.

Irish whiskey Often triple distilled and traditionally lighter in flavor than scotch. There is usually no peat element in Irish whiskey.

Jägermeister German liqueur flavored with fifty-six herbs. Best served cold.

Jamaican rum A heavy bodied dark rum.

Jigger A device for measuring quantities of liquor. See *Basic Bar Equipment*.

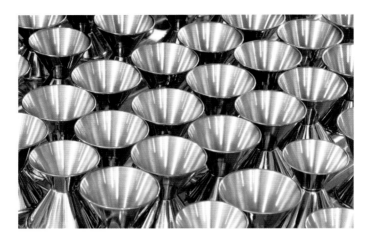

Julep American drink especially popular on Kentucky Derby day. Now commonly made with bourbon, mint and sugar and best served in a silver cup.

Julep Strainer See *Basic Bar Equipment*.

Kahlua A dark coffee flavored liqueur produced in Mexico.

Kirsch, Kirschwasser A brandy distilled from cherries, including the pits.

Kümmel A colorless liqueur made from caraway and cumin.

Layer See *Garnishes*.

Lemon/Lime Wedges See *Garnishes*.

Lemon/Orange Slices See *Garnishes*.

Lemon Spiral See *Garnishes.*

Licor 43 Spanish liqueur flavored with forty-three different herbs and spices. Vanilla is a prominent flavor.

Lillet French wine based apéritif. Available in white (blanc) and red (rouge) varieties.

Liqueur A sweet alcoholic beverage commonly flavored with herbs, spices, fruits, flowers, roots and even cream. Some are descended from old medicine formulas from centuries ago.

Malibu Made in Barbados, this is a mixture of rum and coconut extract.

Maraschino liqueur A clear relatively dry liqueur made from Marasca cherries. It is produced mostly in Croatia and Italy.

Margarita glass See *Glassware.*

Martini glass Stemmed glass with a V-shaped bowl, also known as a cocktail glass. See *Glassware.*

Mescal Mexican spirit distilled from agave. Tequila is a variety of Mescal.

Midori A sweet, green, melon flavored liqueur.

Mint Sprig See *Garnishes.*

Mixing glass Tall, lipped jug used for stirring mixed drinks such as martinis and Manhattans. See *Basic Bar Equipment.*

Muddle Pressing or crushing fruits or herbs.

Muddler Often wooden, this tool is similar to a pestle but longer and used for crushing fruits and herbs. See *Basic Bar Equipment*.

Neat Serving a spirit or liqueur by itself (i.e., no ice or water).

Nocello Walnut and hazelnut liqueur from Italy.

Old Fashioned glass Short glass used for serving liquor or cocktails on ice. Also known as a lowball or a rocks glass. See *Glassware*.

Old Tom gin A gin with sweetening added.

Orange bitters An alcoholic cocktail flavoring agent with orange peel and cardamom as an ingredient among others.

Orange flower water Distillate of fresh orange blossoms. Essential in a Ramos Gin Fizz.

Bitters

Orgeat A sugar syrup flavored with almonds. It sometimes contains rose water.

Ouzo Anise liqueur from Greece.

Parfait amour Very sweet liqueur often flavored with violets among other ingredients.

Paring Knife See *Basic Bar Equipment*.

Pastis Generic term for aniseed flavored French apéritifs with Ricard and Pernod being the best known.

Peach bitters An alcoholic cocktail flavoring agent with peach pits and spices as ingredients.

Peach brandy Sweet, peach flavored liqueur.

Peeler See *Basic Bar Equipment*.

Pernod An anise flavored liqueur. Often used as a replacement for absinthe before the recent reintroduction of the original absinthe.

Pimm's Gin based fruit cup created in 1823 by James Pimm using a secret recipe.

Poire Williams Often colorless brandy distilled from William's pears.

Pony One side of the jigger measuring device, it contains one ounce of liquid.

Port Fortified wine from the Douro Valley in northern Portugal. Comes in many styles.

Pour Spout See *Basic Bar Equipment*.

Pousse-Café Layered drink, sometimes served as a digestif.

Prohibition Period from 1920 to 1933 when alcohol was banned in the United States.

Proof Measure of how much alcohol is in a substance. It is twice the alcohol by volume.

Punch From the Hindi *panch* meaning five, this drink used to be served in large bowls and have five ingredients.

Punt e Mes Italian vermouth with a bittersweet flavor.

Rickey Mixed drink containing a spirit, lime juice and carbonated water.

Rocks glass See *Old Fashioned glass*.

Rum Spirit distilled from sugarcane by products. Can be light, golden or dark in color.

Rye American whiskey made from a mash of 51% to 100% rye. It must be aged for at least two years in new oak barrels. Canadian whisky is often referred to as rye also.

Sake Japanese rice wine.

Sambuca Anise and licorice flavored Italian liqueur.

Sangria Spanish wine punch commonly containing wine, fruits, sugar, spirits and soda water.

Schnapps Historically a Scandinavian term for strong spirits which are colorless and have a light fruit flavor. Nowadays, it more commonly refers to fruit and spice based liqueurs.

Scotch Whisky from Scotland which is distilled from a grain base. Three years of ageing in wooden barrels is the minimum. Commonly available in single malt (product of one distillery) or blended (product of many distilleries).

Shake Method for mixing cocktails using a cocktail shaker filled with ice. Shake hard to combine ingredients well and chill the drink. See *Bartending Techniques*.

Shaker, Boston See *Basic Bar Equipment*.

Shaker, Cobbler See *Basic Bar Equipment*.

Sherry Spanish fortified wine available in different styles.

Shot glass See *Glassware*.

Simple syrup Syrup made from mixing sugar and water.

Sling glass Tall, slim glass commonly used for serving the Singapore Sling.

Sloe gin Gin based red liqueur made from the sloe berry (the fruit of the blackthorn tree).

Snifter Short stemmed glass with a balloon shape. Commonly used for serving brandy.

Soda water Carbonated water.

Sour Mixed drink with three elements: strong, sour and sweet. Usually this will translate as spirit, citrus juice and sugar.

Sour glass See Delmonico glass.

Still Apparatus used in the production of many spirits and liqueurs.

Stir Method of mixing a drink using a long handled spoon. See *Bartending Techniques*.

Straight up Serving spirits or liqueurs in a glass, without ice or water.

Straining, fine See *Bartending Techniques*.

Strega Sweet herbaceous liqueur from Italy.

Swedish Punsch Spicy liqueur with an Arrack base.

Tea (fine) Strainer See *Basic Bar Equipment*.

Tequila Mexican spirit distilled from the blue agave. Different styles are available including silver/blanco, reposado and añejo.

Toddy A mixed drink which is commonly served hot containing spirits, sugar and water.

Toddy glass See *Glassware*.

Tongs *See Basic Bar Equipment.*

Tonic water Carbonated water with a quinine flavor.

Triple Sec Orange flavored liqueur made from curaçao oranges.

Twist Strip of citrus peel used to garnish drinks and provide aroma.

Van der Hum Sweet South African liqueur with a tangerine flavor.

Vermouth A fortified and flavored wine which is usually dry or sweet in style.

Vodka From *voda*, the Slavic word for water. It is a distilled spirit, commonly from grain and occasionally potatoes. Typically light in flavor and aroma.

Whiskey Spirit from many different countries, notably Scotland, Ireland, America and Canada. It is distilled from a grain base. Production techniques vary from country to country but are usually strictly regulated.

Wine glass See *Glassware*.

Whiskey bottle, 1957

Recipes

A

Abbey Cocktail

1¹/₂ ounce (45ml) gin
³/₄ ounce (22ml) Lillet Blanc
³/₄ ounce (22ml) orange juice
2 dashes Angostura bitters

Shake with ice and strain into a cocktail glass.

Abrame

1¹/₄ ounce (37ml) gold rum
1¹/₄ ounce (37ml) slivovitz
¹/₂ ounce (15ml) Amer Picon
¹/₂ ounce (15ml) Cointreau

Shake with ice and strain into a cocktail glass.

Absinthe Cocktail

1¹/₂ ounce (45ml) absinthe
³/₄ ounce (22ml) water
¹/₂ ounce (15ml) anisette
1 dash orange bitters

Shake with ice and strain into a cocktail glass.

Absinthe Suissesse

1 ounce (30ml) absinthe
1 teaspoon (5ml) anisette
1 teaspoon (5ml) simple syrup
1/2 ounce (15ml) egg white

Shake vigorously with ice and strain into a coupe.

Acacia

2 ounces (60ml) gin
1 ounce (30ml) Bénédictine
1/2 teaspoon (2.5ml) kirsch

Shake with ice and strain into a cocktail glass.

Absinthe

Adieu

2 ounces (60ml) cognac
1 ounce (30ml) Grand Marnier
1/2 ounce (15ml) vanilla liqueur

Stir with ice and strain into a cocktail glass. Garnish with an orange twist.

Adonis Cocktail

1 1/2 ounce (45ml) dry sherry
3/4 ounce (22ml) sweet vermouth
1 dash orange bitters

Stir with ice and strain into a cocktail glass.

Affinity Cocktail

3/4 ounce (22ml) Scotch whisky
3/4 ounce (22ml) sweet vermouth
3/4 ounce (22ml) dry vermouth
2 dashes Angostura bitters

Stir with ice and strain into a cocktail glass.
Garnish with a lemon twist.

After Supper Cocktail

1 1/2 ounce (45ml) apricot brandy
1 1/2 ounce (45ml) orange curaçao
3/4 ounce (22ml) lemon juice

Shake with ice and strain into a cocktail glass.

Airmail

1 1/2 ounce (45ml) gold rum
1/2 ounce (15ml) lime juice
1 teaspoon (5ml) honey
Champagne

Shake with ice (except champagne) and strain into an
ice-filled highball glass. Top with champagne.

Alabama Slammer

1/4 ounce (7ml) Southern Comfort
1/4 ounce (7ml) amaretto
1/4 ounce (7ml) sloe gin
1/2 ounce (15ml) orange juice

Shake with ice and strain into a shot glass.

Alabazam

2 ounces (60ml) brandy
3/4 ounce (22ml) lemon juice
1/2 ounce (15ml) orange curaçao
1/2 ounce (15ml) simple syrup
2 dashes Angostura bitters
Soda water

Shake with ice (except soda water) and strain into an
ice-filled highball glass. Top with soda water and
garnish with a lemon slice.

Adapted from *American & Other Drinks* by Leo Engel (1878)

Alamagoozlum

1 ounce (30ml) genever
1 ounce (30ml) water
3/4 ounce (22ml) Jamaican dark rum
3/4 ounce (22ml) green Chartreuse
1/2 ounce (15ml) simple syrup
1/4 ounce (7ml) orange curaçao
3 dashes Angostura bitters
1/2 ounce (15ml) egg white

Shake vigorously with ice and strain into a coupe.

Adapted from *The Gentleman's Companion* by
Charles H. Baker (1939)

Alaska Cocktail

1 1/2 ounce (45ml) gin
3/4 ounce (22ml) yellow Chartreuse
2 dashes orange bitters

Stir with ice and strain into a cocktail glass.
Garnish with a lemon twist.

Alberto

(Created by A. J. Smith)

3/4 ounce (22ml) gin
3/4 ounce (22ml) Lillet Blanc
3/4 ounce (22ml) dry sherry
1 teaspoon (5ml) Cointreau

Stir with ice and strain into a cocktail glass.
Garnish with an orange twist.

Adapted from *Café Royal Cocktail Book* by W. J. Tarling (1937)

Alexander Cocktail

1 ounce (30ml) gin
1 ounce (30ml) white crème de cacao
1 ounce (30ml) cream

Shake with ice and strain into a cocktail glass. Garnish
with grated nutmeg.

Adapted from *The Up-To-Date Bartenders' Guide*
by Harry Montague (1913)

Alfonso Cocktail

3/4 ounce (22ml) Dubonnet rouge
1 sugar cube
Angostura bitters
Champagne

Coat sugar cube in bitters and place in flute with
Dubonnet and one ice cube. Top with champagne.
Garnish with a lemon twist.

Algonquin

1 1/2 ounce (45ml) rye
3/4 ounce (22ml) dry vermouth
3/4 ounce (22ml) pineapple juice

Shake with ice and strain into a cocktail glass.

Alice Mine Cocktail

1 ounce (30ml) Grand Marnier
3/4 ounce (22ml) gin
1/2 ounce (15ml) dry vermouth
1/4 ounce (7ml) sweet vermouth
1 dash Angostura bitters

Stir with ice and strain into a cocktail glass.

Allies

1 1/2 ounce (45ml) gin
1 1/2 ounce (45ml) dry vermouth
1/2 teaspoon (2.5ml) kümmel

Stir with ice and strain into a cocktail glass.

Amalfi Dream

(Created by Salvatore Calabrese, London)

1 1/2 ounce (45ml) vodka
1 ounce (30ml) limoncello
1/2 ounce (15ml) lemon juice

Shake with ice and strain into a cocktail glass.
Garnish with a lemon twist.

Amaretto Sour

2 ounces (60ml) amaretto
1 ounce (30ml) lemon juice
$^1/_4$ ounce (7ml) simple syrup
$^1/_2$ ounce (15ml) egg white
(optional)

Shake vigorously with ice and strain
into an ice-filled Old Fashioned glass.
Garnish with a lemon slice.

Amber Dream Cocktail

1$^1/_2$ ounce (45ml) gin
$^3/_4$ ounce (22ml) sweet vermouth
$^1/_4$ ounce (7ml) yellow Chartreuse
1 dash orange bitters

Stir with ice and strain into a cocktail glass.

Ambulance Cocktail

(Created by H. Verstappen)

1 ounce (30ml) gin
1 ounce (30ml) lemon juice
$^1/_2$ ounce (15ml) Swedish Punsch
2 dashes Angostura bitters

Shake with ice and strain into a cocktail glass.

Adapted from *Barflies & Cocktails* by Harry McElhone (1927)

Amer Picon Cocktail

1¹/₂ ounce (45ml) Amer Picon
³/₄ ounce (22ml) lime juice
¹/₄ ounce (7ml) grenadine

Shake with ice and strain into
a cocktail glass.

If you can get hold of Amer Picon,
be sure to try this drink.

American Beauty

¹/₂ ounce (15ml) brandy
¹/₂ ounce (15ml) dry vermouth
¹/₂ ounce (15ml) grenadine
¹/₂ ounce (15ml) orange juice
1 dash white crème de menthe
1 dash port

Shake with ice (except port) and strain into a small cocktail
glass. Float port on top.

Americano

1 ounce (30ml) Campari
1 ounce (30ml) sweet vermouth
Splash soda water

Build over ice in an Old
Fashioned glass.
Garnish with an orange twist.

A delicious apéritif dating back
to Italy in the 1800s.

Amsterdam Cocktail

1½ ounce (45ml) genever
½ ounce (15ml) Cointreau
¾ ounce (22ml) orange juice
1 dash orange bitters

Shake with ice and strain into a cocktail glass.

Añejo Highball

(Created by Dale DeGroff, New York)

1 ounce (30ml) añejo rum
¾ ounce (22ml) orange curaçao
2 ounces (60ml) ginger beer
1 teaspoon (5ml) lime juice
2 dashes Angostura bitters

Build over ice in a highball glass. Garnish with a
lime wheel and an orange slice.

A cocktail created to pay homage to the bartenders of
Cuba in the 1920s & '30s.

Angel Face

1 ounce (30ml) gin
1 ounce (30ml) apricot brandy
1 ounce (30ml) calvados

Stir with ice and strain into a cocktail glass.

This is perfect for those who like their drinks strong,
dry and fruity.

Angel's Dream Cocktail

1/3 ounce (10ml) maraschino liqueur
1/3 ounce (10ml) crème de violette
1/3 ounce (10ml) cream

Layer the ingredients in the order above in a shot glass.

Angel's Kiss

1/3 ounce (10ml) dark crème de cacao
1/3 ounce (10ml) brandy
1/3 ounce (10ml) cream

Layer the ingredients in the order above in a shot glass.

Angel's Tip

1/2 ounce (15ml) dark crème de cacao
1/2 ounce (15ml) cream

Layer the ingredients in the order above in a shot glass.
Garnish with a cherry on a pick on top of the glass.

Angel's Wing

1/3 ounce (10ml) dark crème de cacao
1/3 ounce (10ml) brandy
1/3 ounce (10ml) cream

Layer the ingredients in the order above in a shot glass.

An Immortal Sour

1 ounce (30ml) applejack
1 ounce (30ml) peach brandy
3/4 ounce (22ml) lime juice
1/2 ounce (15ml) simple syrup
1/2 ounce (15ml) egg white

Shake with ice and strain into a coupe or a cocktail glass.

Adapted from *A Bachelor's Cupboard* by A. Lyman Phillips (1906)

Anisette Cocktail

1 ounce (30ml) gin
1/2 ounce (15ml) anisette
1/2 ounce (15ml) cream
1/2 ounce (15ml) egg white

Shake with ice and strain into a cocktail glass.
Garnish with grated nutmeg.

Ante Cocktail

11/4 ounce (37ml) calvados
1/2 ounce (7ml) Dubonnet rouge
1/4 ounce (7ml) Cointreau
1 dash Angostura bitters

Stir with ice and strain into a cocktail glass.

Appendicitis De Luxe

2 ounces (60ml) gin
1/2 ounce (15ml) lime juice
1/4 ounce (7ml) Grand Marnier
1/2 ounce (15ml) egg white

Shake vigorously with ice and strain into a coupe.

Adapted from *The Fine Art of Mixing Drinks* by
David Embury (1948)

Appetizer Cocktail

1 ounce (30ml) gin
1 ounce (30ml) Dubonnet rouge
3/4 ounce (22ml) orange juice

Shake with ice and strain into a cocktail glass.

Apple Blossom

1 1/2 ounce (45ml) applejack
3/4 ounce (22ml) apple juice
1/2 ounce (15ml) lime juice
1/4 ounce (7ml) maple syrup

Shake with ice and stain into a cocktail glass.
Garnish with a lemon twist.

Apple Blow Fizz

1 1/2 ounce (45ml) applejack
1 ounce (30ml) lemon juice
1/2 ounce (15ml) simple syrup
1/2 ounce (15ml) egg white
Soda water

Shake with ice (except soda water) and strain into an
ice-filled highball glass. Top with soda water and
garnish with an apple slice.

Apple Car

1 1/4 ounce (37ml) applejack
3/4 ounce (22ml) Cointreau
3/4 ounce (22ml) lemon juice

Shake with ice and strain into a
sugar-rimmed (optional) cocktail glass.

This is a tasty variation on the classic Sidecar.

Apple Martini

2 ounces (60ml) vodka or gin
1 ounce (30ml) Berentzen apfelkorn
1/2 ounce (15ml) apple juice

Shake with ice and strain into a cocktail glass.
Garnish with an apple slice.

Apple Martini (left) and Apple Blossom (right)

Apple Mojito

2 ounces (60ml) light rum
3/4 ounce (22ml) lime juice
1/4 ounce (7ml) simple syrup
1 1/2 ounce (45ml) apple juice
8 mint leaves

Gently muddle mint leaves with syrup at bottom of a
highball glass. Add remaining ingredients, crushed ice and
churn with a barspoon. Garnish with a mint sprig
and an apple slice.

Apple Orchard & Cherry Blossom Punch

(Created by Johan Svensson, Drinksfusion, London)

1 ounce (30ml) Armagnac
3/4 ounce (22ml) Poire William eau de vie
2 teaspoons (10ml) Cherry Heering
21/2 ounces (75ml) apple juice
1/2 ounce (15ml) lemon juice
1/2 ounce (15ml) elderflower syrup
6 mint leaves
3 dashes absinthe

Shake with ice and strain into an ice-filled highball glass.
Garnish with a selection of apple and pear slices,
fresh cherry and a sprig of mint.

Apple Pie Cocktail

11/4 ounce (37ml) light rum
11/4 ounce (37ml) sweet vermouth
1/4 ounce (7ml) apricot brandy
1/4 ounce (7ml) lemon juice
2 dashes grenadine

Shake well and strain into a cocktail glass.

Apple Toddy

11/2 ounce (45ml) applejack
1 teaspoon (5ml) simple syrup
Hot apple cider

Build in a heat resistant glass or mug and stir.
Garnish with grated nutmeg.

Applejack Cocktail No. 1

1¹/₂ ounce (45ml) applejack
¹/₂ ounce (15ml) lemon juice
¹/₄ ounce (7ml) grenadine

Shake with ice and strain into a cocktail glass.

Applejack Cocktail No. 2

1¹/₂ ounce (45ml) applejack
³/₄ ounce (22ml) sweet vermouth
1 dash Angostura bitters

Stir with ice and strain into a cocktail glass.

Applejack Rabbit

See Jack Rabbit

Appletree

1¹/₂ ounce (45ml) applejack
¹/₄ ounce (7ml) dry vermouth
1¹/₂ ounce (45ml) apple juice

Build over ice in an Old Fashioned glass.
Garnish with a lemon twist.

Apricot Cocktail

1 ounce (30ml) gin
1/2 ounce (15ml) apricot brandy
1/2 ounce (15ml) lemon juice
1/4 ounce (7ml) grenadine
1 dash Angostura bitters

Shake with ice and strain into a cocktail glass.

Apricot Lady

1 ounce (30ml) light rum
1 ounce (30ml) apricot brandy
1/2 ounce (15ml) lime juice
1/4 ounce (7ml) orange curaçao
1/2 ounce (15ml) egg white.

Shake vigorously with ice and strain into a coupe.

Apricot Pie

1 ounce (30ml) gold rum
1 ounce (30ml) sweet vermouth
1/4 ounce (7ml) apricot brandy
1/4 ounce (7ml) grenadine
1 teaspoon (5ml) lemon juice

Shake with ice and strain into a cocktail glass.
Garnish with an orange twist.

Aqueduct

1¹/₂ ounce (45ml) vodka
¹/₄ ounce (7ml) orange curaçao
¹/₄ ounce (7ml) apricot brandy

Shake with ice and strain into a cocktail glass.
Garnish with an orange twist.

Archbishop Punch

¹/₂ ounce (15ml) Jamaican dark rum
2 ounces (60ml) port
2 ounces (60ml) water
1 ounce (30ml) lime juice
¹/₂ teaspoon (2.5ml) simple syrup

Build over ice in a highball glass.

Argentina

1 ounce (30ml) gin
1 ounce (30ml) dry vermouth
¹/₄ ounce (7ml) Cointreau
¹/₄ ounce (7ml) Bénédictine
1 dash orange bitters
1 dash Angostura bitters

Shake with ice and strain into a cocktail glass.

Armillita Chico

2 ounces (60ml) tequila blanco
3/4 ounce (22ml) lime juice
3/4 ounce (22ml) pomegranate juice
1 teaspoon (5ml) grenadine
2 dashes orange flower water

Shake with ice and strain into a cocktail glass.

Armour Cocktail

1 1/2 ounce (45ml) sherry
1 1/2 ounce (45ml) dry vermouth
1 dash orange bitters

Stir with ice and strain into a cocktail glass.

Army

2 ounces (60ml) gin
1/2 ounce (15ml) sweet vermouth

Stir with ice and strain into a cocktail glass.
Garnish with an orange twist.

FEATURED DRINK

Army & Navy

2 ounces (60ml) gin
1 ounce (30ml) lemon juice
3/4 ounce (22ml) orgeat

Shake with ice and strain into a cocktail glass.

Arsenic & Old Lace

1 1/2 ounce (45ml) gin
1/2 ounce (15ml) pastis
1/2 ounce (15ml) crème de violette
1/4 ounce (7ml) dry vermouth

Stir with ice and strain into a cocktail glass.

Artist's Special

1 ounce (30ml) Scotch whisky
1 ounce (30ml) sherry
1/2 ounce (15ml) lemon juice
1/4 ounce (7ml) grenadine or cherry syrup

Shake with ice and strain into a cocktail glass.

Asil Laymoun Martini (Honey Lemon Martini in Arabic)

(Created by Adam Elmegirab, Evo-lution,
Aberdeen, Scotland, 2008)

1 1/2 ounce (45ml) gin
1 ounce (30ml) lemon juice
1/2 ounce (15ml) orange juice
1/2 ounce (15ml) honey

Shake with ice and strain into a cocktail glass. Garnish with a lemon or orange twist.

Astor Cocktail

2 ounces (60ml) gin
¼ ounce (7ml) lemon juice
¼ ounce (7ml) orange juice

Stir with ice and strain into a cocktail glass.

Astoria

1½ ounce (45ml) gin
¾ ounce (22ml) dry vermouth
1 dash orange bitters

Stir with ice and strain into a cocktail glass.
Garnish with an olive.

Astoria Bianco

(Created by Jim Meehan, New York)

2½ ounces (75ml) gin
¾ ounce (22ml) bianco vermouth
1 dash Fee Brothers orange bitters
1 dash Regan's orange bitters

Stir with ice and strain into a coupe.
Garnish with an orange twist.

Asylum

1 ounce (30ml) gin
1 ounce (30ml) Pernod
1 teaspoon (5ml) grenadine

Build over ice in an Old Fashioned glass and stir.

Atlantic Coast Cocktail

(Created by Alexander Hauck, The Bitter Truth, Germany)

1 ounce (30ml) cognac
1 ounce (30ml) ginger wine
1 teaspoon (5ml) absinthe
2 dashes The Bitter Truth orange bitters

Stir with ice and strain into a cocktail glass.
Garnish with a lemon twist.

Atlas

1 ounce (30ml) calvados
1 ounce (30ml) Demerara rum
¹/₂ ounce (15ml) Cointreau
1 dash Angostura bitters

Stir with ice and strain into a cocktail glass.

Attention

1 ounce (30ml) gin
¹/₂ ounce (15ml) Pernod
¹/₂ ounce (15ml) dry vermouth
¹/₂ ounce (15ml) crème de violette
2 dashes orange bitters

Stir with ice and strain into a cocktail glass.

Atty Cocktail

2 ounces (60ml) gin
1/2 ounce (15ml) dry vermouth
2 dashes crème de violette

Stir with ice and strain into a cocktail glass.
Garnish with a lemon twist.

Adapted from *The Savoy Cocktail Book* by Harry Craddock (1930)

Auld Man's Milk

1 1/2 ounce (45ml) Scotch whisky
1 whole egg
1/2 teaspoon (2.5ml) simple syrup

Shake vigorously with ice and strain into an ice-filled Old
Fashioned glass. Garnish with grated nutmeg.

Aunt Emily

1 ounce (30ml) gin
1 ounce (30ml) applejack
1/2 ounce (15ml) apricot brandy
1/2 ounce (15ml) orange juice
1 teaspoon (5ml) grenadine

Shake with ice and strain into a cocktail glass.

Autumn Leaves

(Created by Jeffrey Morganthaler, Oregon, 2008,
www.jeffreymorgenthaler.com)

3/4 ounce (22ml) rye
3/4 ounce (22ml) apple brandy
3/4 ounce (22ml) sweet vermouth
1/4 ounce (8ml) Strega
2 dashes cinnamon tincture*

Stir with ice and strain into an ice-filled Old Fashioned
glass. Garnish with an orange twist.

*To make cinnamon tincture, soak 4 ounces (110 grams)
whole cinnamon sticks in 16 ounces (473ml) grain alcohol
or 100 proof vodka for three weeks.
Strain solids and bottle.

Avenue Cocktail

(Created by W. G. Crompton)

3/4 ounce (22ml) bourbon
3/4 ounce (22ml) calvados
3/4 ounce (22ml) passion fruit juice
1 teaspoon (5ml) grenadine
1 dash orange flower water

Shake with ice and strain into a cocktail glass.

Adapted from *Café Royal Cocktail Book* by W. J. Tarling (1937)

Aviation No. 1

2 ounces (60ml) gin
3/4 ounce (22ml) lemon juice
2 teaspoons (10ml)
maraschino liqueur

Shake with ice and strain
into a cocktail glass.

Aviation No. 2

2 ounces (60ml) gin
3/4 ounce (22ml) lemon juice
2 teaspoons (10ml) maraschino liqueur
1 teaspoon (5ml) crème de violette

Shake with ice and strain into a cocktail glass.

An early version of this recipe appeared in *Recipes for Mixed Drinks* by Hugo R. Ensslin (1916).

Aviator

1 1/2 ounce (45ml) Dubonnet rouge
1 1/2 ounce (45ml) sherry

Shake with ice and strain into a cocktail glass.
Garnish with a lemon twist.

B

B&B

¹/₂ ounce (15ml) brandy
¹/₂ ounce (15ml) Bénédictine

Build in a brandy snifter without ice.

B52

¹/₃ ounce (10ml) coffee liqueur
¹/₃ ounce (10ml) Irish cream liqueur
¹/₃ ounce (10ml) Grand Marnier

Layer in shot glass in the order above.

B53

¹/₃ ounce (10ml) coffee liqueur
¹/₃ ounce (10ml) Grand Marnier
¹/₃ ounce (10ml) vodka

Layer in shot glass in the order above.

B54

¹/₃ ounce (10ml) amaretto
¹/₃ ounce (10ml) Irish cream liqueur
¹/₃ ounce (10ml) Grand Marnier

Layer in shot glass in the order above.

Baby Woo Woo

$^1/_3$ ounce (10ml) vodka
$^1/_3$ ounce (10ml) peach schnapps
$^1/_3$ ounce (10ml) cranberry juice

Shake with ice and strain into a shot glass.

Bacardi Cocktail

2 ounces (60ml) Bacardi
light rum
1 ounce (30ml) lime juice
2 dashes grenadine

Shake with ice and strain into
a cocktail glass.

The Bacardi is a cocktail so good
that it was the subject
of a legal battle!

Bacardi Special

1$^1/_2$ ounce (45ml) Bacardi Superior light rum
$^1/_2$ ounce (15ml) gin
1 ounce (30ml) lime juice
$^1/_2$ ounce (15ml) grenadine

Shake with ice and strain into a cocktail glass.

Bahama Mama

1/2 ounce (15ml) dark rum
1/2 ounce (15ml) 151 proof rum
1/2 ounce (15ml) coconut rum
1/4 ounce (7ml) coffee liqueur
4 ounces (120ml) pineapple juice
1 ounce (30ml) lemon juice

Shake with ice and strain into an ice-filled highball glass.

Ballantine Cocktail

1 1/2 ounce (45ml) gin
3/4 ounce (22ml) dry vermouth
1 dash absinthe

Stir with ice and strain into a cocktail glass.

Adapted from *Drinks* by Jacques Straub (1914)

Baltimore Egg Nog

1 ounce (30ml) brandy
1/2 ounce (15ml) Madeira
1/2 ounce (15ml) Jamaican
dark rum
1 teaspoon (5ml) simple syrup
1 1/2 ounce (45ml) milk
1 egg yolk

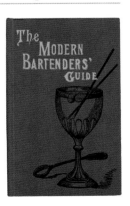

Shake with ice and strain into
a large wine glass.
Dust with grated nutmeg.

Adapted from *Modern Bartender's Guide*
by O. H. Byron (1884)

Bamboo Cocktail

1 1/2 ounce (45ml) dry vermouth
1 1/2 ounce (45ml) dry sherry
1 dash Angostura bitters
1 dash orange bitters

Stir with ice and strain into a cocktail glass.
Garnish with an orange twist.

A mild apéritif, the Bamboo Cocktail is both
dry and complex in flavor.

Adapted from *Drinks* by Jacques Straub (1914)

Banana Cow

1 1/4 ounce (37ml) light rum
3/4 ounce (22ml) crème de bananes
1 ounce (30ml) cream
1 dash grenadine

Shake with ice and strain into a cocktail glass. Garnish
with a banana slice and sprinkle with nutmeg.

Banana Daiquiri

1 1/2 ounce (45ml) light rum
1/2 ounce (15ml) triple sec
1 1/2 ounce (45ml) lime juice
1 banana

Put ingredients in a blender with 1 cup (240ml) of crushed
ice and blend. Serve in a wine glass. Garnish with a cherry.

Barbara Cocktail

1 1/2 ounce (45ml) vodka
3/4 ounce (22ml) white crème de cacao
1/2 ounce (15ml) cream

Shake with ice and strain into a cocktail glass.
Garnish with a dusting of cocoa.

Barbary Coast Cocktail

1/2 ounce (15ml) gin
1/2 ounce (15ml) light rum
1/2 ounce (15ml) Scotch whisky
1/2 ounce (15ml) white crème de cacao
1/2 ounce (15ml) cream

Shake with ice and strain into a cocktail glass.

Barbican

3 ounces (75ml) Scotch whisky
1/2 ounce (15ml) Drambuie
1 ounce (30ml) passion fruit juice

Shake with ice and strain into a cocktail glass.

Barnacle Bill Cocktail

3/4 ounce (22ml) yellow Chartreuse
3/4 ounce (22ml) parfait amour
3/4 ounce (22ml) pastis

Stir with ice and strain into a small cocktail glass.

Barry Cocktail

1 1/2 ounce (45ml) gin
1 1/2 ounce (45ml) sweet vermouth
1/2 teaspoon (2.5ml) crème de menthe
2 dashes Angostura bitters

Stir with ice and strain into a cocktail glass.

Adapted from *American Bar-Tender* by William Boothby (1891)

Barton Special Cocktail

1 1/2 ounce (45ml) applejack
3/4 ounce (22ml) Scotch whisky
1/2 ounce (15ml) gin

Stir with ice and strain into a cocktail glass.
Garnish with a lemon twist.

FEATURED DRINK

Basil Grande

1 ounce (30ml) Chambord
1 ounce (30ml) Grand Marnier
2 ounces (60ml) cranberry juice
4 strawberries
4 basil leaves

Muddle the strawberries and basil leaves in the base of
the shaker. Add everything else and shake with ice.
Double strain into a cocktail glass. Garnish with a
basil leaf and a grind of black pepper.

This is a sweet, fruity drink created at one of the Living
Room bars, a chain of restaurant-bars in the U.K.

Batanga

(Created by Don Javier Delgado Corona)

1³/4 ounce (50ml) silver tequila
¹/4 ounce (7ml) lime juice
Cola

Build in a salt-rimmed highball glass filled with ice.

A long refreshing drink, the Batanga was created by one of Mexico's legendary bartenders whose preference is to stir the drink with a knife before serving.

Batida Morango

2 ounces (60ml) cachaça
1 ounce (30ml) lime juice
¹/2 ounce (15ml) simple syrup
6 strawberries

Put ingredients in a blender with 1 cup (240ml) of crushed ice and blend. Serve in a wine glass. Garnish with a strawberry.

Bay Breeze

1¹/2 ounce (45ml) vodka
3 ounces (90ml) pineapple juice
1 ounce (30ml) cranberry juice

Shake with ice and strain into an ice-filled highball glass.

Beach Cocktail

(Created by Wallace Clements)

1¹/2 ounce (45ml) gin
1¹/2 ounce (45ml) grapefruit juice
1 teaspoon (5ml) maple syrup
1 dash grenadine

Shake with ice and strain into a cocktail glass.

Adapted from *Barflies & Cocktails* by Harry McElhone (1927)

Beachcomber Cocktail

1¹/2 ounce (45ml) light rum
³/4 ounce (22ml) Cointreau
1 ounce (30ml) lime juice
¹/2 teaspoon (2.5ml) maraschino liqueur

Shake with ice and strain into a cocktail glass.

Bebbo Cocktail

1¹/2 ounce (45ml) gin
1 ounce (30ml) lemon juice
¹/2 ounce (15ml) honey
2 teaspoons (10ml) orange juice
1 dash Angostura bitters

Shake with ice and strain into a cocktail glass.

Adapted from *Vintage Spirits and Forgotten Cocktails*
by Ted Haigh (2004)

Beehive

1¹/₂ ounce (45ml) bourbon
2 ounces (60ml) grapefruit juice
³/₄ ounce (22ml) honey

Shake with ice and strain into a cocktail glass.
Garnish with a grapefruit twist.

Bee's Kiss

1 ounce (30ml) light rum
¹/₂ ounce (15ml) dark rum
¹/₂ ounce (15ml) cream
¹/₂ ounce (15ml) honey

Shake with ice and strain into a small cocktail glass.

Bee's Knees Cocktail

1¹/₂ ounce (45ml) gin
¹/₂ ounce (15ml) honey
¹/₂ ounce (15ml) lemon juice

Shake with ice and strain into a cocktail glass.

Beginner

1¹/₂ ounce (45ml) kümmel
1 ounce (30ml) dry vermouth
1 dash absinthe
1 teaspoon (5ml) simple syrup
2 dashes orange bitters

Shake with ice and strain into a cocktail glass.

Adapted from *The Flowing Bowl* by William Schmidt (1891)

Beja Flor

2 ounces (60ml) cachaça
1 ounce (30ml) triple sec
1 ounce (30ml) crème de bananes

Shake with ice and strain into a cocktail glass.
Garnish with a banana slice.

Bellini

1 ounce (30ml) white peach purée
5 ounces (150ml) prosecco

Pour peach purée into a flute, add prosecco and stir.

A light, fruity
drink created by
Giuseppe Cipriani at
the legendary
Harry's Bar in
Venice, Italy.

Bennett Cocktail

(Robert Vermeire: "This cocktail, which is very popular in Chile, is called after a well-known and popular millionaire of that country.")

1 1/2 ounce (45ml) gin
3/4 ounce (22ml) lime juice
1 teaspoon (5ml) simple syrup
2 dashes Angostura bitters

Shake with ice and strain into a cocktail glass.

Adapted from *Cocktails: How To Mix Them* by
Robert Vermeire (1922)

Bentley

1 1/2 ounce (45ml) applejack
1 1/2 ounce (45ml) Dubonnet rouge

Stir with ice and strain into a cocktail glass.

Berkeley Hotel Cocktail

(Created by "Dick" of the Berkeley Hotel, London)

3/4 ounce (22ml) gin
3/4 ounce (22ml) dry vermouth
3/4 ounce (22ml) Strega

Stir with ice and strain into a small cocktail glass.

Adapted from *Anthology of Cocktails* by Booth's Gin (1930s)

Bermudiana Rose

1 1/2 ounce (45ml) gin
1/2 ounce (15ml) apricot brandy
1/2 ounce (15ml) grenadine
1/2 ounce (15ml) lemon juice

Shake with ice and strain into a cocktail glass.

Berry Wall

1 1/2 ounce (45ml) gin
1 1/2 ounce (45ml) sweet vermouth
1 teaspoon (5ml) orange curaçao

Shake with ice and strain into a cocktail glass. Garnish
with a lemon twist.

Adapted from *The Savoy Cocktail Book* by Harry Craddock (1930)

Betty Cocktail

1 ounce (30ml) gin
1 ounce (30ml) light rum
1/2 ounce (15ml) Cointreau

Stir with ice and strain into a cocktail glass.

Between the Sheets

1 ounce (30ml) brandy
1 ounce (30ml) light rum
1 ounce (30ml) Cointreau
1/2 ounce (15ml) lemon juice

Shake with ice and strain into a cocktail glass.

Beuser & Angus Special

(Created by Goncalo de Souza Monteiro, Germany)

1 1/2 ounce (45ml) green Chartreuse
2 teaspoons (10ml) maraschino liqueur
3/4 ounce (22ml) lime juice
1/2 ounce (15ml) egg white
3 dashes The Bitter Truth orange flower water

Shake vigorously with ice and strain into a crushed ice-filled Old Fashioned glass. Dash the orange flower water on top of the drink.

Biffy Cocktail

1 1/2 ounce (45ml) gin
1/2 ounce (15ml) applejack
1 ounce (30ml) lemon juice

Shake with ice and strain into a cocktail glass.

Big 4 Mint Julep

2 ounces (60ml) bourbon
1/4 ounce (7ml) gold rum
6 mint leaves
1 teaspoon (5ml) simple syrup

In the bottom of a highball glass muddle mint with syrup. Add crushed ice, bourbon and stir. Top with crushed ice and pour rum on top. Garnish with a mint sprig dusted in sugar, a raspberry and a strawberry.

Adapted from *The Mixicologist* by C.F. Lawlor (1895)

FEATURED DRINK

Bijou Cocktail

¾ ounce (22ml) Plymouth gin
¾ ounce (22ml) green Chartreuse
¾ ounce (22ml) sweet vermouth
2 dashes orange bitters

Stir with ice and strain into a cocktail glass.
Garnish with a cherry and a lemon twist.

Adapted from *Bartender's Manual* by Harry Johnson (1900)

Bishop Cocktail

1 ounce (30ml) bourbon
1/2 ounce (15ml) sweet vermouth
1 ounce (30ml) orange juice
1 dash yellow Chartreuse

Shake with ice and strain into a cocktail glass.

Biter Cocktail

1 1/2 ounce (45ml) gin
3/4 ounce (22ml) green Chartreuse
3/4 ounce (22ml) lemon juice
A few drops of absinthe

Shake with ice and strain into a cocktail glass.

Adapted from *The Savoy Cocktail Book* by Harry Craddock (1930)

Black Bomber

1 1/2 ounce (45ml) calvados
3/4 ounce (22ml) light rum
3/4 ounce (22ml) Swedish Punsch

Shake with ice and strain into a cocktail glass.

Adapted from *The Standard Cocktail Guide* by Crosby Gaige (1944)

Black Feather

(Created by Robert Hess, 2000)

2 ounces (60ml) brandy
1 ounce (30ml) dry vermouth
1/2 ounce (15ml) Cointreau
1 dash of bitters

Stir with ice and strain into a cocktail glass.
Garnish with a lemon twist.

Black Jack Cocktail

1 1/2 ounce (45ml) Scotch whisky
1 ounce (30ml) coffee liqueur
1/2 ounce (15ml) triple sec
1/2 ounce (15ml) lemon juice

Shake with ice and strain into a cocktail glass.

Black Russian (American)

2 ounces (60ml) vodka
1 ounce (30ml) coffee liqueur

Build in an ice-filled Old Fashioned glass.

Black Russian (English)

1 ounce (30ml) vodka
1 ounce (30ml) coffee liqueur
Cola

Build over ice in a highball glass.

Black Stripe

2 ounces (60ml) Jamaican dark rum
2 teaspoons (10ml) molasses
4 ounces (120ml) boiling water

Dissolve molasses in the boiling water in an Irish coffee glass and add rum. Dust with nutmeg.

Adapted from *The Modern Bartender's Guide* by O. H. Byron (1884)

Black Velvet

2 ounces (60ml) stout
2 ounces (60ml) champagne

Build in a flute.

Blackberry Fizz

(Created by Jonathan Pogash for Madison and Vine Wine Bar and American Bistro in New York)

3/4 ounce (45ml) gin
3/4 ounce (45ml) Lillet Blanc
3 fresh blackberries
1/4 ounce (7ml) lemon juice
1/4 ounce (7ml) simple syrup
3 ounces (90ml) champagne

Muddle the blackberries in the lemon juice and simple syrup. Add the gin and Lillet and shake with ice, then strain into a flute. Top with champagne and garnish with a fresh blackberry.

Jonathan recommends using Bombay Sapphire for the gin and Moët & Chandon for the champagne.

Adapted from *The Essential Bartender's Guide* by Robert Hess (2008)

Blackberry Margarita

1 1/2 ounce (45ml) tequila blanco
1/2 ounce (15ml) crème de mûre
1 teaspoon (5ml) Cointreau
3/4 ounce (22ml) lime juice

Blend with ice and pour into a coupe.
Garnish with a blackberry.

Blackstar

(Created by Jim Meehan, New York)

2 ounces (60ml) vodka
1/4 ounce (7ml) Borsci sambuca
3/4 ounce (22ml) lime juice
3/4 ounce (22ml) grapefruit juice
1/4 ounce (7ml) simple syrup

Shake with ice and strain into a coupe.
Garnish with a star anise pod.

Blackthorn

1 1/2 ounce (45ml) Irish whiskey
1 1/2 ounce (45ml) dry vermouth
2 dashes Angostura bitters
2 dashes absinthe

Stir with ice and strain into a cocktail glass.

Adapted from *Bartender's Manual* by Harry Johnson (1900)

Blanche Cocktail

¾ ounce (22ml) Cointreau
¾ ounce (22ml) anisette
¾ ounce (22ml) white curaçao

Shake with ice and strain into a small cocktail glass.

Adapted from *Barflies & Cocktails* by Harry McElhone (1927)

Blenton Cocktail

2 ounces (60ml) gin
1 ounce (30ml) dry vermouth
1 dash Angostura bitters

Shake with ice and strain into a cocktail glass.

Blinker Cocktail

2 ounces (45ml) rye whiskey
1 ounce (30ml) grapefruit juice
1 teaspoon (5ml) raspberry
syrup/grenadine

Shake with ice and strain into
a cocktail glass. Garnish with
a lemon twist.

Adapted from
The Official Mixer's Manual by
Patrick Gavin Duffy (1934)

Blood & Sand

3/4 ounce (22ml) Scotch whisky
3/4 ounce (22ml) Cherry Heering
3/4 ounce (22ml) sweet vermouth
3/4 ounce (22ml) orange juice

Shake with ice and strain into a cocktail glass.

Blood & Sand was created in 1922 to pay homage to the Rudolph Valentino film of the same name.

Blood & Sand Revisited

(Created by Jörg Meyer, Le Lion • Bar de Paris, Hamburg, Germany)

1 1/2 ounce (45ml) Islay whisky
1 ounce (30ml) sweet vermouth
1 ounce (30ml) wild black cherry liqueur
2 orange wedges

Muddle orange in a cocktail shaker. Add remaining ingredients and shake with ice. Double strain into a cocktail glass. Garnish with a marasca cherry.

Blood Bronx

1 1/2 ounce (45ml) gin
1/4 ounce (7ml) dry vermouth
1/2 ounce (15ml) blood orange juice

Shake with ice and strain into a cocktail glass. Garnish with a blood orange wedge.

Bloodhound No. 1

1½ ounce (45ml) gin
¾ ounce (22ml) sweet vermouth
¾ ounce (22ml) dry vermouth
4 raspberries

Muddle the raspberries in the bottom of the shaker.
Shake with ice and strain into a cocktail glass.
Garnish with a raspberry.

Adapted from *"Cocktail Bill" Boothby's World Drinks and How to Mix Them* by William Boothby (1930)

Bloodhound No. 2

1½ ounce (45ml) gin
¾ ounce (22ml) sweet vermouth
¾ ounce (22ml) dry vermouth
2 diced strawberries

Muddle the strawberries in the bottom of a shaker.
Shake with ice and strain into a cocktail glass. Garnish
with a strawberry on the rim of the glass.

Adapted from *ABC of Mixing Cocktails* by Harry McElhone (1922)

FEATURED DRINK

Blood Orange

*(Created by Jamie Boudreau, Seattle,
www.SpiritsandCocktails.com)*

1½ (45ml) ounce gin
½ ounce (15ml) Amaro Montenegro
½ ounce (15ml) Campari
1 ounce (30ml) orange juice

Shake with ice and strain into a cocktail glass.

FEATURED DRINK

Bloodhound No. 2

Bloody Bull

2 ounces (60ml) vodka
3 ounces (90ml) tomato juice
2 ounces (60ml) beef boullion
1/2 ounce (15ml) lemon juice
1 dash hot sauce

Softly shake with ice and strain into an ice-filled highball
glass. Add salt and black pepper to taste.
Garnish with a lemon wedge.

Bloody Caesar

1¹/₂ ounce (45ml) vodka
3 ounces (90ml) clamato juice
¹/₂ ounce (15ml) lemon juice
Worcestershire sauce to taste
Tabasco sauce to taste
Black pepper to taste
Celery salt to taste

Softly shake with ice and strain into a highball glass.
Garnish with a celery stalk and a wedge of lemon.

Bloody Maria

1¹/₂ ounce (45ml) tequila blanco
3 ounces (90ml) tomato juice
¹/₂ ounce (15ml) lemon juice
Worcestershire sauce to taste
Tabasco sauce to taste
Black pepper to taste
Celery salt to taste

Softly shake with ice and strain into a tall glass.
Garnish with a celery stalk and a wedge of lemon.

Bloody Mary

1½ ounce (45ml) vodka
3 ounces (90ml) tomato juice
½ ounce (15ml) lemon juice
Worcestershire sauce to taste
Tabasco sauce to taste
Black pepper to taste
Celery salt to taste

Softly shake with ice and strain into a highball glass.
Garnish with a celery stalk and a wedge of lemon.

Every bartender has his or her own opinion on how this
drink should be made. This is ours.

Bloomsbury

(Created by Robert Hess, 2003)

2 ounces (60ml) gin
½ ounce (15ml) Licor 43
½ ounce (15ml) Lillet Blanc
2 dashes Peychaud's bitters

Stir with ice and strain into a cocktail glass.
Garnish with a lemon twist.

Blue Bird

2 ounces (60ml) gin
4 dashes Angostura bitters
5 dashes orange curaçao

Stir with ice and strain into a cocktail glass.

Adapted from *The Savoy Cocktail Book* by Harry Craddock (1930)

Bloody Mary

Blue Blazer

2¹/2 ounces (75ml) Scotch whisky
2¹/2 ounces (75ml) boiling water

Preheat two metal mugs with handles.
Pour the scotch into one and the water into the other.
Ignite the scotch and pour into the water and then
repeatedly pour from one mug to the other while on fire.
Lemon twist and sugar are optional. Exercise extreme
caution when making this drink!

Blue Hawaii

3/4 ounce (22ml) light rum
3/4 ounce (22ml) vodka
1/2 ounce (15ml) blue curaçao
3 ounces (90ml) pineapple juice
1/2 ounce (15ml) lemon juice
1/2 ounce (15ml) simple syrup

Shake with ice and strain into a highball or hurricane glass.
Garnish with a slice of pineapple and a cherry.

Blue Lagoon

2 ounces (60ml) vodka
1 1/2 ounce (45ml) blue curaçao
1/2 ounce (15ml) lemon juice
Soda water

Shake everything (except soda water) and strain into a
highball glass full of ice. Top with soda water.

Blue Moon

1 1/2 ounce (45ml) gin
3/4 ounce (22ml) lemon juice
1/4 ounce (7ml) crème de violette

Shake with ice and strain into a cocktail glass.

Blue Train

1 1/2 ounce (45ml) gin
3/4 ounce (22ml) Cointreau
3/4 ounce (22ml) lemon juice
1 drop blue food coloring

Shake with ice and strain into a cocktail glass.

Adapted from *The Savoy Cocktail Book* by Harry Craddock (1930)

Blueberry Martini

1 1/2 ounce (45ml) vodka
1 ounce (30ml) crème de myrtille
15 blueberries

Muddle blueberries in bottom of a shaker. Add remaining ingredients and shake with ice. Strain into a cocktail glass and garnish with blueberries.

Boadas

³/₄ ounce (22ml) light rum
³/₄ ounce (22ml) Dubonnet rouge
³/₄ ounce (22ml) orange curaçao

Stir with ice and strain into a cocktail glass.
Garnish with a cherry.

FEATURED DRINK

Bobby Burns

1¹/₂ ounce (45ml) blended Scotch whisky
1¹/₂ ounce (45ml) sweet vermouth
¹/₄ ounce (7ml) Bénédictine

Stir with ice and strain into a cocktail glass.
Garnish with a lemon twist.

The herbal notes of the Bénédictine marry beautifully
with the scotch and vermouth.

Boilermaker

1 ounce (30ml) bourbon
Beer

Drop the shot of bourbon into the glass of beer or
serve it on the side.

Boisson du Monde

(Created by Gustavo Brizuela, Cuvee, Cordoba, Argentina)

1 ounce (30ml) vanilla vodka
1/2 ounce (15ml) Drambuie
1/2 ounce (15ml) simple syrup
1/4 ounce (7ml) Jägermeister

Shake with ice (except Jägermeister) and strain into a large shot glass. Add Jägermeister and garnish with chopped chives and ground black pepper.

Bonnie Prince Daiquiri

(Created by Calum Lawrie, Edinburgh)

1 1/2 ounce (45ml) light rum
1/2 ounce (15ml) Drambuie
3/4 ounce (22ml) lime juice
1 plum
2 teaspoons (10ml) simple syrup

Cut plum into quarters and muddle with syrup in the base of a shaker. Add remaining ingredients and shake with ice. Strain into a cocktail glass. Garnish with a thistle stem.

This delightful variation on the daiquiri was created by one of Scotland's finest bartenders.

FEATURED DRINK

Boomerang

3/4 ounce (22ml) Swedish Punsch
3/4 ounce (22ml) Canadian Club whisky
3/4 ounce (22ml) dry vermouth
1/4 ounce (7ml) lemon juice
1 dash Angostura bitters

Shake with ice and strain into a cocktail glass.
Garnish with a lemon twist.

Adapted from *The Savoy Cocktail Book* by Harry Craddock (1930)

Boothby Cocktail

*(Created around 1910 by William Boothby at the
Palace Hotel, San Francisco)*

2 ounces (60ml) bourbon or rye
¾ ounce (22ml) sweet vermouth
2 dashes orange bitters
2 dashes Angostura bitters
½ ounce (15ml) champagne

Stir with ice (except champagne) and strain into a cocktail glass. Garnish with a cherry and float champagne on top.

Bosom Caresser No. 1

2 ounces (60ml) brandy
1 teaspoon (5ml) raspberry syrup
1/2 ounce (15ml) milk
1/2 ounce (15ml) lightly beaten egg

Shake vigorously with ice and strain into a cocktail glass.

Adapted from *Recipes of American and Other Iced Drinks*
by Charlie Paul (1902)

Bosom Caresser No. 2

1 1/2 ounce (45ml) brandy
3/4 ounce (22ml) orange curaçao
1 egg yolk
1 teaspoon grenadine

Shake vigorously with ice and strain into a small wine glass.

Adapted from *The Savoy Cocktail Book* by Harry Craddock (1930)

Boston Cocktail

1 ounce (30ml) gin
1 ounce (30ml) apricot brandy
1 ounce (30ml) lemon juice
1/4 ounce (7ml) grenadine

Shake with ice and strain into a small cocktail glass.

Boston Flip

1 1/2 ounce (45ml) rye whiskey
1 1/2 ounce (45ml) Madeira
1 whole egg
1 teaspoon (5ml) simple syrup

Shake vigorously with ice and strain into a small wine glass. Dust with grated nutmeg.

Boulevard Cocktail

1 1/2 ounce (45ml) gin
1/4 ounce (7ml) dry vermouth
3/4 ounce (22ml) orange juice

Shake with ice and strain into a cocktail glass.

Boulevardier Cocktail

1 1/2 ounce (45ml) bourbon
1 ounce (30ml) Campari
1 ounce (30ml) sweet vermouth

Stir with ice and strain into a cocktail glass.
Garnish with a lemon twist.

Adapted from *Barflies & Cocktails* by Harry McElhone (1927)

Bourbon Scaffa

1 1/2 ounce (45ml) bourbon
3/4 ounce (22ml) Bénédictine
1 dash Angostura bitters

Stir with ice and strain into a cocktail glass.

Bourbon Stone Sour

1 1/2 ounce (45ml) bourbon
3/4 ounce (22ml) lemon juice
1 ounce (30ml) orange juice
3/4 ounce (22ml) simple syrup

Shake with ice and strain into a cocktail glass.
Garnish with an orange slice.

Brain Duster

1 ounce (30ml) absinthe
1/2 ounce (15ml) bourbon
1/2 ounce (15ml) sweet vermouth
1/2 teaspoon (2.5ml) simple syrup
Soda water

Stir with ice (except soda water) and strain into a flute.
Top with soda water.

*Adapted from Modern American Drinks by
George Kappeler (1895)*

Brain-Storm Cocktail

1 1/2 ounce (45ml) Irish whiskey
2 dashes Bénédictine
2 dashes dry vermouth

Stir with ice and strain into a small cocktail glass.
Squeeze an orange peel on top.

Bramble

(Created by Dick Bradsell, London)

2 ounces (60ml) gin
1/2 ounce (15ml) crème de mûre
1 ounce (30ml) lemon juice
2 teaspoons (10ml) simple syrup

Build over crushed ice in an Old Fashioned glass.
Stir and crown with the crème de mûre. Garnish with a
lemon slice and two raspberries.

The Bramble has been very popular in London since its
creation in the 1980s.

FEATURED DRINK

Brandy Alexander

1 ounce (30ml) brandy
1 ounce (30ml) dark crème de cacao
1 ounce (30ml) cream

Shake with ice and strain into
a cocktail glass.
Dust with nutmeg.

Brandy Cocktail

2 ounces (60ml) brandy
1 teaspoon (5ml) simple syrup
2 dashes orange bitters

Mix syrup with a small amount of brandy and bitters in the bottom of an Old Fashioned glass. Add one ice cube, more brandy and keep stirring. Gradually add more ice and brandy while stirring. Garnish with an orange twist.

Adapted from *Drinks* by Jacques Straub (1914)

Brandy Crusta

1 1/2 ounce (45ml) brandy
1/4 ounce (7ml) maraschino liqueur
1/4 ounce (7ml) Cointreau
1/4 ounce (7ml) lemon juice

Shake with ice and strain into a small wine glass which has been rimmed with sugar. Pare half a lemon (all in one piece) and place inside the rim of the glass.

FEATURED DRINK

Brandy Daisy

See Daisy

Brandy Flip

See Flip

Brave Bull

1¹/₂ ounce (45ml) blanco tequila
1 ounce (30ml) coffee liqueur

Stir with ice and strain into an ice-filled Old Fashioned
glass. Garnish with a lemon twist.

Brazil

1¹/₂ ounce (45ml) dry vermouth
1¹/₂ ounce (45ml) sherry
4 dashes absinthe
4 dashes Angostura bitters

Stir with ice and strain into a cocktail glass.
Garnish with a cherry and a lemon twist.

Adapted from *Bartender's Manual* by Harry Johnson (1900)

FEATURED DRINK

Breakfast Martini

(Created by Salvatore Calabrese, London)

2 ounces (60ml) gin
¹/₄ ounce (7ml) Cointreau
¹/₄ ounce (7ml) lemon juice
2 teaspoons (10ml) rindless orange marmalade

Shake with ice and strain into a cocktail glass.
Garnish with an orange spiral.

This may be Salvatore Calabrese's best known creation.

Broadway Thirst

2 ounces (60ml) blanco tequila
1 ounce (30ml) orange juice
1 ounce (30ml) lemon juice
2 teaspoons (10ml) sugar syrup

Shake with ice and strain into a cocktail glass.

Bronx

1¹/₂ ounce (45ml) gin
³/₄ ounce (22ml) orange juice
¹/₄ ounce (7ml) sweet vermouth
¹/₄ ounce (7ml) dry vermouth

Shake with ice and strain into a cocktail glass.

Bronx River

1¹/₂ ounce (45ml) gin
³/₄ ounce (22ml) sweet vermouth
¹/₄ ounce (7ml) lemon juice
1 teaspoon (5ml) simple syrup

Shake with ice and strain into a cocktail glass.

Bronx Terrace

1¹/₄ ounce (37ml) gin
1¹/₄ ounce (37ml) dry vermouth
¹/₂ ounce (15ml) lime juice

Shake with ice and strain into a cocktail glass.

Adapted from *Jack's Manual* by Jack Grohusko (1908)

Brooklyn

2 ounces (60ml) rye or bourbon
³/₄ ounce (22ml) sweet vermouth
1 dash Amer Picon
1 dash maraschino liqueur

Stir with ice and strain into a cocktail glass.

If you select rye over bourbon, you'll have a
tastier cocktail.

Adapted from *Jack's Manual* by Jack Grohusko (1908)

Brooklynite

2 ounces (60ml) Jamaican dark rum
³/₄ ounce (22ml) lime juice
¹/₂ ounce (15ml) honey
1 dash Angostura bitters

Shake with ice and strain into a cocktail glass.

Brown Cow

1 1/2 ounce (45ml) coffee liqueur
2 ounces (60ml) milk

Build over ice in an Old Fashioned glass.

Brown Squirrel

1 ounce (30ml) amaretto
1 ounce (30ml) dark crème de cacao
1 ounce (30ml) light cream

Shake with ice and strain into a cocktail glass.

Brunswick Sour

1 1/2 ounce (45ml) light rum
3/4 ounce (22ml) lime juice
1 teaspoon (5ml) simple syrup
1/2 ounce (15ml) red wine

Shake with ice (except wine) and strain into a flute.
Float wine on top and serve.

FEATURED DRINK

Brut Cocktail

2 ounces (60ml) dry vermouth
1 ounce (30ml) Amer Picon
1 dash Angostura bitters

Stir with ice and strain into a cocktail glass.

Adapted from *ABC of Mixing Cocktails* by Harry McElhone (1922)

Buckeye

2¹/₂ ounces (75ml) gin
¹/₂ ounce (15ml) dry vermouth
Black olive

Stir with ice and strain into a cocktail glass.
Garnish with a black olive.

Buck's Fizz

1¹/₂ ounce (45ml) champagne
3 ounces (90ml) orange juice

Pour the orange juice into a flute and top with champagne.

Buffalo Fizz

1¹/₂ ounce (45ml) rye whiskey
³/₄ ounce (22ml) sherry
³/₄ ounce (22ml) lemon juice
¹/₄ ounce (7ml) simple syrup
¹/₂ ounce (15ml) egg white
Soda water

FEATURED DRINK

Shake vigorously with ice
(except soda water) and
strain into an ice-filled
highball glass. Top with soda
water and garnish with an
orange slice.

Adapted from *The Hoffman
House Bartender's Guide* by
Charles Mahoney (1905)

Bulldog Cocktail

3/4 ounce (22ml) gin
1 1/2 ounce (45ml) cherry brandy
3/4 ounce (22ml) lime juice

Shake with ice and strain into a cocktail glass.

Bullseye

5 ounces (150ml) beer
5 ounces (150ml) tomato juice

Stir in a highball glass. Garnish with a tomato slice.

Bullshot

1 1/2 ounce (45ml) vodka
3 ounces (90ml) beef bouillon
1/4 ounce (7ml) lemon juice
Worcestershire sauce to taste
Tabasco sauce to taste
Black pepper to taste
Celery salt to taste

Shake with ice and strain into an ice-filled highball glass.
Garnish with a wedge of lime.

Bunny Hug

1 ounce (30ml) gin
1 ounce (30ml) Scotch whisky
1 ounce (30ml) absinthe

Stir with ice and strain into a cocktail glass.

Adapted from
ABC of Mixing Cocktails
by Harry McElhone (1922)

Burnt Fuselage

(Harry McElhone: "Chuck Kerwood takes to the air so frequently that he likes a stiff steadier when he comes down to earth. The famous flying man calls his concoction the 'Burnt Fuselage'.")

1 ounce (30ml) cognac
1 ounce (30ml) Grand Marnier
1 ounce (30ml) dry vermouth

Shake with ice and strain into a cocktail glass.

Adaped from *Barflies & Cocktails* by Harry McElhone (1927)

C

C.F.H. Cocktail

1 ounce (30ml) gin
1/2 ounce (15ml) applejack
1/2 ounce (15ml) Swedish Punsch
1/2 ounce (15ml) lemon juice
1/2 ounce (15ml) grenadine

Shake with ice and strain into a cocktail glass.

Cable Car

*(Created by Tony Abou-Ganim for the Starlight Room,
San Francisco, 1993)*

1 1/2 ounce (45ml) spiced rum
3/4 ounce (22ml) orange curaçao
1 ounce (30ml) lemon juice
1/2 ounce (15ml) simple syrup

Shake with ice and then strain into a cocktail glass which
has been rimmed with a cinnamon sugar mixture.
Garnish with an orange twist.

Tony recommends making this drink with Captain
Morgan's Spiced Rum and Marie Brizard orange curaçao.

Adapted from *The Essential Bartender's Guide*
by Robert Hess (2008)

Café Arroz

(Created by Jim Meehan, New York)

1 1/2 ounce (45ml) reposado tequila
1/2 ounce (15ml) coffee liqueur
2 ounces (60ml) horchata (orgeat)

Shake with ice and strain into a coupe.
Garnish with grated cinnamon.

Café de Paris

1 3/4 ounce (50ml) gin
1/4 ounce (7ml) anisette
1 teaspoon (5ml) cream
1/2 ounce (15ml) egg white

Shake vigorously with ice and strain into a cocktail glass.

Adapted from *ABC of Mixing Cocktails* by Harry McElhone (1922)

Café Royal Appetiser

(Created by W. J. Tarling)

1 1/4 ounce (37ml) gin
1 1/4 ounce (37ml) Dubonnet rouge
3/4 ounce (22ml) orange juice

Shake with ice and strain into a cocktail glass.

Adapted from *Café Royal Cocktail Book* by W. J. Tarling (1937)

Café Royal Special

(Created by W. J. Tarling)

³/₄ ounce (22ml) gin
³/₄ ounce (22ml) sloe gin
³/₄ ounce (22ml) dry vermouth
³/₄ ounce (22ml) lemon juice

Shake with ice and strain into a cocktail glass.

Adapted from *Café Royal Cocktail Book* by W. J. Tarling (1937)

Caipirinha

2 ounces (60ml) cachaça
¹/₂ ounce (15ml) sugar
1 lime

Wash the lime and cut it into eighths. Put limes and sugar into an Old Fashioned glass and muddle. Add the cachaça and stir. Fill the glass with crushed ice, and stir again.

The Caipirinha is the national cocktail of Brazil.

FEATURED DRINK

Caipirissima

Same as the Caipirinha, but replace cachaça with light rum.

Caipirovska

Same as the Caipirinha, but replace cachaça with vodka.

California Iced Tea

1/2 ounce (15ml) vodka
1/2 ounce (15ml) tequila
1/2 ounce (15ml) light rum
1/2 ounce (15ml) gin
1/2 ounce (15ml) triple sec
3/4 ounce (22ml) lemon juice
1/2 ounce (15ml) simple syrup
Orange juice

Shake with ice (except orange juice) and strain into an ice-filled highball glass. Top with orange juice and garnish with a lemon and orange slice.

Calvados Cocktail

11/2 ounce (45ml) calvados
11/2 ounce (45ml) orange juice
3/4 ounce (22ml) Cointreau
3/4 ounce (22ml) orange bitters

Shake with ice and strain into a cocktail glass.

Calypso Coffee

1¹/₂ ounce (45ml) dark rum
4 ounces (120ml) coffee
³/₄ ounce (22ml) simple syrup
Whipping cream

Lightly whip cream to just under stiff. Build in an Irish coffee glass and float cream on top.

Calypso Cooler

2 ounces (60ml) gold rum
1 ounce (30ml) pineapple juice
¹/₂ ounce (15ml) lime juice
¹/₂ teaspoon (2.5ml) simple syrup
Soda water

Shake with ice (except soda water) and strain into an ice-filled highball glass. Top with soda water and garnish with a cherry and a pineapple spear.

Camberley

1¹/₄ ounce (37ml) gin
¹/₂ ounce (15ml) Grand Marnier
¹/₂ ounce (15ml) Calvados
¹/₄ ounce (7ml) orange juice
¹/₄ ounce (7ml) grenadine

Shake with ice and strain into a cocktail glass.

Cameron's Kick

1 ounce (30ml) Scotch whiskey
1 ounce (30ml) Irish whiskey
1/2 ounce (15ml) lemon juice
1/4 ounce (7ml) orgeat

Shake with ice and strain into a cocktail glass.

Adapted from *ABC of Mixing Cocktails* by Harry McElhone (1922)

Campari Classic

2 ounces (60ml) Campari
Soda water

Build over ice in an Old Fashioned glass.

Campari Cooler

1 ounce (30ml) Campari
1 ounce (30ml) peach schnapps
1 1/2 ounce (45ml) orange juice
1 1/2 ounce (45ml) cranberry juice
1/2 ounce (15ml) lime juice
7-Up

Shake with ice (except 7-Up) and strain into an ice-filled
highball glass. Top with 7-Up and garnish
with an orange slice.

Camparinette

(Created by "Albert" of the Chatam, Paris)

1¹/₂ ounce (45ml) gin
³/₄ ounce (22ml) Campari
³/₄ ounce (22ml) sweet vermouth

Stir with ice and strain into a cocktail glass.
Garnish with a lemon twist.

Adapted from *Cocktails de Paris* by RIP (1929)

FEATURED DRINK

Camparinha

2 ounces (60ml) Campari
¹/₂ ounce (15ml) sugar
1 lime

Wash the lime and cut it into eighths. Put limes and sugar into an Old Fashioned glass and muddle. Add the Campari and stir. Fill glass with crushed ice, and stir again.

Camparosa

2 ounces (60ml) Campari
Grapefruit juice

Build over ice in a highball glass.
Garnish with an orange slice.

Campden

1¹/2 ounce (45ml) gin
¹/4 ounce (7ml) Cointreau
¹/4 ounce (7ml) Lillet Blanc

Shake with ice and strain into a cocktail glass.

Adapted from *The Savoy Cocktail Book* by Harry Craddock (1930)

Canadian Apple

1¹/2 ounce (45ml) Canadian Club
¹/2 ounce (15ml) applejack
¹/2 ounce (15ml) lemon juice
1 teaspoon (5ml) simple syrup

Shake with ice and strain into a cocktail glass.
Dust with cinnamon.

Canadian Breakfast Martini

(Created by Calum Lawrie, Edinburgh)

1¹/2 ounce (45ml) Canadian Club
¹/2 ounce (15ml) Grand Marnier
2 teaspoons (10ml) maple syrup
1 teaspoon (5ml) melon juice
1 dash orange bitters

Shake with ice and strain into a cocktail glass.
Garnish with an orange twist.

Canadian Cocktail

1 1/2 ounce (45ml) Canadian Club
1/4 ounce (7ml) orange curaçao
1/2 ounce (15ml) lemon juice
1/2 teaspoon (2.5ml) simple syrup
2 dashes orange bitters

Shake with ice and strain into a cocktail glass.

Cancoup

1 1/2 ounce (45ml) Canadian Club
1/2 ounce (15ml) Campari
1/2 ounce (15ml) dry vermouth

Stir with ice and strain into a cocktail glass.
Garnish with a lemon twist.

Canvan

3/4 ounce (22ml) Canadian Club
3/4 ounce (22ml) Van der Hum
3/4 ounce (22ml) lemon juice

Shake with ice and strain into a cocktail glass.

Cape Codder

1 1/2 ounce (45ml) vodka
Cranberry juice

Build over ice in a highball glass. Garnish with
a lime wedge.

Caprice Cocktail

1½ ounce (45ml) gin
½ ounce (15ml) Bénédictine
½ ounce (15ml) dry vermouth
1 dash orange bitters

Stir with ice and strain into a cocktail glass.

Cardinal

1 ounce (30ml) gin
¾ ounce (22ml) Campari
¾ ounce (22ml) dry vermouth

Stir with ice and strain into a cocktail glass.
Garnish with a lemon twist.

FEATURED DRINK

Carol Channing

(Created by Dick Bradsell, London)

½ ounce (15ml) crème de framboise
½ ounce (15ml) framboise eau de vie
1 teaspoon (5ml) simple syrup
Champagne

Build in a flute and garnish with a raspberry.

Dick Bradsell created this drink in 1984 to honor the
American comedienne's appearance in the 1967 film
Thoroughly Modern Millie.

Casino

2 ounces (60ml) gin
1 teaspoon (5ml) lemon juice
1 teaspoon (5ml) maraschino liqueur
2 dashes orange bitters

Shake with ice and strain into a cocktail glass.
Garnish with a cherry.

Celebrasion

(Created by Greg Boehm)

2 ounces (60ml) cachaça
1/2 ounce (15ml) Lillet Blanc
1/2 ounce (15ml) celery simple syrup
1/2 ounce (15ml) lime juice
4 or 5 mint leaves
1 dash orange bitters

Shake with ice and double strain into a coupe. To make celery simple syrup, simply place chopped celery in a shallow dish and cover with simple syrup. After 24 hours, strain.

Celebration Special

(Created by C. Toni Watkins)

3/4 ounce (22ml) gin
3/4 ounce (22ml) Cointreau
3/4 ounce (22ml) goldwasser
3/4 ounce (22ml) lemon juice

Shake with ice and strain into a cocktail glass.

Adapted from *Café Royal Cocktail Book* by W. J. Tarling (1937)

Champagne Cocktail

1/2 ounce (15ml) brandy (optional)
1 sugar cube
4 dashes Angostura bitters
Champagne

Coat sugar cube in bitters and place in a flute.
Top with champagne and twist an orange peel over the
surface and discard. Float brandy on top (optional).

One of the few cocktails to appear in Jerry Thomas' 1862
book *The Bar-Tender's Manual*. This version
has been modernized.

Champs Elysee's Cocktail

1 1/2 ounce (45ml) cognac
3/4 ounce (22ml) yellow Chartreuse
3/4 ounce (22ml) lemon juice
1 teaspoon (5ml) simple syrup
1 dash Angostura bitters

Shake with ice and strain into a cocktail glass.

Adapted from *Café Royal Cocktail Book* by W. J. Tarling (1937)

Chanticleer

1 ounce (30ml) gin
1 1/2 ounce (45ml) dry vermouth
1/2 ounce (15ml) Cointreau
1/2 ounce (15ml) egg white

Shake vigorously with ice and strain into a cocktail glass.

Adapted from *Old Waldorf Astoria Bar Book* by
Albert Stevens Crockett (1934)

Champagne Cocktail

C

Charlie's Own

(Created by Charlie Paul)

1 1/2 ounce (45ml) brandy
1/2 ounce (15ml) yellow Chartreuse
1 teaspoon (5ml) strawberry syrup
1 whole egg
Champagne

Shake vigorously with ice (except champagne) and strain
into an ice-filled Old Fashioned glass. Top with champagne.

Adapted from *American & Other Iced Drinks* by
Charlie Paul (1902)

Chas

(Created by Murray Stenson for the Zig Zag Café, Seattle)

2 1/4 ounces (67ml) bourbon whiskey
1/4 ounce (7ml) amaretto
1/4 ounce (7ml) Bénédictine
1/4 ounce (7ml) Cointreau
1/4 ounce (7ml) orange curaçao

Stir with ice and strain into a cocktail glass.
Garnish with an orange twist.

Adapted from *The Essential Bartender's Guide* by
Robert Hess (2008)

Cherry Blossom

(Created by Jamie Boudreau, Seattle,
www.SpiritsandCocktails.com)

1¼ ounce (37ml) rye
¾ ounce (22ml) kirsch
¼ ounce (7ml) white crème de cacao
1 dash Angostura bitters

Stir with ice and strain into a cocktail glass.
Garnish with two griottine cherries.

Cherry Cobbler

1½ ounce (45ml) gin
½ ounce (15ml) Cherry Heering
½ ounce (15ml) lemon juice
½ teaspoon (2.5ml) simple syrup

Build over crushed ice in an Old Fashioned glass and stir.
Garnish with a cherry and a lemon slice.

Chevalier

1 ounce (30ml) cognac
½ ounce (15ml) Cointreau
1 ounce (30ml) lemon juice
1 dash Angostura bitters

Shake with ice and strain into a cocktail glass.

Chi Chi

2 ounces (60ml) vodka
2 ounces (60ml) pineapple juice
1 ounce (30ml) coconut cream

Blend with crushed ice and pour into a hurricane glass.
Garnish with a cherry and a pineapple spear.

Chicago Cocktail

1 ounce (30ml) brandy
1/4 ounce (7ml) orange curaçao
1 dash Angostura bitters
Champagne

Shake with ice (except champagne) and strain into a
sugar-rimmed cocktail glass. Top with champagne.

Adapted from *The Savoy Cocktail Book* by Harry Craddock (1930)

Chicago Fizz

1 ounce (30ml) Jamaican dark rum
1 ounce (30ml) port
1 ounce (30ml) lemon juice
1/2 ounce (15ml) simple syrup
1/2 ounce (15ml) egg white
Soda water

Shake vigorously with ice (except soda water) and strain
into an ice-filled highball glass. Top with soda water.

Adapted from *Drinks* by Jacques Straub (1914)

Chimayo

1½ ounce (45ml) tequila blanco
¼ ounce (7ml) crème de cassis
1 ounce (30ml) apple juice
¼ ounce (7ml) lemon juice

Shake with ice and strain into
a cocktail glass.
Garnish with an apple slice.

Chinese Lady

(Created by Eddie Clarke)

1½ ounce (45ml) lemon-flavored gin
¾ ounce (22ml) yellow Chartreuse
¾ ounce (22ml) grapefruit juice

Shake with ice and strain into a cocktail glass.

Adapted from *Café Royal Cocktail Book* by W. J. Tarling (1937)

Chiquita

1 ounce (30ml) vodka
½ ounce (15ml) crème de bananes
½ ounce (15ml) lime juice
1 teaspoon (5ml) simple syrup
½ banana

Blend with crushed ice and pour into a hurricane glass.
Garnish with a banana slice.

Cho-Cho

1 1/2 ounce (45ml) brandy
1 ounce (30ml) dry vermouth
1/2 ounce (15ml) orange curaçao
A few drops of absinthe

Stir with ice and strain into a cocktail glass.

Adapted from *Drinks–Long & Short* by
Nina Toye and A. H. Adair (1925)

Chocolate Cocktail

1 1/2 ounce (45ml) port
1/4 ounce (7ml) yellow Chartreuse
1 egg yolk
1 teaspoon (5ml) chocolate powder

Shake with ice and strain into a cocktail glass.
Dust with chocolate powder.

Adapted from *The Savoy Cocktail Book* by Harry Craddock (1930)

Chocolate Flip

3/4 ounce (22ml) brandy
3/4 ounce (22ml) sloe gin
1 teaspoon (5ml) simple syrup
1 whole egg

Shake with ice and strain into a small wine glass.
Dust with nutmeg.

Chocolate Mint Martini

1½ ounce (45ml) vodka
¾ ounce (22ml) white crème de cacao
¾ ounce (22ml) white crème de menthe

Shake with ice and strain into a cocktail glass.
Garnish with a mint sprig.

Chrysanthemum Cocktail

*(Well known and very popular in the American Bar
of the S.S. Europa)*

1½ ounce (45ml) dry vermouth
¾ ounce (22ml) Bénédictine
3 dashes absinthe

Stir with ice and strain into a cocktail glass.
Garnish with an orange twist.

Adapted from *Recipes for Mixed Drinks* by Hugo R. Ensslin (1916)

Cilician Voyage

*(Created by Rick Stutz–www.kaiserpenguin.com
and Marshall Fawley– www.scofflawsden.com, 2008)*

1 ounce (30ml) gin
1 ounce (30ml) Strega
1 ounce (30ml) lime juice
½ ounce (15ml) grapefruit juice
1 dash Fee Brothers Whiskey Barrel Aged Bitters
1 dash Fee Brothers Grapefruit Bitters
Ginger beer

Build over crushed ice in a highball glass and stir before
serving. Garnish with a cinnamon stick, lime twist and
a sprinkle of saffron.

Ciro's Special

(From Ciro's, Hollywood)

1¹/₂ ounce (45ml) dark rum
¹/₂ ounce (15ml) crème de cassis
¹/₂ teaspoon (2.5ml) Grand Marnier
1 ounce (30ml) lime juice

Shake with ice and strain into a cocktail glass.
Garnish with an orange twist.

Adapted from *Bottoms Up* by Ted Saucier (1951)

FEATURED DRINK

Claridge Cocktail

1 ounce (30ml) gin
1 ounce (30ml) dry vermouth
¹/₂ ounce (15ml) apricot brandy
¹/₂ ounce (15ml) triple sec

Stir with ice and strain into a cocktail glass.
Dust with chocolate powder.

Adapted from *ABC of Mixing Cocktails* by Harry McElhone (1922)

Clarito

(Created by "Pichin," Argentina, 1935)

2¹/₄ ounces (67ml) gin
¹/₄ ounce (7ml) dry vermouth

Stir with ice and strain into a cocktail glass.
Garnish with a lemon twist.

Argentina's most famous bartender created this in the
1930s as his version of the Dry Martini.

Adapted from *Tragos Magicos* by Santiago "Pichin"
Policastro (1955)

Cliftonian

(Created by Bert Nutt, London, 1935)

1 ounce (30ml) gin
1 ounce (30ml) Grand Marnier
1/3 ounce (10ml) Swedish Punsch
1/3 ounce (10ml) orange juice

Shake with ice and strain into a cocktail glass.

Adapted from *United Kingdom Bartenders' Guild
Guide To Drinks* (1953)

Clover Club

1 1/2 ounce (45ml) gin
3/4 ounce (22ml) lemon juice
1/2 ounce (15ml) raspberry syrup
1/2 ounce (15ml) egg white

Shake vigorously with ice and strain into a cocktail glass.

You can use grenadine
in place of the raspberry
syrup, if you need to.
You'll still have a light,
fruity drink.

Adapted from
Recipes for Mixed Drinks
by Hugo R. Ensslin (1916)

FEATURED DRINK

Clover Leaf

1 1/2 ounce (45ml) gin
3/4 ounce (22ml) lemon juice
1/2 ounce (15ml) raspberry syrup
4 mint leaves
1/2 ounce (15ml) egg white

Shake vigorously with ice and strain into a cocktail glass.
Garnish with a mint leaf.

Adapted from *Drinks* by Jacques Straub (1914)

Club Cocktail

1 1/2 ounce (45ml) gin
3/4 ounce (22ml) sweet vermouth
1/2 teaspoon (2.5ml) green Chartreuse
2 dashes orange bitters

Stir with ice and strain into a cocktail glass.
Garnish with a cherry.

Go easy on the Chartreuse; otherwise it can easily
overpower the drink.

Adapted from *Hoffman House Bartender's Guide* by
C. S. Mahoney (1905)

Club Rose

1 1/2 ounce (45ml) rye whisky
3/4 ounce (22ml) Calvados
3/4 ounce (22ml) Rose's lime juice
1 dash grenadine
1 dash egg white

Shake vigorously and strain into a cocktail glass.

Adapted from *Shaking in the 60's* by Eddie Clarke (1963)

Coaxer

1 1/2 ounce (45ml) Scotch whisky
3/4 ounce (22ml) lemon juice
2 teaspoons (10ml) simple syrup
1/2 ounce (15ml) egg white

Shake vigorously with ice and strain into a small wine glass.

Adapted from *American & Other Iced Drinks* by
Charlie Paul (1902)

Cobbler

2 1/2 ounces (75ml) liquor of choice
(bourbon, brandy, etc.)
2 teaspoons (10ml) simple syrup

Build over crushed ice in an Old Fashioned glass. Garnish
with two orange slices, one lemon slice and a raspberry.

Adapted from *How To Mix Drinks* by Jerry Thomas (1862)

FEATURED DRINK

Cobina Wright

(Created by Cobina Wright, Society Columnist,
Los Angeles Herald and Express)

2 ounces (60ml) applejack
1 ounce (30ml) lemon juice
1/2 ounce (15ml) honey
3 ounces (90ml) ginger ale

Blend with crushed ice and pour into a highball glass.

Adapted from *Bottoms Up* by Ted Saucier (1951)

Cockpit

(Created by Ferdy Tuohy)

1/2 ounce (15ml) rye
1/2 ounce (15ml) Irish whiskey
1 ounce (30ml) dry vermouth
1 ounce (30ml) sweet vermouth

Stir with ice and strain into a cocktail glass.

Adapted from *Barflies & Cocktails* by Harry McElhone (1927)

Coconut Cannon Ball

2 ounces (60ml) gin or vodka
2 ounces (60ml) coconut milk
1 ounce (30ml) lemon juice
1 teaspoon (5ml) sugar syrup
1 dash orange curaçao

Shake, strain into a cocktail glass. Serve in a glass
half-filled with ice or in a coconut shell.

Coffee Cocktail

2 ounces (60ml) port
1 ounce (30ml) brandy
1 whole egg
1 teaspoon (5ml) simple syrup

Shake vigorously with ice
and strain into a small wine
glass. Dust with nutmeg.

The name comes from the
drink's similar appearance
to coffee and has nothing to
do with the ingredients.

Adapted from *The Bar-Tender's
Guide* by Jerry Thomas (1887)

Coffee Royale

1 1/2 ounce (45ml) brandy
4 ounces (120ml) coffee
3/4 ounce (22ml) simple syrup
Whipped cream

Lightly whip cream to just under stiff. Build in an Irish coffee glass and float cream on top.

Coffey Park Swizzle

(Created by Alexander Day, New York)

1 ounce (30ml) Barbancourt 4 year old rum
1 ounce (30ml) Amontillado sherry
1/4 ounce (7ml) Velvet Falernum
3/4 ounce (22ml) ginger syrup
3/4 ounce (22ml) lime juice

Build over crushed ice in a highball glass and "swizzle" with a barspoon. Add three dashes of Angostura bitters on top of the drink.

Colorado Bulldog

1 ounce (30ml) vodka
1 ounce (30ml) coffee liqueur
3 ounces (90ml) milk
Cola

Shake with ice (except cola) and strain into an ice-filled Old Fashioned glass. Top with a splash of cola and stir.

Comet

(Created by Dorothy Perosino)

1 1/4 ounce (37ml) gin
1 ounce (30ml) Lillet Blanc
1/4 ounce (7ml) triple sec
2 dashes maraschino liqueur

Stir with ice and strain into a cocktail glass.

Adapted from *Café Royal Cocktail Book* by W. J. Tarling (1937)

Comfortable Screw

1 1/2 ounce (45ml) Southern Comfort
Orange juice

Build over ice in a highball glass. Garnish with
an orange slice.

Commodore

(Recipe by Phil Gross, Cincinnati)

2 ounces (60ml) rye
3/4 ounce (22ml) lime juice
1/2 ounce (15ml) simple syrup

Shake with ice and strain into a cocktail glass.

Adapted from *ABC of Mixing Cocktails* by Harry McElhone (1922)

FEATURED DRINK

Commodore Perry

(Created by Don Lee, PDT, New York, 2007)

1 ounce (30ml) cognac
1/2 ounce (15ml) orgeat
1/2 ounce (15ml) pineapple juice
Champagne

Shake with ice (except champagne) and strain into a coupe. Top with champagne.

Compass

1 1/2 ounce (45ml) rye
3/4 ounce (22ml) Bénédictine
3/4 ounce (22ml) sweet vermouth

Stir with ice and strain into a cocktail glass.

Adapted from *My 35 Years Behind Bars* by Johnny Brooks (1954)

Continental Sour

FEATURED DRINK

1 1/2 ounce (45ml) bourbon
1/2 ounce (15ml) Dubonnet rouge
1 ounce (30ml) lemon juice
1/2 ounce (15ml) simple syrup

Shake with ice (except Dubonnet) and strain into a sour glass or an ice-filled Old Fashioned glass. Float Dubonnet on top. Garnish with a lemon slice and a cherry.

Adapted from *My 35 Years Behind Bars* by Johnny Brooks (1954)

Cooperstown

2¹/₂ ounces (75ml) gin
¹/₂ ounce (15ml) dry vermouth
4 mint leaves

Shake with ice and strain into a cocktail glass.
Garnish with a mint leaf.

Adapted from *My 35 Years Behind Bars* by Johnny Brooks (1954)

Copenhagen

See Tom and Jerry

Coronation Cocktail

*(Created by Joseph Rose, Murray Brother's Café,
Newark, New Jersey, 1903)*

1¹/₂ ounce (45ml) sherry
³/₄ ounce (22ml) dry vermouth
¹/₂ teaspoon (2.5ml) maraschino liqueur
2 dashes orange bitters

Stir with ice and strain into a cocktail glass.
Garnish with a lemon twist.

Adapted from *Hoffman House Bartender's Guide*
by C. S. Mahoney (1905)

Corpse Reviver No. 1

1 1/2 ounce (45ml) brandy
3/4 ounce (22ml) applejack
3/4 ounce (22ml) sweet vermouth

Stir with ice and strain into a cocktail glass.

Adapted from *The Savoy Cocktail Book* by Harry Craddock (1930)

Corpse Reviver No. 2

3/4 ounce (22ml) gin
3/4 ounce (22ml) Lillet Blanc
3/4 ounce (22ml) triple sec
3/4 ounce (22ml) lemon juice
1 dash absinthe

Shake with ice and strain into a cocktail glass.

This is probably the finest of the Corpse Reviver
classic recipes.

Adapted from *The Savoy Cocktail Book* by Harry Craddock (1930)

Corpse Reviver No.9

(Created by Jim Meehan, New York)

1 ounce (30ml) aquavit
1 ounce (30ml) Cointreau
1 ounce (30ml) Lillet Blanc
1 ounce (30ml) lime juice
Borsci sambuca

Rinse a coupe with sambuca. Shake remaining
ingredients with ice and strain into the rinsed coupe.

Cosmopolitan

1 1/2 ounce (45ml) citrus vodka
1/2 ounce (15ml) Cointreau
3/4 ounce (22ml) cranberry juice
1/4 ounce (7ml) lime juice
2 dashes orange bitters (optional)

Shake with ice and strain into a cocktail glass.
Garnish with a flamed orange twist.

The Cosmopolitan had its peak of popularity from 1998 to 2004 when it was the drink of choice on the *Sex and the City* television series.

Cosmopolitan Delight

1 1/2 ounce (45ml) brandy
1/2 ounce (15ml) orange curaçao
1/2 ounce (15ml) red wine (claret preferably)
3/4 ounce (22ml) lemon juice
1 teaspoon (5ml) orgeat

Shake with ice (except wine) and strain into an ice-filled Old Fashioned glass. Float wine on top and garnish with a lemon slice, strawberry and cherry.

Adapted from *American & Other Iced Drinks* by Charlie Paul (1902)

Cowboy Martini

(Created by Dick Bradsell, London)

2½ ounces (75ml) gin
½ ounce (15ml) simple syrup
6 mint leaves
2 dashes orange bitters

Shake with ice and strain into a cocktail glass.
Garnish with an orange twist.

Crème de Menthe Frappé

2½ ounces (75ml) green crème de menthe

Pour crème de menthe into a coupe
filled with crushed ice.

Crimson Cocktail

1½ ounce (45ml) sloe gin
¾ ounce (22ml) dry vermouth
2 dashes orange bitters
1 dash Angostura bitters

Shake with ice and strain into a cocktail glass. Garnish
with a tangerine twist and a cherry.

Adapted from *Louis' Mixed Drinks* by Louis Muckensturm (1906)

Crooner

1½ oz (45ml) light rum
¾ oz (22ml) orange juice
¾ oz (22ml) blue curaçao

Shake with ice and strain into
a cocktail glass.

*From 1700 Cocktails For
The Man Behind The Bar
by R. de Fleury (1934)*

Crow's Peck

(Created by Tony Wardle)

1 ounce (30ml) gin
1 ounce (30ml) Swedish Punsch
½ ounce (15ml) Van der Hum
½ ounce (15ml) crème de vanille
3 dashes peach bitters

Shake with ice and strain into a cocktail glass.
Garnish with an orange twist.

Adapted from *Café Royal Cocktail Book* by W. J. Tarling (1937)

Crusta

2 ounces (60ml) spirit (brandy, whiskey or gin)
½ teaspoon (2.5ml) orange curaçao
½ teaspoon (2.5ml) lemon juice
1 teaspoon (5ml) simple syrup

Shake with ice and strain into a small wine glass which has
been rimmed with sugar. Peel half a lemon (all in one
piece) and place inside the rim of the glass.

Crux Cocktail

3/4 ounce (22ml) brandy
3/4 ounce (22ml) triple sec
3/4 ounce (22ml) Dubonnet rouge
3/4 ounce (22ml) lemon juice

Shake with ice and strain into a cocktail glass.

Cuba Libre

1 1/2 ounce (45ml) light rum
3/4 ounce (22ml) lime juice
Cola

Build over ice in a highball glass. Top with cola.
Garnish with a lime wedge.

This delectable drink proves that simplicity works best.

Cuban Cocktail

1 1/2 ounce (45ml) brandy
1/2 ounce (15ml) apricot brandy
1/2 ounce (15ml) lime juice

Shake with ice and strain into
a cocktail glass.

Adapted from
ABC of Mixing Cocktails
by Harry McElhone (1922)

Cuban Manhattan

1 1/2 ounce (45ml) gold rum
3/4 ounce (22ml) sweet vermouth
2 dashes Angostura bitters

Stir with ice and strain into a cocktail glass.
Garnish with a cherry.

Cuban Presidente

See El Presidente

Cuban Special Cocktail

1 1/2 ounce (45ml) light rum
1/2 ounce (15ml) triple sec
3/4 ounce (22ml) lime juice
1/2 ounce (15ml) pineapple juice

Shake with ice and strain into a cocktail glass.
Garnish with a cherry.

Cucumber Martini

1 1/4 ounce (37ml) vodka
1 1/4 ounce (37ml) Żubrówka vodka
2 inch (5cm) slice cucumber, chopped
1 teaspoon (5ml) simple syrup

Muddle cucumber with syrup in base of shaker.
Add remaining ingredients and shake with ice. Strain into
a cocktail glass and garnish with a cucumber slice.

Culross Cocktail

3/4 ounce (22ml) light rum
3/4 ounce (22ml) Lillet Blanc
3/4 ounce (22ml) apricot brandy
3/4 ounce (22ml) lemon juice

Shake with ice and strain into a cocktail glass.

Adapted from *The Savoy Cocktail Book* by Harry Craddock (1930)

Curaçao Punch

1 1/2 ounce (45ml) brandy
3/4 ounce (22ml) Jamaican dark rum
1/2 ounce (15ml) orange curaçao
1 ounce (30ml) lemon juice
1 1/2 ounce (45ml) water

Build over crushed ice in a highball glass. Garnish with
an orange slice, a pineapple spear, a raspberry
and a strawberry.

Adapted from *How To Mix Drinks* by Jerry Thomas (1862)

Czarina

1 1/2 ounce (45ml) vodka
3/4 ounce (22ml) dry vermouth
3/4 ounce (22ml) apricot brandy
1 dash Angostura bitters

Stir with ice and strain into a cocktail glass.

D

Daily Mail

2¹/₂ ounces (75ml) whisky
2 dashes orange curaçao
1 dash amaretto
2 teaspoons (10ml) lemon juice
¹/₂ teaspoon (2.5ml) simple syrup

Shake with ice and strain into an ice-filled Old Fashioned glass. Garnish with a lemon slice.

Daiquiri

2 ounces (60ml) light rum
³/₄ ounce (22ml) lime juice
¹/₂ ounce (15ml) simple syrup

Shake with ice and strain into a coupe. Garnish with a lime slice.

D

Daiquiri (frozen)

2 ounces (60ml) light rum
1/2 ounce (15ml) lime juice
1/4 ounce (7ml) simple syrup

Blend ingredients with crushed ice and pour into a coupe.

Daiquiri De Luxe

2 ounces (60ml) light rum
1 ounce (30ml) citrus juice – 1 part lemon to
3 parts lime
1/2 ounce (15ml) orgeat

Shake with ice and strain into a cocktail glass.

Adapted from *The Fine Art of Mixing Drinks*
by David Embury (1948)

Daisy No. 1

2 ounces (60ml) spirit (brandy, gin, rum or whisky)
1 ounce (30ml) lemon juice
1/4 ounce (7ml) simple syrup
1/4 ounce (7ml) orange curaçao
Soda water

Shake with ice (except soda water) and strain into a high-ball glass filled with crushed ice. Top with soda water.

Adapted from *The Bar-Tender's Guide* by Jerry Thomas (1876)

Daisy No. 2

2 ounces (60ml) spirit (brandy, gin, rum or whiskey)
1 ounce (30ml) lemon juice
1/2 ounce (15ml) grenadine
Soda water

Build over crushed ice in a highball glass. Stir and garnish
with a mint sprig and an orange slice.

FEATURED DRINK

Danish Gin Fizz

2 ounces (60ml) gin
1/2 ounce (15ml) Cherry Heering
1 teaspoon (5ml) kirschwasser
1/2 ounce (15ml) lime juice
1/2 teaspoon (2.5ml) simple syrup
Soda water

Shake everything (except soda water) and strain into a
highball glass full of ice. Top with soda water.

Danish Mary

2 ounces (60ml) aquavit
4 ounces (120ml) tomato juice
1 teaspoon (5ml) lemon juice
1/2 teaspoon (2.5ml) Worcestershire sauce
3 dashes hot sauce
1/2 teaspoon (2.5ml) horseradish (optional)

Softly shake with ice and strain into an ice-filled highball
glass. Add salt and black pepper to taste.
Garnish with a lemon slice and a celery stick.

Danny's Special

(Created by Danny Murphy, Sleepy Hollow Country Club, Tarrytown, NY)

1 ounce (30ml) bourbon
1/2 ounce (15ml) Cointreau
1/4 ounce (7ml) Grand Marnier
1 ounce (30ml) lemon juice

Shake with ice and strain into an ice-filled highball glass.

Adapted from *Esquire Drink Book* edited
by Frederic A. Birmingham (1969)

Darb Cocktail

3/4 ounce (22ml) gin
3/4 ounce (22ml) dry vermouth
3/4 ounce (22ml) apricot brandy
4 dashes lemon juice

Shake with ice and strain into a cocktail glass.

Adapted from *The Savoy Cocktail Book* by Harry Craddock (1930)

Darby Cocktail

1 1/2 ounce (45ml) gin
1/2 ounce (15ml) grapefruit juice
1/2 ounce (15ml) lime juice
1 teaspoon (5ml) simple syrup

Shake with ice and strain into a cocktail glass. Add a
splash of soda water and garnish with a cherry.

Dark 'n Stormy

2 ounces (60ml) Gosling's
Black Seal rum
4 ounces (120ml) ginger beer

Pour into an ice-filled
highball glass.
Garnish with a lime wedge.

For an authentic drink,
be sure to use
Gosling's Black Seal rum.

Dawa

2 ounces (60ml) vodka
1 teaspoon (5ml) honey
1 small lime

Wash the lime, and cut it into quarters. Put limes and
honey into an Old Fashioned glass and muddle. Add the
vodka and stir. Fill with crushed ice and stir.

De Rigueur

1¹/₂ ounce (45ml) whisky
³/₄ ounce (22ml) grapefruit juice
³/₄ ounce (22ml) honey

Shake with ice and strain into a cocktail glass.

Adapted from *The Book of Approved Cocktails*
by the United Kingdom Bartenders' Guild (1936)

Deansgate

1 ounce (30ml) light rum
1/2 ounce (15ml) Drambuie
1/2 ounce (15ml) lime juice

Shake with ice and strain into a cocktail glass.
Garnish with an orange twist.

Death in the Afternoon

(Created by Ernest Hemingway)

1 ounce (30ml) absinthe
Champagne

Build in a flute and stir before serving.

Adapted from *So Red The Nose* by Sterling North
and Carl Kroch (1935)

Deauville Cocktail

3/4 ounce (15ml) brandy
3/4 ounce (15ml) applejack
3/4 ounce (15ml) triple sec
3/4 ounce (15ml) lemon juice

Stir with ice and strain into a cocktail glass.

Deep Sea Cocktail

1¹/₂ ounce (45ml) dry vermouth
1¹/₂ ounce (45ml) Old Tom gin
1 dash absinthe
1 dash orange bitters

Shake with ice and strain into a cocktail glass.
Add an olive and a lemon twist.

Adapted from *The World's Drinks & How To Mix Them*
by William Boothby (1908)

Delicious Sour

1 ounce (30ml) applejack
1 ounce (30ml) peach brandy
³/₄ oz (22ml) lime juice
¹/₂ teaspoon (2.5ml) simple syrup
¹/₂ ounce (15ml) egg white

Shake vigorously with ice and strain into an ice-filled
Old Fashioned glass.

Adapted from *The Flowing Bowl* by William Schmidt (1891)

FEATURED DRINK

Delivery Cocktail

1¹/₂ ounce (45ml) gin
1 ounce (30ml) dry vermouth
1 ounce (30ml) cassis
¹/₂ ounce (15ml) egg white

Shake with ice and strain into a cocktail
glass. Put a dash of orgeat on top.

Adapted from *My 35 Years Behinds Bars*
by Johnny Brooks (1954)

Delmonico

1 ounce (30ml) gin
1/2 ounce (15ml) brandy
1/2 ounce (15ml) dry vermouth
1/2 ounce (15ml) sweet vermouth
1 dash orange bitters

Stir with ice and strain into a cocktail glass.
Garnish with a lemon twist.

Dempsey Cocktail

(Recipe by Fred Martin, Casino, Deauville, 1922)

1 1/2 ounce (45ml) calvados
3/4 ounce (22ml) gin
2 dashes grenadine
1 dash absinthe

Shake with ice and strain into a cocktail glass.

Adapted from *ABC of Mixing Cocktails* by Harry McElhone (1922)

Depth Bomb

1 ounce (30ml) cognac
1 ounce (30ml) calvados
3 dashes lemon juice
3 dashes grenadine

Shake with ice and strain into a cocktail glass.

Adapted from *Livre de Cocktails* by Emile Bauwens (1949)

Derby Cocktail

2 ounces (60ml) bourbon
1/4 ounce (7ml) Bénédictine
1 dash Angostura bitters

Stir with ice and strain into a cocktail glass.
Garnish with a lemon twist.

Derby Fizz

1 1/2 ounce (45ml) blended whiskey
1 teaspoon (5ml) orange curaçao
1/2 ounce (15ml) lemon juice
1 teaspoon (5ml) simple syrup
1 whole egg
Soda water

Shake everything (except soda water) and strain into a
highball glass full of ice. Top with soda water.

Deshler

1 1/2 ounce (45ml) rye
1 ounce (30ml) Dubonnet rouge
1/4 ounce (7ml) Cointreau
2 dashes Peychaud's bitters
1 orange twist (in mixing glass)
1 lemon twist (in mixing glass)

Stir with ice and strain into a cocktail glass.
Garnish with an orange peel.

Detroit Martini

(Created by Dick Bradsell, London)

2 ounces (60ml) vodka
2 teaspoons (10ml) simple syrup
6 mint leaves

Shake with ice and strain into a cocktail glass.
Garnish with a mint leaf.

Dewy D

(Created by Don Lee, PDT, New York, 2008)

2 ounces (60ml) rye
3/4 ounce (22ml) East India sherry
1/2 ounce (15ml) Aperol
2 dashes Angostura bitters

Stir with ice and strain into a cocktail glass.
Garnish with an orange twist.

Diablo

2 ounces (60ml) rum
1/2 ounce (15ml) Cointreau
1/2 ounce (15ml) dry vermouth
2 dashes Angostura bitters

Stir with ice and strain into a cocktail glass.
Garnish with a twist of orange peel.

Diamond Fizz

2 ounces (60ml) gin
1 ounce (30ml) lemon juice
1 teaspoon (5ml) simple syrup

Shake with ice and strain into an ice-filled highball glass.
Top with champagne.

Diamond Mind Fizz

(Created by Keith Waldbauer, Seattle, 2008,
http://movingatthespeedoflife.blogspot.com)

2 ounces (60ml) rhum agricole
1/2 ounce (15ml) pimento dram (allspice dram)
1/2 ounce (15ml) lime juice
Sparkling wine

Shake with ice (except sparkling wine) and strain into a
flute. Top with sparkling wine and garnish with a lime twist.

FEATURED DRINK

Diki-Diki

(Robert Vermeire: "Diki-Diki is the chief
monarch of the Island Ubian [Southern
Philippines], who is now 37 years old,
weighs 23 lb., and his height is 32 in.
The author introduced this cocktail at the
Embassy Club in London, February, 1922.")

1 ounce (30ml) Calvados
1/2 ounce (15ml) Swedish Punsch
1/2 ounce (15ml) grapefruit juice

Shake with ice and strain
into a cocktail glass.

COCKTAILS
HOW TO MIX THEM

Adapted from *Cocktails: How To Mix Them*
by Robert Vermeire (1922)

Ding Ho

(Created by Robert Hess)

2 ounces (60ml) gin
1/2 ounce (15ml) St-Germain elderflower liqueur
1/2 ounce (15ml) orgeat
1/2 ounce (15ml) lime juice

Shake with ice and strain into an ice-filled Old Fashioned
glass. Garnish with a cherry and a lime wedge.
Serve with straws.

Dinosaur

*(Harry McElhone: "Louis Wilson of the Dingo Bar is all for bigger
and better cocktails. Hence he recommends the Dinosaur.")*

2 ounces (60ml) champagne
1 ounce (30ml) gin
1/2 ounce (15ml) brandy
1/2 ounce (15ml) cherry liqueur
1 dash anisette

Shake with ice (except champagne) and strain into a flute.
Add champagne and stir gently.

Adapted from *Barflies & Cocktails* by Harry McElhone (1927)

Diplomat

1 1/2 ounce (45ml) dry vermouth
3/4 ounce (22ml) sweet vermouth
2 dashes maraschino liqueur
2 dashes Angostura bitters

Stir with ice and strain into a small cocktail glass.
Garnish with a cherry and a lemon twist.

Dirty Martini

2¹/₂ ounces (75ml) vodka or gin
1 teaspoon (5ml) dry vermouth
1 teaspoon (5ml) olive brine

Stir with ice and strain into a cocktail glass.
Garnish with an olive.

Dirty Mother

1¹/₂ ounce (45ml) brandy
1¹/₂ ounce (45ml) coffee liqueur
¹/₂ ounce (15ml) milk

Stir with ice and strain into an ice-filled
Old Fashioned glass. Top with milk.

Dizzy Sour

1¹/₂ ounce (45ml) bourbon
¹/₂ ounce (15ml) dark rum
3 dashes Bénédictine
³/₄ ounce (45ml) lemon juice
1 teaspoon (5ml) simple syrup

Shake all of the ingredients (except the rum) with ice and
strain into a sour glass or a cocktail glass. Float the rum on
top. Garnish with a chunk of pineapple.

Doctor Cocktail No. 1

1 ounce (30ml) Swedish Punsch
2 ounces (60ml) lime juice

Shake with ice and strain into a cocktail glass.

Doctor Cocktail No. 2

1 ounce (30ml) Swedish Punsch
1 ounce (30ml) orange juice
1 ounce (30ml) lemon juice

Shake with ice and strain into a cocktail glass.

Adapted from *ABC of Mixing Cocktails* by Harry McElhone (1922)

Dolores

3/4 ounce (45ml) brandy
3/4 ounce (45ml) cherry flavored brandy
3/4 ounce (45ml) white crème de cacao
1/2 ounce (15ml) egg white

Shake with ice and strain into a cocktail glass.

DOM Cocktail

2 ounces (60ml) gin
1/2 ounce (15ml) Bénédictine
1 ounce (30ml) orange juice

Shake with ice and strain into a cocktail glass.

Don Raphael

*(Created by Mario Kappes, Le Lion • Bar de Paris,
Hamburg, Germany)*

**2 ounces (60ml) Spanish brandy
1 ounce (30ml) Pedro Ximenez sherry**

Stir with ice and strain into a cocktail glass.
Garnish with an orange twist.

Don't Give Up the Ship

**1 1/2 ounce (45ml) gin
1/2 ounce (15ml) Dubonnet rouge
1/4 ounce (7ml) Fernet Branca
1/4 ounce (7ml) orange curaçao**

Stir with ice and strain into a small
cocktail glass.

FEATURED DRINK

Dorchester Cocktail

(Created by "Ernest" of the Dorchester Hotel, London)

**1 1/2 ounce (45ml) gin
1/2 ounce (15ml) Lillet Blanc
1/4 ounce (7ml) Dubonnet rouge
1/2 teaspoon (2.5ml) orange curaçao**

Stir with ice and strain into a cocktail glass.
Garnish with an orange twist.

Adapted from *An Anthology of Cocktails* by Booth's Gin (1930s)

Double-Barrel Cocktail

1/2 ounce (15ml) whiskey
1/2 ounce (15ml) dry vermouth
1/2 ounce (15ml) sweet vermouth
2 dashes Angostura bitters
2 dashes orange bitters

Stir with ice and strain into a small cocktail glass.

Adapted from *Modern American Drinks*
by George J. Kappeler (1895)

Douglas Fairbanks

2 ounces (60ml) gin
1 ounce (30ml) apricot brandy
3/4 ounce (22ml) lime juice
1/2 ounce (15ml) egg white

Shake with ice and strain into a flute.

Adapted from *Sloppy Joe's Cocktails Manual: Season 1934*
by Jose Abeal and Valentin Garcia (1934)

Dr. Fink

2 ounces (60ml) gin
1 1/2 ounce (45ml) Pernod or Herbsaint
1 teaspoon (5ml) lemon juice
1 teaspoon (5ml) simple syrup
Soda water

Shake with ice (except soda water) and strain into an ice-filled highball glass. Top with soda water and garnish with a lemon slice.

Adapted from *Bartender's Guide* by Trader Vic (1947)

Dr. Funk

1 1/2 ounce (45ml) light rum
1/4 ounce (7ml) dark rum
1 teaspoon (5ml) absinthe
3/4 ounce (22ml) lime juice
1/2 ounce (15ml) grenadine
Soda water

Shake with ice (except soda water and dark rum) and strain into an ice-filled highball glass. Top with soda water and float dark rum on top. Garnish with a lime wedge.

FEATURED DRINK

Dream Cocktail

(Contributed by Bruce Reynolds)

2 ounces (60ml) brandy
1 ounce (30ml) orange curaçao
1 dash absinthe

Stir with ice and drain into a cocktail glass.

Adapted from *Barflies & Cocktails* by Harry McElhone (1927)

Dreaming Eyes

1½ ounce (45ml) gin
¾ ounce (22ml) crème de violette
½ ounce (15ml) lemon juice
1 teaspoon (5ml) simple syrup
½ ounce (15ml) egg white

Shake vigorously with ice and strain into a cocktail glass.

Adapted from *My 35 Years Behind Bars* by Johnny Brooks (1954)

Dry Manhattan

2 ounces (60ml) rye
1 ounce (30ml) dry vermouth
2 dashes Angostura bitters

Stir with ice and strain into a cocktail glass. Garnish
with a lemon twist.

Dry Martini

2½ ounces (75ml) gin
½ ounce (15ml) dry vermouth
2 dashes orange bitters (optional but recommended)

Stir with ice and strain into a cocktail glass. Garnish with a
lemon twist or an olive.

Don't be afraid to add orange bitters to this drink for
an interesting variation.

Adapted from *How to Mix Fancy Drinks*
by Joseph R. Peebles Sons Co. (1903)

Dry Whistle

(Courtesy of Lindy's, New York)

1¹/₂ ounce (45ml) light rum
¹/₂ ounce (15ml) Cointreau
¹/₂ ounce (15ml) lime juice

Shake with ice and strain into a cocktail glass or coupe.
Garnish with a lime wedge.

Adapted from *Bottoms Up* by Ted Saucier (1951)

Dubonnet Cocktail

1¹/₂ ounce (45ml) gin
1¹/₂ ounce (45ml) Dubonnet rouge
1 dash orange bitters

Stir with ice and strain into a cocktail glass.

Duchess

¹/₂ ounce (15ml) absinthe
¹/₂ ounce (15ml) dry vermouth
¹/₂ ounce (15ml) sweet vermouth

Stir with ice and strain into a small cocktail glass.

Adapted from *Drinks* by Jacques Straub (1914)

Duck and Dodge

(Created by Gilbert White)

³/₄ ounce (22ml) cognac
³/₄ ounce (22ml) dry vermouth
³/₄ ounce (22ml) mandarin juice or orange juice

Shake with ice and strain into a cocktail glass.

Adapted from *Barflies & Cocktails* by Harry McElhone (1927)

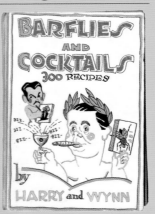

BARFLIES AND COCKTAILS 300 RECIPES

by HARRY and WYNN

Duck Under

1¹/₂ ounce (45ml) gin
1¹/₂ ounce (45ml) Cointreau
2 dashes grapefruit juice

Stir with ice and strain into a cocktail glass.

Duke

¹/₂ ounce (15ml) Cointreau
¹/₂ teaspoon (2.5ml) maraschino liqueur
2 teaspoons (10ml) lemon juice
1 teaspoon (5ml) orange juice
¹/₂ ounce (15ml) lightly beaten egg
1 dash of Angostura bitters
Champagne

Shake with ice (except champagne) and strain into a flute.
Fill with champagne.

Dunhill's Special Cocktail

1 ounce (30ml) gin
1 ounce (30ml) sherry
1 ounce (30ml) dry vermouth
¹/₄ ounce (7ml) orange curaçao
1 dash Pernod

Stir with ice and strain into a cocktail glass.
Garnish with an olive.

Adapted from *Jones' Complete Barguide* by Stan Jones (1977)

Duplex

**1½ ounce (45ml) sweet vermouth
1½ ounce (45ml) dry vermouth
2 dashes orange bitters**

Shake with ice and strain into a small cocktail glass.

Adapted from *Drinks*
by Jacques Straub (1914)

Durkee

**1½ ounce (45ml) Jamaican dark rum
¾ ounce (22ml) orange curaçao
½ lemon
1 teaspoon (5ml) sugar**

Cut half a lemon into quarters and place in a mixing glass. Add the sugar and muddle well. Fill the glass ⅔ full with crushed ice. Add the rum and orange curaçao and stir. Pour into a highball glass, top with soda water and stir again gently.

Dusty Martini

**2¼ ounces (67ml) gin
¼ ounce (7ml) Scotch whisky**

Stir with ice and strain into a cocktail glass. Garnish with an olive.

Eagle Fizz

1½ ounce (45ml) gin
½ teaspoon (2.5ml) crème de vanille
2 ounces (60ml) milk
1 ounce (30ml) lemon juice
¾ ounce (22ml) simple syrup
½ ounce (15ml) egg white
3 dashes orange flower water
Soda water

Shake vigorously with ice (except soda water) and strain
into an ice-filled highball glass. Top with soda water.

This is similar to a Ramos Gin Fizz but with a hint of vanilla.

Adapted from *Hoffman House Bartender's Guide*
by C. S. Mahoney (1905)

Eagle's Dream

1½ ounce (45ml) gin
½ ounce (15ml) crème de violette
¾ ounce (22ml) lemon juice
½ ounce (15ml) egg white
1 teaspoon (5ml) simple syrup

Shake vigorously with ice and strain into a cocktail glass.
Garnish with a cherry.

Adapted from *ABC of Mixing Cocktails* by Harry McElhone (1922)

Earl Grey Fizz

(Created by Henry Besant, London)

1/2 ounce (15ml) Żubrówka vodka
1/2 ounce (15ml) strong cold Earl Grey tea
1 teaspoon (5ml) simple syrup
Champagne

Build in a flute. Garnish with a string of red currants.

Earl Grey Mar-Tea-Ni

(Created by Audrey Saunders, New York)

1 1/2 ounce (45ml) gin
1 ounce (30ml) strong cold Earl Grey tea
3/4 ounce (22ml) lemon juice
1/2 ounce (15ml) simple syrup
1/2 ounce (15ml) egg white

Shake vigorously with ice and strain into a cocktail glass.
Garnish with a lemon twist.

Eastern Smash

(Created by Tomek Roehr, Alkoteka, Poland)

2 ounces (60ml) Żołądkowa Gorzka vodka
1 ounce (30ml) lemon juice
1/2 ounce (15ml) simple syrup
6 mint leaves

Shake with ice and strain into an ice-filled Old Fashioned
glass. Garnish with a mint sprig.

East India Cocktail

2¹/₂ ounces (75ml) brandy
1 teaspoon (5ml) orange curaçao
1 teaspoon (5ml) pineapple juice
2 dashes Angostura bitters
2 dashes maraschino liqueur

Stir with ice and strain into a cocktail glass.
Garnish with a lemon twist.

Adapted from *Bartender's Manual* by Harry Johnson (1888)

Eddie Brown

1³/₄ ounce (50ml) gin
³/₄ ounce (22ml) Lillet Blanc
1 teaspoon (5ml) apricot brandy

Shake with ice and strain into a cocktail glass.

Adapted from *The Savoy Cocktail Book* by Harry Craddock (1930)

Egg Sour

1¹/₂ ounce (45ml) brandy
¹/₄ ounce (7ml) orange curaçao
1 ounce (30ml) lemon juice
¹/₂ ounce (15ml) simple syrup
1 egg yolk

Shake vigorously with ice and strain into a
small wine glass.

Adapted from *Bartender's Manual* by Harry Johnson (1900)

Eggnog

1 ounce (30ml) brandy
1/2 ounce (15ml) dark rum
1 1/2 ounce (45ml) milk
1 whole egg
1 teaspoon (5ml) simple syrup

Shake with ice and strain into an ice-filled (optional)
highball glass. Dust with nutmeg.

This is the classic drink to serve during any festive period.

Eight Bells

(Created by Eddie Clarke, London, 1947)

1 1/2 ounce (45ml)
Jamaican dark rum
1/2 ounce (15ml)
Van der Hum
1/2 ounce (15ml) dry
vermouth
1/4 ounce (7ml) lemon juice
1/4 ounce (7ml) orange juice
1 dash Angostura bitters

Shake with ice and strain
into a cocktail glass.
Dust with nutmeg.

Adapted from *Shaking In The 60's* by Eddie Clarke (1963)

El Burro

(Created by Jim Meehan, New York)

1 1/2 ounce (45ml) reposado tequila
1/4 ounce (7ml) absinthe
3/4 ounce (22ml) lime juice
3/4 ounce (22ml) pineapple juice
1/2 ounce (15ml) simple syrup
1 ounce (30ml) ginger beer

Shake with ice (except ginger beer) and strain into an
ice-filled highball glass. Top with ginger beer. Garnish with
a piece of candied ginger speared to a lime wheel.

El Diablo

1 1/2 ounce (45ml) tequila blanco
1/2 ounce (15ml) crème de cassis
1/2 ounce (15ml) lime juice
Ginger ale

Build over ice in a highball glass.
Garnish with a lime wedge.

Adapted from *Trader Vic's Book Of Food & Drink*
by Trader Vic (1946)

El Floridita No. 1

1 1/2 ounce (45ml) light rum
1 teaspoon (5ml) maraschino liqueur
1/2 ounce (15ml) grapefruit juice

Shake (or blend) with ice and strain into a cocktail glass.

Pink grapefruit juice works well in this Cuban drink.

El Floridita No. 2

1 1/2 ounce (45ml) light rum
1/2 ounce (15ml) sweet vermouth
1/2 teaspoon (2.5ml) white crème de cacao
1 teaspoon (5ml) grenadine
1/2 ounce (15ml) lime juice

Shake with ice and strain into a cocktail glass.

Adapted from *The Joy Of Mixology* by Gary Regan (2003)

El Floradita No. 2

El Presidente

1½ ounce (45ml) gold rum
¾ ounce (22ml) orange curaçao
¾ ounce (22ml) dry vermouth
1 dash grenadine

Shake with ice and strain into a cocktail glass. Garnish
with a cherry and an orange twist.

Adapted from *Bar La Florida Cocktails* (Havana, Cuba, 1935)

El Puente
(Created by Jim Meehan, New York)

2 ounces (60ml) mezcal
½ ounce (15ml) St-Germain elderflower liqueur
½ ounce (15ml) lime juice
½ ounce (15ml) grapefruit juice
1 teaspoon (5ml) agave syrup
3 cucumber slices

Muddle the cucumber with agave and lime juice in a
shaker. Add remaining ingredients and shake with ice.
Strain into a coupe and garnish with a grapefruit twist.

Elderflower & Bisongrass Cobbler
(Created by George Sinclair, London, 2008)

1¼ ounce Żubrówka vodka
½ ounce (15ml) St-Germain elderflower liqueur
2 teaspoons (10ml) simple syrup
2 lemon twists

Muddle lemon twists with syrup in the bottom of an Old
Fashioned glass. Add crushed ice, liquor and stir. Top with
crushed ice and garnish with a lemon twist.

Elderflower Fizz

3/4 ounce (22ml) elderflower cordial
2 teaspoons (10ml) simple syrup
Champagne

Build in a flute. Garnish with a lemon twist.

Elderflower Martini

(Created by Henry Besant, London)

1 1/2 ounce Żubrówka vodka
3/4 ounce (22ml) apple juice
1/2 ounce (15ml) elderflower cordial

Stir with ice and strain into a cocktail glass.
Garnish with a lemon twist.

Elderthorn

(Created by Robert Hess, 2007)

1 ounce (30ml) cognac or brandy
1/2 ounce (15ml) St-Germain elderflower liqueur
1/2 ounce (15ml) Cynar

Stir with ice and strain into a small cocktail glass.

FEATURED DRINK

E

Electric Iced Tea

$1/2$ ounce (15ml) vodka
$1/2$ ounce (15ml) gin
$1/2$ ounce (15ml) triple sec
$1/2$ ounce (15ml) bourbon
$3/4$ ounce (22ml) lemon juice
$1/2$ ounce (15ml) simple syrup
Cola

Shake with ice (except cola) and strain into an ice-filled highball glass. Top with cola and garnish with a lemon slice.

Elegante

(Created by Tony Conigliaro, London,
http://drinkfactory.blogspot.com/)

1 ounce (30ml) vodka
1 ounce (30ml) prosecco
1 ounce (30ml) lemon juice
2 teaspoons (10ml) simple syrup
1 scoop lemon sorbet

Blend with crushed ice and pour into a highball glass. Garnish with lemon strings.

Elephants Sometimes Forget

1 ounce (30ml) gin
$3/4$ ounce (22ml) cherry brandy
$1/4$ ounce (7ml) dry vermouth
$3/4$ ounce (22ml) lemon juice
1 dash orange bitters

Shake with ice and strain into a cocktail glass.

Elk's Fizz

(Created by Peter F. Sindar, St. Paul, Minnesota, 1901)

1½ ounce (45ml) rye
½ ounce (15ml) port
1 ounce (30ml) lemon juice
¾ ounce (22ml) simple syrup
½ ounce (15ml) egg white
Soda water

Shake vigorously with ice (except soda water) and strain into an ice-filled highball glass. Top with soda water and garnish with a pineapple spear.

Adapted from *Hoffman House Bartender's Guide* by C. S. Mahoney (1905)

Elk's Own

1 ounce (30ml) Canadian Club
1 ounce (30ml) port
½ ounce (15ml) lemon juice
2 teaspoons (10ml) simple syrup
½ ounce (15ml) egg white

Shake vigorously with ice and strain into a cocktail glass.

Adapted from *ABC of Mixing Cocktails* by Harry McElhone (1922)

Embassy Jubilee

1½ ounce (45ml) gin
1½ ounce (45ml) Lillet Blanc
2 dashes Bénédictine
2 dashes orange flower water

Shake with ice and strain into a cocktail glass.

Emerald

1 1/2 ounce (45ml) Irish whiskey
3/4 ounce (22ml) sweet vermouth
2 dashes orange bitters

Stir with ice and strain into a cocktail glass.
Garnish with an orange twist.

Emerson

1 ounce (30ml) gin
3/4 ounce (22ml) sweet vermouth
1/4 ounce (7ml) maraschino liqueur
1/2 ounce (15ml) lime juice

Shake with ice and strain into a cocktail glass.

Empire Glory

(Created by W. J. Tarling)

1 1/2 ounce (45ml) Canadian Club
3/4 ounce (22ml) Stone's Original Green Ginger Wine
3/4 ounce (22ml) lemon juice
2 teaspoons (10ml) grenadine

Shake with ice and strain into a cocktail glass.

Adapted from *Café Royal Cocktail Book* by W. J. Tarling (1937)

Empire Punch

¼ ounce (7ml) brandy
¼ ounce (7ml) Bénédictine
¼ ounce (7ml) orange curaçao
3 ounces (90ml) red wine
Champagne

Build over ice in a highball glass. Garnish with a lemon
slice, a raspberry and a strawberry.

Endeavour

(Created by C.F. Chisnall)

1 ounce (30ml) bourbon
1 ounce (30ml) green Chartreuse
1 ounce (30ml) Lillet Blanc
1 dash Angostura bitters

Shake with ice and strain into a cocktail glass.
Garnish with an orange twist.

Adapted from *The Book of Approved Cocktails*
by the United Kingdom Bartenders' Guild (1934)

English Cobbler

2 ounces (60ml) Jamaican dark rum
1 ounce (30ml) strong cold tea
½ ounce (15ml) lemon juice
2 teaspoons (10ml) simple syrup

Build over crushed ice in a highball glass. Garnish with
a lemon slice, a raspberry and a strawberry.

Adapted from *The Fine Art Of Mixing Drinks*
by David Embury (1948)

FEATURED DRINK

English Rose Cocktail

1 1/2 ounce (45ml) gin
1/2 ounce (15ml) dry vermouth
1/2 ounce (15ml) apricot juice or nectar
1/4 ounce (7ml) lemon juice
1 teaspoon (5ml) grenadine

Shake with ice and strain into a sugar-rimmed cocktail glass.

Adapted from *Old Mr. Boston Official Bartender's Guide* by Leo Cotton (1935)

Espresso Martini

(Created by Dick Bradsell, London, 1984)

1 1/2 ounce (45ml) vodka
3/4 ounce (22ml) coffee liqueur
1 ounce (30ml) fresh espresso
1 dash simple syrup

FEATURED DRINK

Shake with ice and strain into a cocktail glass. Garnish with three coffee beans.

This is a delicious pick-me-up drink whenever you need a caffeine boost.

Esquire Martini

(Created by Dick Bradsell, London)

1¼ ounce (37ml) vodka
1¼ ounce (37ml) raspberry vodka
½ ounce (15ml) parfait amour

Stir with ice and strain into a cocktail glass.
Garnish with a blackberry.

Eureka

1½ ounce (45ml) calvados
1 ounce (30ml) sloe gin
1 teaspoon (5ml) sherry
¾ ounce (22ml) lemon juice

Shake with ice and strain into a cocktail glass.

Adapted from *Bar La Florida Cocktails* (Havana, Cuba, 1935)

European Union

(Created by Alexander Day, New York)

1½ ounce (45ml) Old Tom gin
1 ounce (30ml) sweet vermouth
½ ounce (15ml) Calvados
1 teaspoon (5ml) Strega
2 dashes The Bitter Truth Jerry Thomas' Own
Decanter Bitters

Stir with ice and strain into a cocktail glass.

Everything But

1/2 ounce (15ml) gin
1/2 ounce (15ml) bourbon
1 teaspoon (5ml) apricot brandy
1/2 ounce (15ml orange juice
1/2 ounce (15ml) lemon juice
1 whole egg
2 teaspoons (10ml) simple syrup

Shake vigorously with ice and strain into a cocktail glass.

Adapted from *The Savoy Cocktail Book* by Harry Craddock (1930)

Express Cocktail

1 1/4 ounce (37ml) Scotch whisky
1 1/4 ounce (37ml) sweet vermouth
2 dashes orange bitters

Stir with ice and strain into a cocktail glass.

Eye Opener

1 1/2 ounce (45ml) light rum
1/4 ounce (7ml) absinthe
1/4 ounce (7ml) crème de noyaux
1/4 ounce (7ml) orange curaçao
1 teaspoon (5ml) simple syrup
1 egg yolk

Shake vigorously with ice and strain into a cocktail glass.

Adapted from *The Savoy Cocktail Book* by Harry Craddock (1930)

Fairbank Cocktail

*(Likely named for Senator Charles Fairbanks,
Theodore Roosevelt's vice-president. If so, the missing 's' in
the name of the cocktail is a mystery.)*

**1¹/₂ ounce (45ml) gin
¹/₂ ounce (15ml) dry vermouth
2 teaspoons (10ml) crème de noyaux
2 dashes orange bitters**

Stir with ice and strain into a cocktail glass.
Garnish with an orange twist.

Adapted from *Cocktails: How To Mix Them*
by Robert Vermeire (1922)

Fairmont

(Created at Fairmont Hotel, San Francisco)

**1¹/₂ ounce (45ml) light rum
³/₄ ounce (22ml) Grand Marnier
³/₄ ounce (22ml) lime juice**

Shake with ice and strain into a cocktail glass.
Garnish with a lemon twist.

Adapted from *Bottoms Up* by Ted Saucier (1951)

Fairy Belle

1 1/2 ounce (45ml) gin
3/4 ounce (22ml) apricot brandy
1 teaspoon (5ml) grenadine
1/2 ounce (15ml) egg white

Shake vigorously with ice and strain into a cocktail glass.

Fallen Angel

1 1/2 ounce (45ml) gin
1 teaspoon (5ml) green crème de menthe
3/4 ounce (22ml) lemon juice
1 dash Angostura bitters

Shake with ice and strain into a cocktail glass.

Adapted from *The Savoy Cocktail Book* by Harry Craddock (1930)

Fancy Cocktail

2 ounces (60ml) liquor (brandy, gin, etc.)
1/2 ounce (15ml) orange curaçao
2 dashes Angostura bitters
1/2 teaspoon (2.5ml) simple syrup

Shake with ice and strain into a cocktail glass.
Garnish with a lemon twist.

Fancy Cocktail

Fifth Avenue

1/3 ounce (10ml) white crème de cacao
1/3 ounce (10ml) apricot brandy
1/3 ounce (10ml) cream

Layer in a shot glass in the order above.

Adapted from *The Savoy Cocktail Book* by Harry Craddock (1930)

Fifty Fifty

1 1/4 ounce (37ml) gin
1 1/4 ounce (37ml) dry vermouth

Stir with ice and strain into a cocktail glass.
Garnish with a lemon twist.

This is a simple martini which really highlights the
quality of the vermouth used.

Adapted from *The Savoy Cocktail Book* by Harry Craddock (1930)

Fin de Siècle Cocktail

1 1/2 ounce (45ml) Plymouth Gin
1 ounce (30ml) sweet vermouth
1 teaspoon (5ml) Amer Picon
1 dash orange bitters

Stir with ice and strain into a cocktail glass.

Adapted from *The How & When* by Hyman Gale
and Gerald F. Marco (1937)

First One

1 1/2 ounce (45ml) gin
1/2 ounce (15ml) white crème de menthe
3/4 ounce (22ml) lemon juice
1 teaspoon (5ml) simple syrup
1 dash orange bitters

Shake with ice and strain into a cocktail glass.
Garnish with a lemon twist.

Adapted from *The Flowing Bowl* by William Schmidt (1891)

Fish House Punch

1 1/2 ounce (45ml) Jamaican dark rum
3/4 ounce (22ml) cognac
1 teaspoon (5ml) peach brandy
1 ounce (30ml) lemon juice
1 teaspoon (5ml) simple syrup
Soda water

Build over ice in a highball glass.

FEATURED DRINK

Fisherman's Prayer

1 1/2 ounce (45ml) gold rum
1/2 ounce (15ml) raspberry syrup
3/4 ounce (22ml) lemon juice

Shake with ice and strain into an ice-filled Old Fashioned
glass. Garnish with a lemon slice and raspberries.

Adapted from *American & Other Iced Drinks*
by Charlie Paul (1902)

Fitz-G-Honeymooner

(Created by Ed and Pegeen Fitzgerald, TV & radio personalities)

1 1/2 ounce (45ml) light rum
1/2 ounce (15ml) orange curaçao
3/4 ounce (22ml) lemon juice
1 teaspoon (5ml) honey

Shake with ice and strain into a cocktail glass.
Garnish with a lemon twist.

Adapted from *Bottoms Up* by Ted Saucier (1951)

Fix

2 ounces (60ml) liquor of choice
(bourbon, brandy, etc.)
1 ounce (30ml) lemon juice
3/4 ounce (22ml) simple syrup

Shake with ice and strain into a crushed ice-filled
Old Fashioned glass. Garnish with a lemon slice,
a raspberry and a strawberry.

Fizz

1 1/2 ounce (45ml) liquor of choice
(bourbon, brandy, etc.)
1 ounce (30ml) lemon juice
3/4 ounce (22ml) simple syrup
Soda water

Shake with ice (except soda water) and strain into an
ice-filled highball glass. Top with soda water and
garnish with a lemon slice.

Flamingo

1 1/2 ounce (45ml) light rum
3/4 ounce (22ml) pineapple juice
3/4 ounce (22ml) lime juice
1 dash grenadine

Blend with crushed ice and pour into a coupe.

Adapted from *Bottoms Up* by Ted Saucier (1951)

Flash of Lightning

1 1/2 ounce (45ml) brandy
1/2 ounce (15ml) raspberry syrup
3/4 ounce (22ml) lemon juice
Pinch cayenne pepper

Shake with ice and strain into an ice-filled Old Fashioned
glass. Garnish with a lemon slice and raspberries.

Adapted from *American & Other Iced Drinks*
by Charlie Paul (1902)

Flatliner

1/2 ounce (15ml) tequila blanco
1/2 ounce (15ml) sambuca
4 dashes Tabasco

Pour sambuca into a shot glass and layer tequila on top.
Dash Tabasco over the surface and it will settle
in the middle.

Flip

1¹/2 ounce (45ml) liquor
(rum, whiskey, brandy, sherry, port etc.)
1 whole egg
1 teaspoon (5ml) simple syrup

Shake vigorously with ice and strain into a small wine glass. Dust with nutmeg.

Flirtini

¹/2 ounce (15ml) vodka
¹/2 ounce (15ml) Cointreau
³/4 ounce (22ml) pineapple juice
Champagne

Shake with ice (except champagne) and strain into a cocktail glass. Top with champagne and garnish with a cherry.

FEATURED DRINK

Floradora Cooler

1¹/2 ounce (45ml) gin
¹/2 ounce (15ml) raspberry syrup
³/4 ounce (22ml) lime juice
Ginger ale

Build over ice in a highball glass. Stir well and garnish with a lime wedge.

Adapted from *Drinks* by Jacques Straub (1914)

Flying Grasshopper

3/4 ounce (22ml) vodka
3/4 ounce (22ml) white crème de cacao
3/4 ounce (22ml) green crème de menthe
3/4 ounce (22ml) cream

Shake with ice and strain into a cocktail glass.

Fog Cutter

1 1/2 ounce (45ml) light rum
1 ounce (30ml) brandy
1/2 ounce (15ml) gin
1/4 ounce (7ml) sherry
2 ounces (60ml) orange juice
1 ounce (30ml) lemon juice
1/2 ounce (15ml) orgeat

Shake with ice (except sherry) and strain into an ice-filled hurricane glass. Float sherry on top.

Football Hero

1 1/2 ounce (45ml) gin
3/4 ounce (22ml) dry vermouth
3/4 ounce (22ml) sweet vermouth
1 dash Bénédictine

Shake with ice and strain into a cocktail glass.

Adapted from *What'll You Have?* by Julien J. Proskauer (1933)

Ford Cocktail

1 1/4 ounce (37ml) gin
1 1/4 ounce (37ml) sweet vermouth
1 teaspoon (5ml) Bénédictine
3 dashes orange bitters

Stir with ice and strain into a cocktail glass.
Garnish with an orange twist.

Adapted from *Modern American Drinks*
by George Kappeler (1895)

Forty Eight

(Created by Bert Nutt, 1948)

1 1/2 ounce (45ml) gin
1/2 ounce (15ml) dry vermouth
1/2 ounce (15ml) apricot brandy
1/2 ounce (15ml) orange curaçao
1 ounce (30ml) lemon juice

Shake with ice and strain into a cocktail glass.

Adapted from *United Kingdom Bartenders' Guild
Guide To Drinks* (1953)

Fourth Degree

³/4 ounce (22ml) gin
³/4 ounce (22ml) dry vermouth
³/4 ounce (22ml) sweet vermouth
¹/4 ounce (7ml) absinthe

Stir with ice and strain into a cocktail glass.
Garnish with a lemon twist.

Adapted from *ABC of Mixing Cocktails* by Harry McElhone (1922)

Fourth Estate

³/4 ounce (22ml) gin
³/4 ounce (22ml) dry vermouth
³/4 ounce (22ml) sweet vermouth
3 dashes absinthe

Stir with ice and strain into a cocktail glass.

Adapted from *The Bartender's Book* by Jack Townsend
and Tom Moore McBride (1951)

Fox Shot

1¹/2 ounce (45ml) gin
³/4 ounce (22ml) brandy
³/4 ounce (22ml) sweet vermouth
3 dashes Angostura bitters

Stir with ice and strain into a cocktail glass.

Adapted from *Drinks* by Jacques Straub (1914)

Fox Trot

1 1/2 ounce (45ml) light rum
1/2 ounce (15ml) orange curaçao
1/2 ounce (15ml) lemon juice

Shake with ice and strain into a cocktail glass.

Frank Sullivan

3/4 ounce (22ml) brandy
3/4 ounce (22ml) Cointreau
3/4 ounce (22ml) Lillet Blanc
3/4 ounce (22ml) lemon juice

Shake with ice and strain into a cocktail glass.

Fräulein Frankfurt

(Awarded Diploma, International Competition, Germany, 1937)

1 ounce (30ml) gin
1/3 ounce (10ml) cherry brandy
1/3 ounce (10ml) crème de noyaux
1/3 ounce (10ml) lemon juice

Shake with ice and strain into a cocktail glass.

Adapted from *Shaking in the 60's* by Eddie Clarke (1963)

Freddy Fudpucker

1 1/2 ounce (45ml) tequila blanco
1/2 ounce (15ml) Galliano
Orange juice

Build over ice (except Galliano) in a highball glass.
Float Galliano on top.

French 75

1 ounce (30ml) gin
1/2 ounce (15ml) lemon juice
1 teaspoon (5ml) simple syrup
Champagne

Shake with ice
(except champagne) and
strain into a flute. Top with
champagne and garnish
with a cherry.

For an interesting variation,
try substituting
cognac for gin.

French Maid

(Created by Jim Meehan, New York)

1 1/2 ounce (45ml) cognac
1/4 ounce (7ml) falernum
3/4 ounce (22ml) lime juice
3/4 ounce (22ml) simple syrup
8 mint leaves
3 cucumber slices
Ginger beer

Muddle the cucumber with mint and simple syrup in a
shaker. Add remaining ingredients (except ginger beer)
and shake with ice. Strain into an ice-filled highball glass
and top with ginger beer. Garnish with a mint sprig
and a cucumber wheel.

French Martini

1 1/2 ounce (45ml) vodka
1/2 ounce (15ml) Chambord
1 ounce (30ml) pineapple juice

Shake with ice and strain into a cocktail glass.

French Quarter

(Created by Robert Hess, 2004: "Using the Bordeaux cocktail as inspiration, I created this drink specifically to pair with the Trout Almandine served at Antoine's Restaurant in New Orleans.")

2 1/2 ounces (75ml) brandy
3/4 ounce (22ml) Lillet Blanc

Stir with ice and strain into a cocktail glass.
Garnish with a thin quarter wheel of lemon.

Adapted from *The Essential Bartender's Guide* by Robert Hess (2008)

French Quarter Punch

(Created by Charles Joly, Chief Mixologist, The Drawing Room, Chicago, 2008)

FEATURED DRINK

1 ounce (30ml) golden rum
1/2 ounce (15ml) cognac
1/2 ounce (15ml) falernum
3/4 ounce (22ml) lime juice
1/4 ounce (7ml) agave syrup
1 dash peach bitters
1 dash orange bitters

Shake with ice (except bitters) and strain into a Collins glass filled with crushed ice. Dust with grated nutmeg and add bitters to the top of the drink. Garnish with three lime wheels on the rim of the glass.

French's Fillup

(Created by Windsor French, columnist, Cleveland Press)

1/2 ounce (15ml) Grand Marnier
1/4 ounce (7ml) cognac
1/4 ounce (7ml) crème de vanille
1 egg yolk
Champagne

Shake with ice (except champagne) and strain into a coupe. Top with champagne.

Adapted from *Bottoms Up* by Ted Saucier (1951)

Fresh Bloody Mary

(Created by Adam Elmegirab, Evo-lution, Aberdeen, Scotland, 2008)

1 1/2 ounce (45ml) citrus vodka
2 teaspoons (10ml) lemon juice
1 teaspoon (5ml) simple syrup
6 cherry tomatoes
6 basil leaves
1 teaspoon diced, deseeded red chili
Pinch of salt
Pinch of ground black pepper

Muddle tomatoes in base of shaker, add remaining ingredients, ice and shake. Double strain into a cocktail glass and garnish with a cherry tomato on the rim of the glass.

FEATURED DRINK

Frisco

1 1/2 ounce (45ml) gin
1 ounce (30ml) grapefruit juice
4 mint leaves

Shake with ice and strain into a cocktail glass.
Garnish with a mint leaf.

Adapted from *My 35 Years Behind Bars* by Johnny Brooks (1954)

Frozen Daiquiri

2 ounces (60ml) light rum
1 ounce (30ml) lime juice
1/2 ounce (15ml) simple syrup

Blend with crushed ice and pour into a coupe or
an Old Fashioned glass.

Frozen Margarita

1 1/2 ounce (45ml) tequila blanco or reposado
3/4 ounce (22ml) triple sec
3/4 ounce (22ml) lime juice

Blend with crushed ice and pour into a coupe or an Old
Fashioned glass. Salt rim optional.

Frozen Mud Slide

3/4 ounce (22ml) vodka
3/4 ounce (22ml) Baileys Irish Cream
3/4 ounce (22ml) coffee liqueur
3/4 ounce (22ml) cream

Blend with crushed ice and pour into
an Old Fashioned glass.

Frozen Scotch El Borracho

(Created at El Borracho Restaurant, New York)

1 1/2 ounce (45ml) Scotch whisky
1 teaspoon (5ml) Cointreau
3/4 ounce (22ml) lemon juice
1 teaspoon (5ml) simple syrup
1 dash Angostura bitters
1 pineapple wedge

Blend with crushed ice and pour into a coupe.
Garnish with a pineapple spear.

Adapted from *Bottoms Up* by Ted Saucier (1951)

Fuego Manzana

(Created by Danny Smith, London)

1¹/2 ounce (45ml) light rum
1/2 ounce (15ml) pomme vert (apple liqueur)
1/2 ounce (15ml) apple juice
1/4 ounce (7ml) lime juice
1 teaspoon (5ml) simple syrup
1/2 inch (12mm) red chili pepper
1/2 green apple

Deseed chili and muddle with syrup in the base of a shaker.
Chop up apple and muddle in shaker. Add remaining
ingredients and shake with ice. Strain into a cocktail glass
and garnish with chili on rim.

Danny's drink is equally beautiful if you substitute
tequila for the rum.

Futurity

1¹/4 ounce (37ml) sloe gin
1¹/4 ounce (37ml) sweet vermouth
1/2 teaspoon (2.5ml) grenadine
3 dashes Angostura bitters

Shake with ice and strain into a cocktail glass

Adapted from *Bottoms Up* by Ted Saucier (1951)

Fuzzy Navel

1¹/2 ounce (45ml) peach schnapps
Orange juice

Build over ice in a highball glass. Garnish with
an orange slice.

Gangadine Cocktail

1½ ounce (45ml) gin
½ ounce (15ml) white crème de menthe
¼ ounce (7ml) absinthe
1 teaspoon (5ml) crème de framboise

Shake with ice and strain into a cocktail glass.

Gaslight

1½ ounce (45ml) Scotch whisky
½ ounce (15ml) sweet vermouth
¼ ounce (7ml) orange curaçao
1 dash Drambuie

Stir with ice (except Drambuie) and strain into a cocktail glass. Float Drambuie and garnish with an orange twist.

Gaxiola

(Created by William Gaxton, actor)

1½ ounce (45ml) Spanish brandy
½ ounce (15ml) lime juice
2 teaspoons (10ml) simple syrup
2 dashes orange flower water

Shake with ice and strain into a cocktail glass.
Garnish with a lime twist.

Adapted from *Bottoms Up* by Ted Saucier (1951)

G-CAT (Gin, Cranberry & Tonic)

(As popularized by James Prichard of the Manor Arms, Clapham, London)

1 1/2 ounce (45ml) gin
1 ounce (30ml) cranberry juice
Tonic water

Build over ice in a highball glass.
Garnish with a lime wedge.

Genou de Apis

(Created by Søren Krogh Sørensen, Le Lion • Bar de Paris, Hamburg, Germany)

2 ounces (60ml) gin
1 ounce (30ml) honeyed chestnut liqueur
3/4 ounce (22ml) lemon juice

Shake with ice and strain into an ice-filled Old Fashioned glass. Garnish with a lemon twist and a roasted chestnut on the side.

Georgia Mint Julep

1 1/2 ounce (45ml) brandy
1 ounce (30ml) peach brandy
1 teaspoon (5ml) simple syrup
6 mint leaves

Lightly press syrup and mint together with a muddler. Fill an Old Fashioned glass with crushed ice and add liquor. Stir to mix. Top with more ice and garnish with mint sprig.

Adapted from *The Bar-Tender's Guide* by Jerry Thomas (1887)

Gibson

2¹/₂ ounces (75ml) gin or vodka
¹/₂ ounce (15ml) dry vermouth
2 cocktail onions

Stir with ice and strain into a
cocktail glass.
Garnish with onions.

Adapted from *Cocktails: How To Mix
Them* by Robert Vermeire (1922)

FEATURED DRINK

Gimlet

2 ounces (60ml) gin or vodka
³/₄ ounce (22ml) Rose's lime juice

Shake with ice and strain into a cocktail glass. Garnish
with a lime twist.

Gin and Cin

*(Created by Blair "Trader Tiki" Reynolds, Portland, 2007,
http://www.tradertiki.com)*

2 ounces (60ml) gin
1 ounce (30ml) cinnamon syrup
¹/₂ ounce (15ml) lemon juice
2 dashes Fee Brothers old fashioned bitters
¹/₄ teaspoon freshly grated ginger
Ginger beer

Shake with ice (except ginger beer) and strain into an ice-
filled highball glass. Top with ginger beer and garnish with
ginger slices and powdered cinnamon.

Gin & It

1³/₄ ounce (50ml) gin
³/₄ ounce (22ml) sweet vermouth

Stir with ice and strain into a cocktail glass or
an ice-filled Old Fashioned glass.

Gin & Tonic

1¹/₂ ounce (45ml) gin
Tonic

Build over ice in a highball glass. Garnish with a lime wedge.

Gin Basil Smash

(Created by Jörg Meyer, Le Lion • Bar de Paris, Hamburg, Germany)

2 ounces (60ml) gin
1 ounce (30ml) lemon juice
¹/₂ ounce (15ml) simple syrup
10 green or red basil leaves with sprigs

Muddle basil and simple syrup in shaker. Add remaining
ingredients and shake with ice. Double strain into an ice-
filled Old Fashioned glass and garnish with a basil leaf.

Gin Buck

1¹/₂ ounce (45ml) gin
¹/₄ ounce (7ml) lemon juice
Ginger ale

Build over ice in a highball glass.
Garnish with a lemon slice.

Gin Fix

2 ounces (60ml) gin or genever
1 ounce (30ml) lemon juice
¹/₂ ounce (15ml) simple syrup
¹/₄ ounce (7ml) pineapple syrup (optional)

Build over crushed ice in an Old Fashioned glass.
Stir before serving and garnish with a lemon slice.

Adapted from *How To Mix Drinks* by Jerry Thomas (1862)

Gin Fizz

1¹/₂ ounce (45ml) gin
1 ounce (30ml) lemon juice
³/₄ ounce (22ml) simple syrup
Soda water

Shake with ice (except soda water) and strain into an
ice-filled highball glass. Top with soda water and
garnish with a lemon slice.

Adapted from *The Bar-Tender's Guide* by Jerry Thomas (1876)

Gin Garden

1¹/₂ ounce (45ml) gin
1 ounce (30ml) apple juice
¹/₂ ounce (10ml) elderflower cordial
2 inch (5cm) slice cucumber

Chop up a cucumber and muddle in the bottom of a
cocktail shaker. Add remaining ingredients and shake
with ice. Strain into a cocktail glass and garnish with
a cucumber slice.

FEATURED DRINK

Gin Rickey

1¹/₂ ounce (45ml) gin
¹/₃ ounce (10ml) lime juice
Soda water

Build over ice in a highball glass.
Garnish with a lime wedge.

FEATURED DRINK

Gin Sling

2 ounces (60ml) gin
1 ounce (30ml) water
1 teaspoon (5ml) simple syrup

Build over ice in an Old Fashioned glass.
Garnish with an orange twist or nutmeg dusting.

Adapted from *How To Mix Drinks* by Jerry Thomas (1862)

G

Gin Sour

2 ounces (60ml) gin
1 ounce (30ml) lemon juice
1/2 ounce (15ml) simple syrup
1/2 ounce (15ml) egg white (optional)

Shake with ice and strain into a sour glass or an
ice-filled Old Fashioned glass. Garnish with
a lemon slice and a cherry.

Gin Zoom

2 ounces (60ml) gin
1 teaspoon (5ml) honey
1 teaspoon (5ml) cream

Shake vigorously and strain into an ice-filled
Old Fashioned glass.

Adapted from *The Artistry of Mixing Drinks*
by Frank Meier (1936)

Gloom Chaser

(Created by "Charlie," Ermitage Bar, Champs-Élysées, Paris)

1 1/2 ounce (45ml) light rum
1/2 ounce (15ml) Grand Marnier
1/2 ounce (15ml) orange curaçao
3/4 ounce (22ml) lemon juice
1 teaspoon (5ml) grenadine

Shake with ice and strain into a cocktail glass.

Adapted from *Barflies & Cocktails* by Harry McElhone (1927)

Gloria Cocktail

(À la Pendennis Club, Louisville, Kentucky)

1 1/2 ounce (45ml) Plymouth gin
3/4 ounce (22ml) lemon juice
1/2 ounce (15ml) grenadine
1/2 ounce (15ml) egg white
4 mint leaves

Shake vigorously with ice and strain into a cocktail glass.

Adapted from *The World's Drinks & How To Mix Them*
by William Boothby (1908)

Goddaughter

2 ounces (60ml) vodka
1 ounce (30ml) amaretto
1 ounce (30ml) cream

Shake with ice and strain into an ice-filled
Old Fashioned glass.

Godfather

2 ounces (60ml) Scotch whisky
1 ounce (30ml) amaretto

Stir with ice and strain into an ice-filled
Old Fashioned glass.

The Godfather is sweet, nutty and very easy to make.

FEATURED DRINK

Godfrey, The

(Created by Salvatore Calabrese, London)

**1 ounce (30ml) cognac
1/2 ounce (15ml) crème de mûre
1/2 ounce (15ml) Grand Marnier
1/2 ounce (15ml) lemon juice
4 blackberries**

Shake vigorously with ice and strain into a crushed ice-filled Old Fashioned glass. Top with more crushed ice and garnish with a blackberry and a mint sprig.

Godmother

**2 ounces (60ml) vodka
1 ounce (30ml) amaretto**

Stir with ice and strain into an ice-filled Old Fashioned glass.

Godson

2 ounces (60ml) Scotch whisky
1 ounce (30ml) amaretto
1 ounce (30ml) cream

Shake with ice and strain into an ice-filled
Old Fashioned glass.

Golden Cadillac

1 1/4 ounce (37ml) Galliano
1 ounce (30ml) white crème de cacao
1 1/2 ounce (45ml) cream

Shake with ice and strain into a cocktail glass.

Golden Dawn

(Created by Tom Buttery)

3/4 ounce (22ml) gin
3/4 ounce (22ml) Calvados
3/4 ounce (22ml) apricot brandy
3/4 ounce (22ml) orange juice
1 dash grenadine

Shake with ice (except grenadine) and strain into a
cocktail glass. Add a dash of grenadine which will
sink to the bottom.

Adapted from *Café Royal Cocktail Book* by W. J. Tarling (1937)

Golden Fizz

1½ ounce (45ml) gin
1 ounce (30ml) lemon juice
¾ ounce (22ml) simple syrup
1 egg yolk
Soda water

Shake with ice (except soda water) and strain into an ice-filled highball glass. Top with soda water and garnish with a lemon slice.

Golden Gleam

(Created by Chas. A. Tuck)

1½ ounce (45ml) brandy
1 ounce (30ml) Grand Marnier
¾ ounce (22ml) lemon juice
¼ ounce (7ml) orange juice

Shake with ice and strain into a cocktail glass.

Adapted from *Café Royal Cocktail Book* by W. J. Tarling (1937)

Golden Glove

2 ounces (60ml) light rum
1 teaspoon (5ml) Cointreau
½ ounce (15ml) lime juice
1 teaspoon (5ml) simple syrup

Shake with ice and strain into a cocktail glass.

Golden Slipper

1/2 ounce (15ml) yellow Chartreuse
1/2 ounce (15ml) goldwasser
1 egg yolk

In a shot glass, add Chartreuse, carefully layer egg yolk on top and layer goldwasser on top of yolk.

Adapted from *Bartender's Manual* by Harry Johnson (1900)

Good Morning Fizz

1 1/2 ounce (45ml) gin
2 teaspoons (10ml) absinthe
1 ounce (30ml) lemon juice
3/4 ounce (22ml) simple syrup
1/2 ounce (15ml) egg white
Soda water

Shake vigorously with ice (except soda water) and strain into an ice-filled highball glass. Top with soda water and garnish with a lemon slice.

Gotham

(Created by Robert Hess, 2002)

2 ounces (60ml) brandy
1/2 teaspoon (2.5ml) absinthe or pastis
3 dashes peach bitters

Coat a chilled small rocks glass with absinthe or pastis, then add the peach bitters and brandy.
Garnish with a lemon twist. Serve in a rocks glass.

Adapted from *The Essential Bartender's Guide*
by Robert Hess (2008)

Grand Mimosa

1/2 ounce (15ml) Grand Marnier
1 ounce (30ml) orange juice
Champagne

Build in a flute.

Grape & Watermelon Cobbler

(Created by Johan Svensson, Drinksfusion, London)

1 1/2 ounce (45ml) gin
3 ounces (90ml) sauvignon blanc
3 chunks watermelon
2 sprigs cilantro (coriander)
1 dash simple syrup

Muddle melon in the base of a shaker. Add remaining ingredients, shake and strain into an ice-filled highball glass. Garnish with a watermelon wedge on rim.

Grape Vine

2 ounces (60ml) gin
1 ounce (30ml) lemon juice
1 ounce (30ml) white grape juice
1 teaspoon (5ml) grenadine

Shake with ice and strain into a cocktail glass.

Adapted from *1700 Cocktails For The Man Behind The Bar*
by R. de Fleury (1934)

Grappacino

(Created by George Sinclair, London, 2002)

1½ ounce (45ml) grappa
2 teaspoons (10ml) amaretto
2 teaspoons (10ml) simple syrup
1 ounce (30ml) strong espresso

Shake with ice and strain into a cocktail glass.
Garnish with three coffee beans.

FEATURED DRINK

Grasshopper

1 ounce (30ml) green crème de
menthe
1 ounce (30ml) white crème de
cacao
1 ounce (30ml) cream

Shake with ice and strain into a
cocktail glass or coupe.

FEATURED DRINK

Green Deacon

(Created by Jim Meehan, New York)

1½ ounce (45ml) Plymouth gin
¾ ounce (22ml) sloe gin
1 ounce (30ml) grapefruit juice
Absinthe rinse

Rinse a coupe with absinthe. Shake remaining
ingredients with ice and strain into the rinsed coupe.

Green Dragon

1 1/2 ounce (45ml) gin
1/2 ounce (15ml) kümmel
1/2 ounce (15ml) green crème de menthe
1/2 ounce (15ml) lemon juice
2 dashes peach bitters

Shake with ice and strain into a cocktail glass.

Green Glacier

(Created by Jamie Boudreau, Seattle,
www.SpiritsandCocktails.com)

2 ounces (60ml) cognac
3/4 ounce (22ml) green Chartreuse
1/4 ounce (7ml) white crème de cacao
2 dashes Angostura bitters

Stir with ice and strain into a cocktail glass.

Greyhound

1 1/2 ounce (45ml) vodka
Grapefruit juice

Build over ice in a highball glass.

Grosvenor House

(Created at Grosvenor House, Park Lane, London)

1¹/2 ounce (45ml) gin
¹/2 ounce (15ml) dry vermouth
¹/2 teaspoon (2.5ml) Cointreau

Stir with ice and strain into a cocktail glass.

Adapted from *Bottom's Up* by Ted Saucier (1951)

Guava & Wild Strawberry Batida

(Created by Johan Svensson, Drinksfusion, London)

1¹/2 ounce (45m) cachaça
¹/2 ounce (15ml) crème de fraise
1 ounce (30ml) guava purée
¹/2 ounce (15ml) lemon juice
³/4 ounce (22ml) coconut cream
6 strawberries
¹/2 teaspoon (2.5ml) vanilla syrup

Blend with crushed ice and pour into a hurricane glass. Garnish with a strawberry dusted with icing (powdered) sugar and coconut flakes.

Gypsy Serenade

(Created by Mischa Borr, The Waldorf-Astoria, New York)

1 1/2 ounce (45ml) gin
3/4 ounce (22ml) maraschino
liqueur
1/4 ounce (7ml) lemon juice
1/4 ounce (7ml) orange juice

Shake with ice and strain into a
cocktail glass.

Adapted from *Bottom's Up* by Ted
Saucier (1951)

H

Habitant

(Created by Larry Denis, Seignory Club,
The Log Château, Québec)

1½ ounce (45ml) rye
1 ounce (30ml) lemon juice
2 teaspoons (10ml) maple syrup
1 dash Angostura bitters

Shake with ice and strain into a cocktail glass.

Adapted from *Bottom's Up* by Ted Saucier (1951)

Haitian Fight Sour

(Created by Jim Meehan, New York)

1½ ounce (45ml) aged rum
½ ounce (15ml) Bénédictine
¾ ounce (22ml) lime juice
½ ounce (15ml) simple syrup
2 dashes Angostura bitters

Shake with ice and strain into a coupe.
Garnish with a lime wheel.

H

Hannibal Hamlin

1 1/2 ounce (45ml) cognac
1 1/2 ounce (45ml) rum
1/2 ounce (15ml) lemon juice
1/2 ounce (15ml) orange juice
2 teaspoons (10ml) honey

Shake with ice and strain into a cocktail glass.

Adapted from *American en Fancy Drinks Ijsrecepten en Dranken*
by W. Slagter (circa 1920)

FEATURED DRINK

Hannibal Hamlin No. 2

1 1/2 ounce (45ml) arrack
1 1/2 ounce (45ml) cognac
1/2 ounce (15ml) maple syrup
3/4 ounce (22ml) orange juice

Shake with ice and strain into a cocktail glass.

Adapted from *Die Modernen Getraenke* by F. J. Beutel (1919)

Happy Days

(Created by E. L. Horton)

1 1/2 ounce (45ml) gin
1 ounce (30ml) Lillet Blanc
3/4 ounce (22ml) Van der Hum
1/2 ounce (15ml) lemon juice
1 dash peach bitters

Shake with ice and strain into a cocktail glass.

Adapted from *Café Royal Cocktail Book* by W. J. Tarling (1937)

Happy Honey Annie

(Created by Frank Meier for Mr. P. A. Chavane)

1¹/₂ ounce (45ml) brandy
¹/₂ ounce (15ml) grapefruit juice
1 teaspoon (5ml) honey

Shake well and strain into a cocktail glass.

Adapted from *The Artistry Of Mixing Drinks*
by Frank Meier (1936)

Harlem Cocktail

1¹/₂ ounce (45ml) gin
¹/₄ ounce (7ml) maraschino liqueur
³/₄ ounce (22ml) pineapple juice
2 wedges fresh pineapple

Muddle pineapple at the bottom of a shaker. Add remaining
ingredients, shake with ice and strain into a cocktail glass.

Harry M. Stevens Cocktail

³/₄ ounce (22ml) light rum
³/₄ ounce (22ml) dry vermouth
³/₄ ounce (22ml) apricot brandy
³/₄ ounce (22ml) orange juice
¹/₂ teaspoon (2.5ml) orange curaçao
¹/₂ teaspoon (2.5ml) grenadine

Shake with ice and strain into a cocktail glass.
Garnish with a lime twist.

Adapted from the *Hotel Lincoln Cock-tail Book*
(Havana, Cuba, 1937)

Harry's Cocktail

1³/₄ ounce (50ml) gin
³/₄ ounce (22ml) sweet vermouth
1 dash Angostura bitters
4 mint leaves

Shake with ice and strain into a cocktail glass.
Garnish with a mint leaf.

Adapted from *ABC of Mixing Cocktails* by Harry McElhone (1922)

FEATURED DRINK

Harvard

1¹/₂ ounce (45ml) cognac
³/₄ ounce (22ml) sweet vermouth
2 dashes Angostura bitters

Stir with ice and strain into a cocktail glass.

While the Harvard is simply a Manhattan made with
cognac, it's still an excellent digestif.

Adapted from *Modern American Drinks* by George Kappeler (1895)

FEATURED DRINK

Harvard Cooler

1¹/₂ ounce (45ml) applejack
¹/₂ ounce (15ml) lemon juice
1 teaspoon (5ml) simple syrup
Soda water or ginger ale

Build over ice in a highball glass.
Garnish with a lemon twist.

Harvest Punch

(Created by Rick Stutz, 2008, www.kaiserpenguin.com)

1 1/2 ounce (45ml) Jamaican rum
1 ounce (30ml) Barbados rum
1/2 ounce (15ml) apfelkorn
1 teaspoon (5ml) pimento dram (allspice dram)
1 ounce (30ml) grapefruit
1/2 ounce (15ml) cinnamon syrup
1 dash Angostura bitters

Build over crushed ice in an Old Fashioned glass and "swizzle" with a barspoon. Garnish with a cinnamon stick and a grapefruit twist.

Harvey Wallbanger

1 1/2 ounce (45ml) vodka
1/2 ounce (15ml) Galliano
Orange juice

Build over ice in a highball glass. Float the Galliano.

Havana Cocktail

1 ounce (30ml) gin
1 ounce (30ml) Swedish Punsch
1/2 ounce (15ml) apricot brandy
1/2 ounce (15ml) lemon juice

Shake with ice and strain into a cocktail glass.

Adapted from *United Kingdom Bartenders' Guild Guide To Drinks* (1953)

Harvest Punch

Havana Special

1 ounce (30ml) light rum
1 ounce (30ml) Cointreau
1/2 ounce (15ml) peach brandy
1/2 ounce (15ml) grapefruit juice

Shake with ice and strain into a cocktail glass.

Adapted from *My 35 Years Behind Bars* by Johnny Brooks (1954)

Hawaiian Room

1 ounce (30ml) light rum
1/2 ounce (15ml) applejack
1/2 ounce (15ml) triple sec
1/2 ounce (15ml) pineapple juice
1/2 ounce (15ml) lemon juice

Shake with ice and strain into a cocktail glass.

Adapted from *Bottom's Up* by Ted Saucier (1951)

Hearst

1 1/2 ounce (45ml) gin
3/4 ounce (22ml) sweet vermouth
1 dash orange bitters
1 dash Angostura bitters

Stir with ice and strain into a cocktail glass.

Adapted from *Drinks* by Jacques Straub (1914)

FEATURED DRINK

Hedgerow Sling

(Created by Cairbry Hill, London)

1½ ounce (45ml) sloe gin
¾ ounce (22ml) gin
½ ounce (15ml) crème de mûre
½ ounce (15ml) lemon juice
2 teaspoons (10ml) lime juice
2 teaspoons (10ml) simple syrup

Shake with ice and strain into a sling or a cocktail glass.
Garnish with a lemon slice, a raspberry and a strawberry.

Hell Diver

1 ounce (30ml) gin
1 ounce (30ml) Dubonnet rouge
½ ounce (15ml) white crème de cacao
¼ ounce (7ml) absinthe

Stir with ice and strain into a cocktail glass.

Adapted from *How To Properly Mix Drinks* by "Anonymous" (1934)

Hemingway Daiquiri

See Papa Doble.

Henri's Special

(Created at Henri's French Restaurant, New York)

1 1/2 ounce (45ml) calvados
3/4 ounce (22ml) apricot brandy
1/2 ounce (15ml) lime juice

Shake with ice and strain into a cocktail glass.

Adapted from *Bottom's Up* by Ted Saucier (1951)

Henry VIII

(Created by Henry Besant, London)

3/4 ounce (22ml) pepper vodka
2 teaspoons (10ml) crème de peche
Absinthe
Sugar cube
Champagne

Coat sugar cube in absinthe and place in a flute. Add vodka and peche and top with champagne.

The pepper and peach combine to make a fantastic champagne cocktail.

Hey Hey

3/4 ounce (22ml) brandy
3/4 ounce (22ml) Lillet Blanc
3/4 ounce (22ml) Cointreau
3/4 ounce (22ml) lemon juice

Shake with ice and strain into a cocktail glass.

Highball

2 ounces (60ml) liquor of choice
(bourbon, brandy, etc.)
4 ounces (120ml) mixer of choice
(soda water, tonic, etc.)

Build over ice in a highball glass.

Adapted from *The Mixicologist* by C.F. Lawlor (1895)

Hoffman House Cocktail

1½ ounce (45ml) Plymouth gin
¾ ounce (22ml) dry vermouth
2 dashes orange bitters

Stir with ice and strain into a cocktail glass.
Garnish with a lemon twist.

Adapted from *ABC of Mixing Cocktails* by Harry McElhone (1922)

Honeymoon Cocktail

1½ ounce (45ml) applejack
1 ounce (30ml) Bénédictine
2 teaspoons (10ml) orange curaçao
¾ ounce (22ml) lemon juice

Shake with ice and strain into a cocktail glass.

Adapted from *The Savoy Cocktail Book* by Harry Craddock (1930)

Honeysuckle

1¹/2 ounce (45ml) gold rum
¹/2 ounce (15ml) lime juice
2 teaspoons (10ml) honey

Shake with ice and strain into a cocktail glass.

Honolulu Cocktail

³/4 ounce (22ml) gin
³/4 ounce (22ml) Bénédictine
³/4 ounce (22ml) maraschino liqueur

Stir with ice and strain into a cocktail glass.

Adapted from *The Savoy Cocktail Book*
by Harry Craddock (1930)

Hoop La

³/4 ounce (22ml) brandy
³/4 ounce (22ml) Cointreau
³/4 ounce (22ml) Lillet Blanc
³/4 ounce (22ml) lemon juice

Shake with ice and strain into a cocktail glass.

Adapted from *United Kingdom Bartenders' Guild
Guide To Drinks* (1953)

Hoots Mon Cocktail

1½ ounce (45ml) Scotch whisky
¾ ounce (22ml) sweet vermouth
¾ ounce (22ml) Lillet Blanc

Stir with ice and strain into a cocktail glass.

Adapted from *The Savoy Cocktail Book* by Harry Craddock (1930)

Hop Toad

1½ ounce (45ml) apricot brandy
½ ounce (15ml) lemon juice

Shake with ice and strain into a cocktail glass.

Adapted from *The Savoy Cocktail Book* by Harry Craddock (1930)

Horse's Neck

1½ ounce (45ml) bourbon or brandy
Ginger ale
1 entire lemon peel

Using a paring knife, cut off the whole peel from a lemon in one long spiral. Place this in a highball glass and fill with ice. Add liquor and fill with ginger ale.

Adapted from *Modern American Drinks* by George Kappeler (1895)

Horse's Neck

Hot Buttered Rum

2 ounces (60ml) dark rum
1/2 ounce (15ml) simple syrup
1/2 teaspoon (2.5ml) unsalted butter
1 cinnamon stick
1 clove
Ground cinnamon
Boiling water

Place clove, cinnamon stick and syrup in an Irish coffee
glass and add boiling water. Stir and add rum and butter.
Dust with ground cinnamon.

FEATURED DRINK

Hot Kiss

1 1/2 ounce (45ml) cognac
3/4 ounce (22ml) sweet vermouth
1 teaspoon (5ml) orange curaçao

Stir with ice and strain into a cocktail glass.
Garnish with a cherry.

Adapted from *Bar La Florida Cocktails* (Havana, Cuba, 1935)

Hot Shot

1/3 ounce (10ml) Galliano
1/3 ounce (10ml) hot coffee
1/3 ounce (10ml) cream

Layer in the order above in
a shot glass,
floating cream on top.

Hot Toddy

FEATURED DRINK

2 ounces (60ml) scotch, bourbon, brandy or dark rum
1 teaspoon (5ml) honey
1 cinnamon stick
3 cloves
Nutmeg
Boiling water

Place cloves, cinnamon, and honey into an Irish coffee
glass and add boiling water. Stir and add liquor.
Dust with grated nutmeg.

Hotel Atlantico

(Created at Hotel Atlantico, Monte Estoril, Portugal)

1¹/₂ ounce (45ml) brandy
³/₄ ounce (22ml) cherry brandy
³/₄ ounce (22ml) lemon juice

Shake with ice and strain into a cocktail glass.

Adapted from *Bottom's Up* by Ted Saucier (1951)

Hotel du Parc

(Created at Hotel du Parc and Majestic, Vichy, France)

1¹/₂ ounce (45ml) gin
³/₄ ounce (22ml) Cointreau
³/₄ ounce (22ml) tangerine juice

Shake with ice and strain into a cocktail glass.

Adapted from *Bottom's Up* by Ted Saucier (1951)

Hungaria Cocktail

(Created by "Fred," Hungaria, London)

³/₄ ounce (22ml) gin
³/₄ ounce (22ml) dry vermouth
³/₄ ounce (22ml) sweet vermouth
1 dash absinthe

Stir with ice and strain into a cocktail glass.

Adapted from *An Anthology of Cocktails* by Booth's Gin (1930s)

Hurricane

1 ounce (30ml) light rum
1 ounce (30ml) dark rum
1½ ounce (45ml) pineapple juice
1½ ounce (45ml) orange juice
1½ ounce (45ml) passion fruit juice
¾ ounce (22ml) lime juice
1 teaspoon (5ml) grenadine
1 teaspoon (5ml) simple syrup

Shake with ice and strain into an ice-filled hurricane glass. Garnish with a pineapple spear and a cherry.

Fruit juice and rum are a perfect match in this New Orleans classic.

I

I.B.F. Pick Me Up

(Created by Bob Card, Harry's New York Bar, Paris)

1 ounce (30ml) brandy
1 teaspoon (5ml) Fernet Branca
1 teaspoon (5ml) orange curaçao
Champagne

Shake with ice (except champagne) and strain into a
coupe. Top with champagne.

Adapted from *Barflies & Cocktails* by Harry McElhone (1927)

Ichbien Cocktail

1 1/2 ounce (45ml) brandy
1/2 ounce (15ml) orange curaçao
1 egg yolk
4 ounces (120ml) milk

Shake with ice and strain into an ice-filled cocktail glass.
Dust with nutmeg.

Adapted from *The Savoy Cocktail Book*
by Harry Craddock (1930)

Ideal Cocktail

¾ ounce (22ml) gin
¾ ounce (22ml) sweet vermouth
¾ ounce (22ml) dry vermouth
1 teaspoon (5ml) maraschino liqueur
½ ounce (15ml) grapefruit juice

Shake with ice and strain into a cocktail glass.

Adapted from *Bar La Florida Cocktails* (Havana, Cuba, 1935)

Imperial Blueberry Fizz

(Created by Jim Meehan, New York)

1½ ounce (45ml) cognac
½ ounce (15ml) crème de violette
12 blueberries
Champagne

Muddle blueberries and crème de violette in a shaker. Add remaining ingredients (except champagne) and shake with ice. Double strain into a coupe and top with champagne. Garnish with an edible orchid.

Inca

¾ ounce (22ml) gin
¾ ounce (22ml) sherry
½ ounce (15ml) sweet vermouth
½ ounce (15ml) dry vermouth
1 dash orgeat
1 dash Angostura bitters

Shake well and strain into a cocktail glass.

Income Tax Cocktail

1 1/2 ounce (45ml) gin
3/4 ounce (22ml) dry vermouth
3/4 ounce (22ml) sweet vermouth
1/2 ounce (15ml) orange juice
2 dashes Angostura bitters

Shake with ice and strain into a cocktail glass.

Interesting Cocktail, The

(Created by Gary Regan)

2 ounces (60ml) tequila blanco
3/4 ounce (22ml) Aperol
1/4 ounce (7ml) dark crème de cacao
1/4 ounce (7ml) lemon juice
4 grapefruit twists

Add everything to an ice-filled mixing glass. Twist three of
the grapefruit peels over the glass, and drop them in.
Shake with ice and strain into a flute.
Garnish with the remaining grapefruit twist.

Irish Coffee

1 1/2 ounce (45ml) Irish whiskey
4 ounces (120ml) coffee
3/4 ounce (22ml) simple syrup
Whipped cream

Lightly whip cream to just under stiff.
Build in an Irish coffee glass and float cream on top.

The combination of whiskey, coffee and cream make
a perfect after dinner drink.

FEATURED DRINK

Itza Paramount

(Created by C. O'Conner)

1½ ounce (45ml) gin
¾ ounce (22ml) Drambuie
¾ ounce (22ml) Cointreau

Stir with ice and strain into a cocktail glass. Garnish with a cherry.

Adapted from *United Kingdom Bartenders' Guild*
Guide To Drinks (1953)

J

Jack Frost Whiskey Sour

1 1/2 ounce (45ml) applejack
3/4 ounce (22ml) cream
1/2 ounce (15ml) lemon juice
1 teaspoon (5ml) simple syrup
Soda water

Shake vigorously with ice and strain into an ice-filled highball glass. Top with soda water.

Adapted from *The Flowing Bowl* by William Schmidt (1891)

Jack Rabbit

1 1/2 ounce (45ml) applejack
1/4 ounce (7ml) fresh orange juice
1/4 ounce (7ml) lemon juice
1/4 ounce (7ml) maple syrup

Shake with ice and strain into a cocktail glass.

Adapted from *The Fine Art of Mixing Drinks* by David Embury (1948)

Jack Rose

2 ounces (60ml) applejack
3/4 ounce (22ml) lemon juice
1/2 ounce (15ml) grenadine

Shake with ice and strain into a cocktail glass.
Garnish with a lemon twist.

Jack Wallace Cocktail

(As made at the Arrowhead Inn, New York City)

3/4 ounce (22ml) whisky
3/4 ounce (22ml) dry vermouth
3/4 ounce (22ml) lemon juice
3/4 ounce (22ml) grenadine
1/2 ounce (15ml) egg white
1 dash cream

Shake vigorously with ice and strain into a cocktail glass.

Adapted from *The Cocktail Hour* by Louis P. De Gouy (1951)

Jamaica Joe

(Winner of British Rum Cocktail Competition, 1948)

1/2 ounce (15ml) light rum
1/2 ounce (15ml) advocaat
1/2 ounce (15ml) Tia Maria

Shake, strain into a small cocktail glass, and add a dash of
grenadine and a little nutmeg on top.

Adapted from *Shaking in the 60's* by Eddie Clarke (1963)

Jamaican Mule

2 ounces (60ml) spiced rum
1/2 ounce (15ml) lemon juice
1/4 ounce (7ml) simple syrup

Shake with ice and strain into an ice-filled highball glass.
Top with ginger beer.

Japanese Cocktail

2 ounces (60ml) brandy
1/2 ounce (15ml) orgeat
2 dashes Angostura bitters

Stir with ice and strain into a cocktail glass.
Garnish with a lemon twist.

Adapted from *The Bar-Tender's Guide* by Jerry Thomas (1862)

FEATURED DRINK

Japanese Fizz

1 1/2 ounce (45ml) bourbon or rye whisky
1/2 ounce (15ml) port
1/2 ounce (15ml) lemon juice
1 teaspoon (5ml) simple syrup
1/2 ounce (15ml) egg white
Soda water

Shake with ice (except soda water) and strain into a
highball glass full of ice. Top with soda water.
Garnish with a pineapple spear.

Japanese Slipper

1 ounce (30ml) Midori
1 ounce (30ml) Cointreau
1 ounce (30ml) lemon juice

Shake with ice and strain into a cocktail glass.
Garnish with a cherry.

Jasmine

(Created by Paul Harrington)

1 1/2 ounce (45ml) gin
1/4 ounce (7ml) Cointreau
1/4 ounce (7ml) Campari
3/4 ounce (22ml) lemon juice

Shake with ice and strain into a cocktail glass. Garnish
with a lemon twist.

Javana

(Created by John W. Emmerich)

2 ounces (60ml) apricot brandy
3/4 ounce (22ml) arrack
3/4 ounce (22ml) orange juice
1 teaspoon (5ml) gin
1 teaspoon (5ml) Cointreau
2 dashes orange bitters
2 dashes lemon juice

Shake, strain into a cocktail glass. Garnish with
a chunk of pineapple.

Adapted from *The Book of Approved Cocktails* by the United
Kingdom Bartenders' Guild (1934)

Jersey Sour

1 1/2 ounce (45ml) applejack
1/4 ounce (7ml) orange juice
1/4 ounce (7ml) lemon juice
1/4 ounce (7ml) simple syrup

Shake with ice and strain into a cocktail glass.

Jerlovs Tuting

1 1/2 ounce (45ml) aquavit
3/4 ounce (22ml) pale madeira
1/4 ounce (7ml) orange curaçao

Stir with ice and strain into
a cocktail glass.
Garnish with an olive.

Adapted from
Benjamins Cocktailsbok
(Stockholm, 1931)

Jewel

3/4 ounce (22ml) gin
3/4 ounce (22ml) green Chartreuse
3/4 ounce (22ml) sweet vermouth
1 dash orange bitters

Stir with ice and strain into a cocktail glass.
Garnish with a cherry.

Jimmy Rutledge

(Created by Don Lee, PDT, New York, 2007)

1 1/2 ounce (45ml) Four Roses Barrel Strength Bourbon
1/2 ounce (15ml) green Chartreuse
Champagne
1 sugar cube
1 dash Angostura bitters

Coat sugar cube with bitters and place in a coupe. Add
bourbon and crushed ice. Top with champagne
and float Chartreuse.

Joan Miró

1 ounce (30ml) whisky
1 ounce (30ml) Grand Marnier
1 ounce (30ml) dry vermouth

Shake with ice and strain into a cocktail glass.
Garnish with a cherry.

J

Jobourg

1¹⁄₄ ounce (37ml) light rum
1¹⁄₄ ounce (37ml) Dubonnet rouge
2 dashes orange bitters

Stir with ice and strain into a cocktail glass.
Garnish with a lemon twist.

Jockey Club

2 ounces (60ml) gin
¹⁄₂ ounce (15ml) lemon juice
2 teaspoons (10ml) white crème de cacao
1 dash orange bitters
1 dash Angostura bitters

Shake with ice and strain into a cocktail glass.

John Collins

2 ounces (60ml) bourbon (or genever gin)
1 ounce (30ml) lemon juice
³⁄₄ ounce (22ml) simple syrup
Soda water

Shake everything (except soda water) and strain into a
highball glass full of ice. Top with soda water and
garnish with a lemon slice.

FEATURED DRINK

John Perona

(Created by John Perona, El Morocco)

1¹/₂ ounce (45ml) light rum
1¹/₂ ounce (45ml) sweet vermouth
1 dash Campari

Stir with ice and strain into a cocktail glass. Serve with an orange twist and a lemon twist.

Adapted from *Bottoms Up* by Ted Saucier (1951)

Johnny Apple Collins

(Created by Jim Meehan, New York)

1¹/₂ ounce (45ml) bourbon
³/₄ ounce (22ml) apple schnapps
³/₄ ounce (22ml) lemon juice
2 dashes Bitter Truth Jerry Thomas' Own
Decanter Bitters
Bitter lemon soda

Shake with ice (except bitter lemon) and strain into an ice-filled highball glass. Top with bitter lemon and garnish with a lemon twist.

Jolly Pilot Cocktail

1 1/2 ounce (45ml) gin
1/2 ounce (15ml) cognac
1/2 ounce (15ml) triple sec
1/2 ounce (15ml) sherry
1 dash Angostura bitters

Stir and strain into a cocktail glass.
Garnish with a lemon twist
and a pearl onion.

Adapted from *Amateur Mixen* by Harry Schraemli (1956)

Journalist Cocktail

1 ounce (30ml) gin
1/2 ounce (15ml) dry vermouth
1/2 ounce (15ml) sweet vermouth
2 dashes orange curaçao
2 dashes lemon juice

Stir with ice and strain into a cocktail glass.

Adapted from *ABC of Mixing Cocktails* by Harry McElhone (1922)

Jubilee "Hermitage"

(Created by Godfrey Baldini)

1 1/2 ounce (45ml) gin
1/2 ounce (15ml) Grand Marnier
1/4 ounce (7ml) kirsch
3/4 ounce (22ml) grapefruit juice

Shake with ice and strain into a cocktail glass.

Adapted from *Café Royal Cocktail Book* by W. J. Tarling (1937)

Jubilee Beacon

(Created by Fred Gage)

1 1/2 ounce (45ml) light rum
3/4 ounce (22ml) Bénédictine
3/4 ounce (22ml) orange juice
4 dashes orange bitters

Shake with ice and strain into a cocktail glass.

Adapted from *The Book of Approved Cocktails* by
the United Kingdom Bartenders' Guild (1934)

Juliet & Romeo

(Created by Toby Maloney, The Violet Hour, Chicago, 2008)

2 ounces (60ml) Plymouth gin
3/4 ounce (22ml) lime juice
3/4 ounce (22ml) simple syrup
3 dashes Angostura bitters
1 mint sprig
3 drops rose water
3 slices cucumber
1 pinch salt

Muddle cucumber and salt in shaker. Add remaining
ingredients, ice and shake. Strain into a coupe.
Garnish with a mint leaf with one drop of rose water on
the top and three dashes of Angostura surrounding it.

July Revolution

*(Created by Jamie Boudreau, Seattle, 2008,
www.SpiritsandCocktails.com)*

2 ounces (60ml) bourbon
3/4 ounce (22ml) Dubonnet rouge
1/2 ounce (15ml) Pommeau de Normandie
1 dash peach bitters
1 dash Angostura bitters

Stir with ice and strain into a cocktail glass.

June Bug

1/2 ounce (15ml) crème de bananes
1/2 ounce (15ml) Malibu
1/2 ounce (15ml) Midori
1/2 ounce (15ml) lime juice
2 ounces (60ml) pineapple juice

Shake with ice and strain into a cocktail glass.

Jupiter Cocktail

11/2 ounce (45ml) gin
3/4 ounce (22ml) dry vermouth
1 teaspoon (5ml) orange juice
1 teaspoon (5ml) Parfait Amour

Stir with ice and strain into a cocktail glass.

Adapted from *ABC of Mixing Cocktails* by Harry McElhone (1922)

K

Kamikazi

³/4 ounce (22ml) vodka
¹/4 ounce (7ml) triple sec
¹/4 ounce (7ml) lime juice

Shake with ice and strain into a shot glass.

Kenny

1¹/2 ounce (45ml) applejack
¹/4 ounce (7ml) sweet vermouth
³/4 ounce (22ml) lemon juice
2 teaspoons (10ml) grenadine
1 dash Angostura bitters

Shake with ice and strain into a cocktail glass.

Kerry Cooler

1¹/2 ounce (45ml) Irish whiskey
1 ounce (30ml) sherry
1 ounce (30ml) lemon juice
³/4 ounce (22ml) orgeat
Soda water

Shake with ice (except soda water) and strain into an
ice-filled highball glass. Top with soda water and
garnish with a lemon slice.

Key Lime Pie

1¹/2 ounce (45ml) vanilla vodka
1¹/4 ounce (37ml) pineapple juice
¹/2 ounce (15ml) fresh lime juice
¹/4 ounce (7ml) Rose's lime juice
Graham cracker

Shake with ice and strain into a cocktail glass which has been rimmed with crumbled graham cracker.

Kicker

1¹/2 ounce (45ml) light rum
³/4 ounce (22ml) Calvados
¹/4 ounce (7ml) sweet vermouth

Stir with ice and strain into a cocktail glass.

Adapted from *"Cocktail Bill" Boothby's World Drinks and How to Mix Them* by William Boothby (1934)

Kiddie Car

1³/4 ounce (50ml) applejack
¹/4 ounce (7ml) Cointreau
¹/2 ounce (15ml) lime juice

Shake with ice and strain into a cocktail glass.

Kir

1/3 ounce (10ml) crème de cassis
Chilled dry white wine

Swirl the cassis around in a wine glass to coat the inside,
then add the wine.

Kir Royal

1/3 ounce (10ml) crème de cassis
Chilled champagne

Swirl the cassis around
in a flute to coat the inside, then add the champagne.

K

Knickerbocker

1½ ounce (45ml) gold rum
1 teaspoon (5ml) orange curaçao
2 teaspoons (10ml) raspberry syrup
¾ ounce (22ml) lemon juice

Shake with ice and strain into a cocktail glass.
Garnish with a raspberry.

Adapted from *How To Mix Drinks* by Jerry Thomas (1862)

Knickerbein

½ ounce (15ml) vanilla liqueur
½ ounce (15ml) kümmel
1 egg yolk
2 dashes Angostura bitters

Layer in a shot glass. First add the vanilla liqueur, then the
yolk and float the kümmel on top. Dash with bitters.

Adapted from *Modern Bartender's Guide* by O. H. Byron (1884)

Kool Hand Luke

(Created by Jamie Terrell)

1½ ounce (45ml) Jamaican dark rum
1 lime cut into eighths
1 dash Angostura bitters
2 teaspoons (10ml) simple syrup

Muddle lime and syrup at the bottom of an
Old Fashioned glass. Add crushed ice and rum
and bitters. Stir well before serving.

L

La Bicyclette

(Created by Jamie Boudreau, Seattle,
www.SpiritsandCocktails.com)

2 ounces (60ml) Plymouth gin
3/4 ounce (22ml) Cinzano Rosso
1/2 ounce (15ml) St-Germain elderflower liqueur
2 dashes peach bitters

Stir with ice and strain into a cocktail glass.

La Gitana

(Created by George Sinclair, London, 2008)

1 ounce (30ml) Krupnik Honey Vodka liqueur
1/2 ounce (15ml) crème d'abricot
1 ounce (30ml) lemon juice
1/2 ounce (15ml) egg white
2 teaspoons (10ml) simple syrup

Shake vigorously with ice and strain into an ice-filled
highball glass. Garnish with a lemon twist.

L

La Tuna (The Prickly Pear)

1¹/₂ ounce (45ml) tequila blanco
1 teaspoon (5ml) lime juice
4 dashes Angostura bitters
Soda water

Sprinkle salt on top of ice cubes. Stir with ice and strain into an ice-filled Old Fashioned glass. Fill with soda water.

Adapted from *The Food & Drink of Mexico*
by George C. Booth (1964)

La Vie en Rose

1¹/₂ ounce (45ml) gin
1 ounce (30ml) kirsch
³/₄ ounce (22ml) lemon juice
1 teaspoon (5ml) grenadine

Shake with ice and strain into a cocktail glass.
Garnish with a cherry.

L'Aiglon Dubarry

(Created by Billy Wilson, Hollywood)

1¹/₂ ounce (45ml) gin
¹/₂ ounce (15ml) Cointreau
1 teaspoon (5ml) Cherry Heering
³/₄ ounce (22ml) orange juice

Shake with ice and strain into a cocktail glass.
Garnish with an orange twist.

Adapted from *Bottoms Up* by Ted Saucier (1951)

L'amour en Fuite

(Created by Jamie Boudreau, Seattle,
www.SpiritsandCocktails.com)

1 1/2 ounce (45ml) Plymouth gin
3/4 ounce (22ml) Lillet blanc
1/4 ounce (7ml) St-Germain
Absinthe

Rinse a cocktail glass with a small quantity of absinthe.
Stir the drink over ice in a mixing glass and
strain into the rinsed glass.

Lancaster on Hudson

(Created by Tad Carducci, Tippling Bros.)

2 ounces (60ml) bourbon
1 ounce (30ml) lemon juice
3/4 ounce (22ml) maple syrup
1 teaspoon (5ml) Spice and Sassafras Apple Butter
2 dashes absinthe

Shake vigorously with ice and strain into an ice-filled
Old Fashioned glass. Garnish with an apple slice
dusted with fennel pollen.

Lansdowne Coronation Cocktail

(Created by "Carlo," Lansdowne Club, London)

3/4 ounce (22ml) gin
3/4 ounce (22ml) kirsch
3/4 ounce (22ml) blue curaçao
3/4 ounce (22ml) grapefruit juice

Shake with ice and strain into a cocktail glass.

Adapted from *An Anthology of Cocktails* by Booth's Gin (1930s)

Larchmont

(Created by David Embury)

2 ounces (60ml) light rum
3/4 ounce (22ml) Grand Marnier
3/4 ounce (22ml) lime juice
1 teaspoon (5ml) simple syrup

Shake with ice and strain into a cocktail glass.

David Embury named this drink for the
New York town where he lived.

Adapted from *The Fine Art Of Mixing Drinks*
by David Embury (1948)

Last Word

3/4 ounce (22ml) gin
3/4 ounce (22ml) maraschino liqueur
3/4 ounce (22ml) green Chartreuse
3/4 ounce (22ml) lime juice

Shake with ice and strain into
a cocktail glass.

This is a great example of a
drink from long ago that has
recently been rediscovered.
Definitely worth a try.

Adapted from *Bottoms Up*
by Ted Saucier (1951)

Le Coq D'Or Special

(Created by "Jack," Le Coq D'Or, London)

**1¹/₂ ounce (45ml) gin
2 teaspoons (10ml) crème de cassis
³/₄ ounce (22ml) lemon juice
¹/₂ ounce (15ml) egg white**

Shake vigorously with ice and strain into a cocktail glass.

Adapted from *An Anthology of Cocktails* by Booth's Gin (1930s)

Leap Frog

(Created by Jim Meehan, New York)

**2 ounces (60ml) Plymouth gin
¹/₂ ounce (15ml) apricot brandy
³/₄ ounce (22ml) lemon juice
¹/₂ ounce (15ml) simple syrup
1 dash Fee Brothers orange bitters
1 dash Regan's orange bitters
6 mint leaves**

Muddle mint leaves with simple syrup in a shaker.
Add remaining ingredients and shake with ice.
Double strain into a coupe.

FEATURED DRINK

Leap-Year Cocktail

(Created by Harry Craddock, Savoy Hotel, London)

1½ ounce (45ml) gin
½ ounce (15ml) Grand Marnier
½ ounce (15ml) sweet vermouth
¼ ounce (7ml) lemon juice

Shake and strain into a cocktail glass.
Garnish with a lemon twist.

Adapted from *The Savoy Cocktail Book* by Harry Craddock (1930)

Leg Before Wicket

(Created by E. Angerosa)

1½ ounce (45ml) gin
¼ ounce (7ml) Dubonnet rouge
1 teaspoon (5ml) Campari
1 teaspoon (5ml) lime juice

Shake with ice and strain into a cocktail glass.
Garnish with a lemon twist.

Adapted from *Café Royal Cocktail Book* by W. J. Tarling (1937)

Lemon Cocktail

1 1/2 ounce (45ml) bourbon
3/4 ounce (22ml) lemon juice
1/2 ounce (15ml) simple syrup
2 dashes Peychaud's bitters
2 dashes orange bitters

Shake with ice and strain into a cocktail glass.

FEATURED DRINK

This 100+ year old recipe proves that lemon and bourbon are a great combination.

Adapted from *Hoffman House Bartender's Guide* by C. S. Mahoney (1905)

Lemon Drop

1/3 ounce (10ml) citrus vodka
1/3 ounce (10ml) Cointreau
1/3 ounce (10ml) lemon juice

Shake with ice and strain into a shot glass.

Leo's Special

(Created by Leo Schwabl)

3/4 ounce (22ml) dry vermouth
1/4 ounce (7ml) apricot brandy
Champagne

Shake with ice (except champagne) and strain into a coupe.
Top with champagne and garnish with a lemon twist.

Adapted from *Café Royal Cocktail Book* by W. J. Tarling (1937)

FEATURED DRINK

Liberal

1 1/2 ounce (45ml) bourbon
1/2 ounce (15ml) sweet vermouth
1/4 ounce (7ml) Amer Picon
1 dash orange bitters

Stir with ice and strain into a cocktail glass.

Adapted from *Modern American Drinks*
by George Kappeler (1895)

Liberty

1 3/4 ounce (50ml) applejack
3/4 ounce (22ml) light rum
1 dash simple syrup

Stir with ice and strain into a cocktail glass.

Little King

(Created by Otto Sogolow, cartoonist)

1 ounce (30ml) gin
1/2 ounce (15ml) apricot brandy
1/2 ounce (15ml) applejack
1/2 ounce (15ml) lemon juice

Shake with ice and strain into a cocktail glass.

Adapted from *Bottoms Up* by Ted Saucier (1951)

Livener

3/4 ounce (22ml) brandy
1/4 ounce (7ml) lemon juice
1 teaspoon (5ml) raspberry syrup
2 dashes Angostura bitters
Champagne

Shake with ice (except champagne) and strain into a
coupe. Top with champagne and garnish
with a lemon twist.

Adapted from *American & Other Iced Drinks*
by Charlie Paul (1902)

London Buck

1 1/2 ounce (45ml) gin
1/2 ounce (15ml) lemon juice
Ginger ale

Build over ice in a highball glass.
Garnish with a lemon slice.

FEATURED DRINK

London Pride

(Created by C.T. Read)

1 1/2 ounce (45ml) gin
3/4 ounce (22ml) crème de violette
3/4 ounce (22ml) passion fruit juice

Shake with ice and strain into a cocktail glass.

Adapted from *Café Royal Cocktail Book* by W. J. Tarling (1937)

Lone Tree

1 1/2 ounce (45ml) gin
3/4 ounce (22ml) sweet vermouth

Stir with ice and strain into a cocktail glass.

Adapted from *The World's Drinks & How To Mix Them*
by William Boothby (1908)

Lone Tree Cooler

1 1/2 ounce (45ml) gin
1/2 ounce (15ml) dry vermouth
1 teaspoon (5ml) simple syrup
Soda water or ginger ale

Build over ice in a highball glass.
Garnish with a lemon slice.

Long Beach Iced Tea

1/2 ounce (15ml) vodka
1/2 ounce (15ml) gin
1/2 ounce (15ml) tequila blanco
1/2 ounce (15ml) triple sec
1/2 ounce (15ml) light rum
3/4 ounce (22ml) lemon juice
1/2 ounce (15ml) simple syrup
Cranberry juice

Shake with ice (except cranberry juice) and strain into an ice-filled highball glass. Top with cranberry juice and garnish with a lime wedge.

Long Island Iced Tea

1/2 ounce (15ml) vodka
1/2 ounce (15ml) gin
1/2 ounce (15ml) tequila blanco
1/2 ounce (15ml) triple sec
1/2 ounce (15ml) light rum
3/4 ounce (22ml) lemon juice
1/2 ounce (15ml) simple syrup
Cola

Shake with ice (except cola) and strain into an ice-filled highball glass. Top with cola and garnish with a lemon slice.

Long Range Cocktail

1½ ounce (45ml) brandy
¾ ounce (22ml) sweet vermouth
¼ ounce (7ml) absinthe
2 dashes Peychaud's bitters

Stir with ice and strain into a cocktail glass.
Garnish with a lemon twist.

Adapted from *Modern American Drinks*
by George Kappeler (1895)

Long Vodka

1½ ounce (45ml) vodka
¾ ounce (22ml) Rose's lime juice
3 dashes Angostura bitters
7-Up

Coat the inside of a highball glass with Angostura bitters.
Add ice and build drink. Garnish with a lime wedge.

Loretto Lemonade

(Created by Jamie Terrell, London)

1½ ounce (45ml) bourbon
½ ounce (15ml) Midori
½ ounce (15ml) lime juice
2 ounces (60ml) apple juice
Ginger beer

Shake with ice (except ginger beer) and strain into an
ice-filled highball glass. Top with ginger beer and
garnish with a mint sprig and a lime wedge.

FEATURED DRINK

Loudspeaker

3/4 ounce (22ml) gin
3/4 ounce (22ml) brandy
1/2 ounce (15ml) Cointreau
1/2 ounce (15ml) lemon juice

Shake with ice and strain into a cocktail glass.

Adapted from *The Savoy Cocktail Book* by Harry Craddock (1930)

Lublin Fix

(Created by Tomek Roehr, Alkoteka, Poland)

2 ounces (60ml) Żołądkowa Gorzka vodka
3/4 ounce (22ml) lemon juice
1/2 ounce (15ml) simple syrup
1/4 ounce (7ml) sour cherry liqueur
1 dash The Bitter Truth aromatic bitters

Shake with ice and strain into a coupe.
Garnish with a sour cherry.

Lucky Jim

2 1/2 ounces (75ml) vodka
1 teaspoon (5ml) dry vermouth
2 teaspoons (10ml)
Cucumber juice

Stir with ice and strain into a
cocktail glass.
Float a cucumber slice on top
with the peel on.

Adapted from *On Drink*
by Kingsley Amis (1972)

Luigi

(Created by Luigi Naintre, Embassy Club, London)

1 ounce (30ml) gin
1/2 ounce (15ml) dry vermouth
1/2 teaspoon (2.5ml) Cointreau
3/4 ounce (22ml) tangerine juice
1/2 teaspoon (2.5ml) grenadine

Shake with ice and strain into a cocktail glass.
Garnish with a lemon twist.

Adapted from *Cocktails: How To Mix Them*
by Robert Vermeire (1922)

Lynchburg Lemonade

1 1/2 ounce (45ml) Jack Daniels
3/4 ounce (22ml) Cointreau
3/4 ounce (22ml) lemon juice
7-Up

Shake with ice (except 7-Up) and strain into an ice-filled
highball glass. Top with 7-Up and garnish with
a lemon slice.

M

Mac Special

(Created by Bill McDermott, Château Frontenac, Québec)

1½ ounce (45ml) brandy
½ ounce (15ml) dark rum
½ teaspoon (2.5ml) Cointreau
½ ounce (15ml) lemon juice
1 dash grenadine

Shake with ice and strain into a cocktail glass.

Adapted from *Bottoms Up* by Ted Saucier (1951)

Macau

1 ounce (30ml) brandy
1 ounce (30ml) port
1 ounce (30ml) dry vermouth

Stir and strain into a cocktail glass.

Adapted from *Cocktails & Wines* by Lai Che San (1974)

Madras

1½ ounce (45ml) vodka
2 ounces (60ml) orange juice
3 ounces (90ml) cranberry juice

Build over ice in a highball glass.
Garnish with an orange slice.

M

Magic Key

1 1/2 ounce (45ml) applejack
3/4 ounce (22ml) orange juice
1/3 ounce (10ml) Cointreau
1/3 ounce (10ml) absinthe

Shake with ice and strain into a cocktail glass.

Adapted from *My 35 Years Behind Bars* by Johnny Brooks (1954)

FEATURED DRINK

Mai Tai

(Created by Trader Vic)

1 ounce (30ml) light rum
1 ounce (30ml) gold rum
1/2 ounce (15ml) orange curaçao
1/2 ounce (15ml) orgeat
1/2 ounce (15ml) fresh lime juice
1/2 ounce (15ml) dark rum

Shake all (except the dark rum) with ice. Strain into an ice-filled Old Fashioned glass. Float the dark rum, then garnish with a maraschino cherry.

Mai Tai

(Donn Beach style)

1¼ ounce (37ml) Jamaican dark rum
¾ ounce (22ml) gold rum
½ ounce (15ml) falernum
½ ounce (15ml) Cointreau
1 ounce (30ml) grapefruit juice
¾ ounce (22ml) lime juice
2 dashes Angostura bitters
1 dash absinthe

Shake with ice and strain into an ice-filled
Old Fashioned glass. Garnish with a mint sprig.

Maiden's Blush

1 1/2 ounce (45ml) gin
1/2 ounce (15ml) orange curaçao
1/2 ounce (15ml) lemon juice
1 dash grenadine

Shake with ice and strain into a cocktail glass.

Adapted from *The Savoy Cocktail Book* by Harry Craddock (1930)

Maiden's Prayer

1 ounce (30ml) gin
1 ounce (30ml) triple sec
1/2 ounce (15ml) lemon juice
1/2 ounce (15ml) orange juice

Shake with ice and strain into a cocktail glass.

Adapted from *The Savoy Cocktail Book* by Harry Craddock (1930)

FEATURED DRINK

Mamie Taylor

2 ounces (60ml) Scotch whisky
2 lime wedges
Ginger ale

Build over ice in a highball glass, squeezing in the juice
from the lime wedges. Garnish with a fresh lime wedge.

Man in Black

(Created by Jim Wrigley, London, for Johnny Cash)

2 ounces (60ml) bourbon
1 ounce (30ml) coffee liqueur
2 dashes Angostura bitters

Mix a small amount of bourbon and bitters in the bottom of an Old Fashioned glass. Add one ice cube, more whisky and keep stirring. Gradually add more ice, coffee liqueur and bourbon while stirring.

FEATURED DRINK

Manhattan

1¹/₂ ounce (45ml) rye or bourbon
³/₄ ounce (22ml) sweet vermouth
2 dashes Angostura bitters

Stir with ice and strain into a cocktail glass. Garnish with a cherry.

Adapted from *Modern Bartender's Guide* by O. H. Byron (1884)

FEATURED DRINK

Manhattan (Dry)

1¹/₂ ounce (45ml) rye or bourbon
³/₄ ounce (22ml) dry vermouth
2 dashes Angostura bitters

Stir with ice and strain into a cocktail glass.
Garnish with a lemon twist.

Adapted from *Modern Bartender's Guide* by O. H. Byron (1884)

Manhattan (Perfect)

1¹/2 ounce (45ml) rye or bourbon
¹/4 ounce (7ml) sweet vermouth
¹/4 ounce (7ml) dry vermouth
2 dashes Angostura bitters

Stir with ice and strain into a cocktail glass.
Garnish with a cherry and a lemon twist.

FEATURED DRINK

Maple Leaf

1¹/2 ounce (45ml) bourbon
³/4 ounce (22ml) lemon juice
2 teaspoons (10ml) maple syrup

Shake with ice and strain into a cocktail glass.

Marco-Antonio

2 ounces (60ml) gin
¹/3 ounce (10ml) grapefruit juice
1 teaspoon (5ml) maraschino liqueur
¹/4 ounce (7ml) egg white

Shake vigorously with ice and strain into a cocktail glass.

Adapted from *Bar La Florida Cocktails* (Havana, Cuba, 1935)

Mardi Gras Cocktail

(Created by Alexander Hauck, The Bitter Truth, Germany)

2 ounces (60ml) bourbon
1/2 ounce (15ml) apricot brandy
2 dashes The Bitter Truth lemon bitters

Stir with ice and strain into a cocktail glass.
Garnish with a lemon twist.

Margaret Rose

3/4 ounce (22ml) gin
3/4 ounce (22ml) Calvados
1/3 ounce (10ml) Cointreau
1/3 ounce (10ml) lemon juice
1 dash grenadine

Shake with ice and strain into a cocktail glass.

Adapted from *United Kingdom Bartenders' Guild
Guide To Drinks* (1953)

Margarita

1 1/2 ounce (45ml) tequila
blanco or reposado
3/4 ounce (22ml) triple sec
3/4 ounce (22ml) lime juice

Shake with ice and strain into a
cocktail glass or an
ice-filled Old Fashioned glass.
Salt rim optional.

FEATURED DRINK

M

Marguerite

2 ounces (60ml) Plymouth gin
3/4 ounce (22ml) dry vermouth
1 dash orange bitters

Stir with ice and strain into a cocktail glass.

Adapted from *Stuart's Fancy Drinks & How To Mix Them*
by Thomas Stuart (1896)

Markee

(Created by Giovanni Burdi at Match EC1, London)

1 1/2 ounce (45ml) bourbon
1/2 ounce (15ml) Chambord
2 ounces (60ml) cranberry juice
1/2 ounce (15ml) lemon juice
1 teaspoon (5ml) simple syrup

Shake with ice and strain into a cocktail glass.
Garnish with a raspberry.

Marmalade Cocktail

2 ounces (60ml) gin
1/2 ounce (15ml) orange marmalade
1/4 ounce (7ml) lemon juice

Shake with ice and strain into a cocktail glass.
Garnish with an orange twist.

Adapted from *The Savoy Cocktail Book* by Harry Craddock (1930)

Martin Casa

(Created at Café Martin, Montreal)

2 ounces (60ml) Jamaican dark rum
1/2 ounce (15ml) Cointreau
1/2 ounce (15ml) apricot brandy
3/4 ounce (22ml) lime juice

Shake with ice and strain into a cocktail glass.

Adapted from *Bottoms Up* by Ted Saucier (1951)

Martinez

11/4 ounce (37ml) gin
11/4 ounce (37ml) sweet vermouth
1 teaspoon (5ml) orange curaçao or
maraschino liqueur
2 dashes Angostura bitters

Stir with ice and strain into a cocktail glass.
Garnish with a lemon twist.

Adapted from *Modern Bartender's Guide* by O. H. Byron (1884)

Martini (dry)

21/2 ounces (75ml) gin or vodka
1/2 ounce (15ml) dry vermouth

Stir with ice and strain into a cocktail glass.
Garnish with a lemon twist or an olive.

Dry Martini (left), Sweet Martini (right).

Martini (extra dry)

2¹/₂ ounces (75ml) gin or vodka
1 dash dry vermouth

Stir with ice and strain into a cocktail glass.
Garnish with a lemon twist or an olive.

Martini (sweet)

2¹/₂ ounces (75ml) gin or vodka
¹/₂ ounce (15ml) sweet vermouth

Stir with ice and strain into a cocktail glass.
Garnish with a lemon twist or a cherry.

Mary Morandeyra

1 ounce (30ml) sloe gin
1 ounce (30ml) sweet vermouth
1 teaspoon (5ml) maraschino liqueur
1 ounce (30ml) grapefruit juice

Shake with ice and strain into a cocktail glass.

Adapted from *Bar La Florida Cocktails* (Havana, Cuba, 1935)

Mary Pickford

13/4 ounce (50ml) light rum
1 teaspoon (5ml) maraschino liqueur
1 ounce (30ml) pineapple juice
2 dashes grenadine

Shake with ice and strain into a cocktail glass.

Adapted from *The Savoy Cocktail Book* by Harry Craddock (1930)

Masson Sour

(Created by Jeff Masson)

11/2 ounce (45ml) añejo rum
1/2 ounce (15ml) port
3/4 ounce (22ml) lemon juice
2 teaspoons (10ml) honey
1/2 ounce (15ml) egg white

Shake vigorously with ice and strain into an ice-filled
Old Fashioned glass. Garnish with a black grape
and a lemon slice.

Matinée Martini

(Created by Stephan Berg, The Bitter Truth, Germany)

2 ounces (60ml) gin
11/2 teaspoon (7.5ml) The Bitter Truth
Orange Flower Water
1 teaspoon (5ml) ginger syrup
3 sage leaves

Muddle the sage leaves with the ginger syrup in the base of
a shaker. Add everything else and shake with ice. Double
strain into a cocktail glass. Garnish with a lemon twist.

Maxim

1³/₄ ounce (50ml) gin
¹/₂ ounce (15ml) dry vermouth
¹/₄ ounce (7ml) white crème de cacao

Stir with ice and strain into a cocktail glass.

Mayfair Cocktail

(Created by Robert Vermeire, Embassy Club, London)

1¹/₂ ounce (45ml) gin
¹/₂ ounce (15ml) apricot brandy
³/₄ ounce (22ml) orange juice
1 dash clove syrup

Shake with ice and strain into a cocktail glass.

Adapted from *Cocktails: How To Mix Them*
by Robert Vermeire (1922)

FEATURED DRINK

Mediterranean Fizz

*(Created by Adam Elmegirab, Evo-lution,
Aberdeen, Scotland, 2008)*

1¹/₂ ounce (45ml) vodka
³/₄ ounce (22ml) lemon juice
¹/₂ ounce (15ml) vanilla syrup
8 white grapes
6 basil leaves
Soda water

Muddle grapes in the base of a shaker, add remaining
ingredients (except soda water), ice and shake. Top with
soda water and double strain into an ice-filled highball
glass. Garnish with a basil leaf.

Meehoulong

1 1/2 ounce (45ml) sloe gin
3/4 ounce (22ml) dry vermouth
3/4 ounce (22ml) sweet vermouth
1 dash orange bitters

Stir with ice and strain into a cocktail glass.
Garnish with a lemon twist.

Adapted from *Cocktails: How To Mix Them*
by Robert Vermeire (1922)

Melon Ball

1 ounce (30ml) vodka
1 ounce (30ml) Midori
Orange juice or pineapple juice

Build over ice in a highball glass.
Garnish with an orange slice and a melon slice.

Merry Widow

1 1/2 ounce (45ml) gin
3/4 ounce (22ml) dry vermouth
1 dash Bénédictine
1 dash absinthe
1 dash Angostura bitters

Stir with ice and strain into a cocktail glass.
Garnish with a lemon twist.

Adapted from *The Savoy Cocktail Book*
by Harry Craddock (1930)

Meteor

(Created by Harry Craddock, American Bar, Dorchester Hotel, London)

1 1/2 ounce (45ml) rye or bourbon
1/4 ounce (7ml) sweet vermouth
1/4 ounce (7ml) absinthe

Stir with ice and strain into a cocktail glass.

Adapted from *Bottoms Up* by Ted Saucier (1951)

Metropole

1 1/4 ounce (37ml) brandy
1 1/4 ounce (37ml) dry vermouth
1 dash Peychaud's bitters
1 dash orange bitters

Stir with ice and strain into a cocktail glass.
Garnish with a cherry.

Metropolitan (old recipe)

1 1/2 ounce (45ml) cognac
3/4 ounce (22ml) sweet vermouth
2 dashes simple syrup
2 dashes Angostura bitters

Stir with ice and strain into a cocktail glass.
Garnish with a cherry.

Metropolitan (modern)

1 1/2 ounce (45ml) Absolut Kurant
1/2 ounce (15ml) Cointreau
3/4 ounce (22ml) cranberry juice
1/2 ounce (15ml) lime juice

Shake with ice and strain into a cocktail glass.
Garnish with a flamed orange peel.

Miami Beach

1 ounce (30ml) Scotch whisky
3/4 ounce (22ml) dry vermouth
3/4 ounce (22ml) grapefruit juice

Shake with ice and strain into a cocktail glass.

Miami Cocktail

1 1/2 ounce (45ml) light rum
1/2 ounce (15ml) lime juice
1 teaspoon (5ml) white crème de menthe

Shake with ice and strain into a cocktail glass.

Miami Iced Tea

1/2 ounce (15ml) vodka
1/2 ounce (15ml) gin
1/2 ounce (15ml) light rum
1/2 ounce (15ml) peach schnapps
1 ounce (30ml) cranberry juice
7-Up

Build over ice in a highball glass.
Garnish with a lemon slice.

Mikado Cocktail

1³/₄ ounce (50ml) brandy
¹/₄ ounce (7ml) crème de noyeaux
¹/₄ ounce (7ml) orange curaçao
¹/₄ ounce (7ml) orgeat
2 dashes Angostura bitters

Stir with ice and strain into a cocktail glass.
Garnish with a cherry and a lemon twist.

Adapted from *Cocktails: How To Mix Them*
by Robert Vermeire (1922)

Milk Punch

2 ounces (60ml) cognac
1 ounce (30ml) añejo rum
¹/₂ ounce (15ml) simple syrup
4 ounces (120ml) milk

Shake with ice and strain into a large wine glass.
Dust with nutmeg.

Adapted from *How To Mix Drinks*
by Jerry Thomas (1862)

FEATURED DRINK

Millionaire

1¹/2 ounce (45ml)
Jamaican dark rum
³/4 ounce (22ml) sloe gin
³/4 ounce (22ml)
apricot brandy
³/4 ounce (22ml)
lime juice

Shake with ice and strain
into a coupe.

Adapted from
The Savoy Cocktail Book
by Harry Craddock (1930)

Mimosa

1¹/2 ounce (45ml) orange juice
Champagne

Build in a flute.

Adapted from *The Artistry of Mixing Drinks* by Frank Meier (1936)

Mint Julep

2 ounces (60ml) bourbon
2 teaspoons (10ml) simple syrup
6 mint leaves

In the bottom of a highball glass
muddle mint with syrup.
Add crushed ice, bourbon
and stir. Top with crushed
ice and garnish with
a mint sprig.

You will definitely
impress your guests if
you serve your juleps in a
frosty silver cup.

Mitch Martini

(Created by Giovanni Burdi, Match EC1, London)

1 1/2 ounce (45ml) Żubrówka vodka
3/4 ounce (22ml) apple juice
1 teaspoon (5ml) passion fruit syrup
1 teaspoon (5ml) crème de peche

Shake with ice and strain into a cocktail glass.
Garnish with a lemon twist.

Mix '06

(created by Robert Hess, 2006)

1 ounce (30ml) gin
1/2 ounce (15ml) Bénédictine
1/4 ounce (7ml) Campari
1 dash Peychaud's bitters
Ginger ale

Shake everything with ice (except ginger ale) and strain into an ice-filled highball glass. Top with ginger ale. Garnish with a lime twist.

Mockingbird

2 ounces (60ml) gin
1/2 ounce (15ml) light rum
1/2 ounce (15ml) kirsch
1 dash absinthe

Shake with ice and strain into a cocktail glass.

Adapted from *My 35 Years Behind Bars* by Johnny Brooks (1954)

Modern Cocktail

1 3/4 ounce (50ml) Scotch whisky
1/4 ounce (7ml) Jamaican dark rum
1 teaspoon (5ml) absinthe
1/4 ounce (7ml) lemon juice
1 dash orange bitters

Shake with ice and strain into a cocktail glass.

Mojito

2 ounces (60ml)
light rum
1 ounce (30ml) lime juice
1/2 ounce (15ml)
simple syrup
8 mint leaves
Soda water (optional but
not recommended)

In the bottom of a highball
glass muddle mint with
syrup. Add crushed ice, rum,
lime and stir. Top with
crushed ice and garnish with
a mint sprig.

FEATURED DRINK

Monkey Gland

(Created by Harry McElhone)

1 1/2 ounce (45ml) gin
3/4 ounce (22ml) orange juice
1 dash absinthe
1 teaspoon (5ml) grenadine

Shake with ice and strain into a cocktail glass.

Adapted from *ABC of Mixing Cocktails* by Harry McElhone (1922)

FEATURED DRINK

Montana Cocktail

1 1/2 ounce (45ml) brandy
1/2 ounce (15ml) dry vermouth
1 teaspoon (5ml) port
1 teaspoon (5ml) anisette
2 dashes Angostura bitters

Stir with ice and strain into a cocktail glass.

Adapted from *Drinks* by Jacques Straub (1914)

Morning After Cocktail

(Created by J.P. Mitchell)

1 1/2 ounce (45ml) Fernet Branca
1/2 ounce (15ml) white crème de menthe
1/4 ounce (7ml) crème de cassis

Shake with ice and strain into a cocktail glass.

Adapted from *Barflies & Cocktails* by Harry McElhone (1927)

Morning Coffee / Steve's Coffee

*(Created by Steve Jaffe who says "People like to order this as
Steve's drink because they know that I know what they mean and
they don't have to let it be known they want a drink with liquor
in it—they just want me [wink, wink] to make it.")*

1/4 ounce (7ml) Tia Maria
1/4 ounce (7ml) crème de bananes
Coffee
Cream (optional)

Stir liqueurs into hot coffee and add cream if desired.

Morning Glory Fizz

1 1/2 ounce (45ml) Scotch whisky
2 dashes absinthe
1/2 ounce (15ml) simple syrup
1/2 ounce (15ml) egg white
1/2 ounce (15ml) lime juice
1/4 ounce (7ml) lemon juice
Soda water

Shake vigorously with ice (except soda water) and strain into an ice-filled highball glass. Top with soda water.

Adapted from *Bartender's Manual* by Harry Johnson (1882)

Morro Castle

1 1/2 ounce (45ml) gold rum
3/4 ounce (22ml) dry vermouth
3/4 ounce (22ml) pineapple juice
3 dashes grenadine

Shake with ice and strain into a cocktail glass.

Adapted from *My 35 Years Behind Bars* by Johnny Brooks (1954)

Moscow Mule

(Created at Cock 'n' Bull Tavern, Hollywood)

1½ ounce (45ml)
vodka
½ lime
Ginger beer

Build over ice in a high-ball glass, squeezing in lime and dropping it in for garnish.

It's been traditional to serve this drink in a copper mug. However, they can be hard to find today.

Adapted from *Bottom's Up* by Ted Saucier (1951)

Moth Cocktail

1½ ounce (45ml) gin
½ ounce (15ml) dry vermouth
1 dash absinthe
2 pickled onions

Stir with ice and strain into a cocktail glass.
Garnish with pickled onions.

Adapted from *One Hundred Ways* by John Boyle Stafford (1932)

Mountain

1 1/2 ounce (45ml) rye
1/4 ounce (7ml) dry vermouth
1/4 ounce (7ml) sweet vermouth
1/4 ounce (7ml) lemon juice
1/2 ounce (15ml) egg white

Shake vigorously with ice and strain into a cocktail glass.

Mr. & Mrs.

(Created by Walter Kiernan, radio commentator)

1 1/2 ounce (45ml) rye
3/4 ounce (22ml) lemon juice
2 teaspoons (10ml) grenadine
1/2 ounce (15ml) egg white

Shake vigorously with ice and strain into a cocktail glass.

Adapted from *Bottom's Up* by Ted Saucier (1951)

Mr. Jack

(Created by Charly Artale, B-Boulevard Bar, Cordoba, Argentina)

2 ounces (60ml) Jack Daniels
1 ounce (30ml) Grand Marnier
1 ounce (30ml) apple juice

Stir with ice and strain into a cocktail glass. Garnish with a cinnamon stick which has been soaked in Jack Daniels.

Mr. Wardle

(Created by Michelle Mantynen, 2008)

4 ounces (120ml) Sandeman Founders Reserve Port
1 ounce (30ml) Aperol
1 teaspoon (5ml) pimento dram (allspice dram)
1 ounce (30ml) pineapple juice
1 slice orange

Muddle orange in a toddy glass. Heat remaining ingredients in a pan and pour over an orange slice.

Mudslide

3/4 ounce (22ml) vodka
3/4 ounce (22ml) Baileys Irish Cream
3/4 ounce (22ml) coffee liqueur
3/4 ounce (22ml) cream

Shake with ice and strain into an ice-filled
Old Fashioned glass.

Mulata Daiquiri

1 1/2 ounce (45ml) gold rum
1/2 ounce (15ml) white crème de cacao
1/2 ounce (15ml) lime juice
1/2 teaspoon (2.5ml) simple syrup

Shake with ice and strain into a cocktail glass.

This drink was originally made with Bacardi Elixir,
a liqueur that was made by macerating prunes and
cherry stones in rum.

Mule

1 1/2 ounce (45ml) gin
1/2 ounce (15ml) crème de cassis
3/4 ounce (22ml) lemon juice

Shake with ice and strain into a cocktail glass.

Murderer's Cocktail

(Created by Bob Coates who advises: "Exits should be plainly marked and fire extinguishers provided at all times when this cocktail is served.")

3/4 ounce (22ml) Calvados
3/4 ounce (22ml) Swedish Punsch
3/4 ounce (22ml) dark rum
2 dashes absinthe
1 dash Angostura bitters

Shake with ice and strain into a cocktail glass.

Adapted from *Barflies & Cocktails*
by Harry McElhone (1927)

My Old Pal

(Created by "Sparrow" Robertson)

3/4 ounce (22ml) Canadian Club
3/4 ounce (22ml) Campari
3/4 ounce (22ml) sweet vermouth

Build over ice in an Old Fashioned glass.

Adapted from *Barflies & Cocktails*
by Harry McElhone (1927)

Myrtle Bank Special

(Created at Myrtle Bank Hotel, Kingston, Jamaica)

1 1/2 ounce (45ml) gin
3/4 ounce (22ml) sweet
vermouth
3/4 ounce (22ml) pineapple
juice

Shake with ice and strain into
a cocktail glass.

Adapted from *Bottom's Up*
by Ted Saucier (1951)

N

Nacional Cocktail

(As prepared at the Hotel Nacional, Cuba)

3 ounces (90ml) light rum
1/2 ounce (15ml) lime juice
1/2 ounce (15ml) pineapple juice
1 teaspoon (5ml) simple syrup

Shake well and strain into a coupe.

Adapted from *The Cocktail Hour* by Louis P. De Gouy (1951)

Napoleon

1 1/2 ounce (45ml) gin
3/4 ounce (22ml) orange curaçao
1/4 ounce (7ml) Fernet Branca
1/4 ounce (7ml) Dubonnet rouge

Stir with ice and strain into a cocktail glass.
Garnish with a lemon twist.

Negroni

1 ounce (30ml) gin
1 ounce (30ml) sweet vermouth
1 ounce (30ml) Campari

Build over ice in an Old Fashioned glass. Stir well
before serving and garnish with an orange slice.

Adapted from *Bottoms Up* by Ted Saucier (1951)

Negroni Tredici

(Created by Toby Maloney, The Violet Hour, Chicago, 2009)

2 ounces (60ml) gin
1 ounce (30ml) sweet vermouth
1/4 ounce (7ml) Cynar
1/4 ounce (7ml) Campari
13 drops Regan's orange bitters

Stir with ice and strain into an ice-filled Old Fashioned glass. Garnish with a lemon and an orange twist.

Nerøs

(Created by Søren Krogh Sørensen, Le Lion • Bar de Paris, Hamburg, Germany)

2 ounces (60ml) scotch
3/4 ounce (22ml) dandelion liqueur
3/4 ounce (22ml) freshly squeezed
Granny smith apple juice

Stir scotch and dandelion liqueur with ice and strain into an ice-filled Old Fashioned glass. Top with apple juice.

Neutral Ground

(Created by Rhiannon Enlil, Old Absinthe House, New Orleans.)

2 ounces (60ml) Sazerac rye whiskey
1/2 ounce (15ml) Bénédictine
1/2 ounce (15ml) dry amontillado sherry
3 dashes Regan's orange bitters

Stir with ice and strain into a cocktail glass. Garnish with an orange twist.

New Orleans Gin Fizz

See Ramos Gin Fizz

New Waldorf

1¹/₂ ounce (45ml) gin
³/₄ ounce (22ml) sweet vermouth
³/₄ ounce (22ml) dry vermouth
1 pineapple wedge

Muddle pineapple in the base of a shaker. Add remaining ingredients and shake with ice. Strain into a cocktail glass.

Adapted from *Bottoms Up* by Ted Saucier (1951)

New York Cavalcade

(Created by Louis Sobol, syndicated New York Journal-American columnist)

1¹/₂ ounce (45ml) light rum
1 ounce (30ml) Grand Marnier
³/₄ ounce (22ml) lemon juice
1 teaspoon (5ml) grenadine

Blend with crushed ice and pour into a coupe.

Adapted from *Bottoms Up* by Ted Saucier (1951)

New York Sour

2 ounces (60ml) bourbon or rye
3/4 ounce (22ml) red wine
1 ounce (30ml) lemon juice
1/2 ounce (15ml) simple syrup

Shake with ice (except red wine) and strain into a sour glass or an ice-filled Old Fashioned glass. Float red wine and garnish with a lemon slice and a cherry.

Newark

(Created by Jim Meehan, New York)

2 ounces (60ml) bonded apple brandy
1 ounce (30ml) sweet vermouth
1/4 ounce (7ml) Fernet Branca
1/4 ounce (7ml) maraschino liqueur

Shake with ice and strain into a coupe.

Nielka

1 1/2 ounce (45ml) vodka
1/2 ounce (15ml) dry vermouth
1 ounce (30ml) orange juice

Shake with ice and strain into a cocktail glass.

Adapted from *Drinks – Long & Short*
by Nina Toye and A. H. Adair (1925)

No Name

1 ounce (30ml) gin
1/2 ounce (15ml) Grand Marnier
1/2 ounce (15ml) kirsch
1 ounce (30ml) lemon juice

Shake with ice and strain into a cocktail glass.

Nooner, The

(Created by Charles Joly, Chief Mixologist,
The Drawing Room, Chicago, 2007)

2 ounces (60ml) bourbon
1/2 ounce (15ml) Navan
1/4 ounce (7ml) maple syrup
1/2 teaspoon freshly
grated ginger
3 dashes orange bitters

Shake with ice (except bitters)
and double strain into a coupe.
Add bitters and garnish with
flamed orange peel.

Norsk Mulata

(Created by George Sinclair, London, 2008)

1 1/2 ounce (45ml) aquavit
3/4 ounce (22ml) dark crème de cacao
3/4 ounce (22ml) lemon juice

Shake with ice and strain into a cocktail glass.
Garnish with a lemon twist.

Novara

(Created by Jamie Boudreau, Seattle,
www.SpiritsandCocktails.com)

1 1/2 ounce (45ml) Plymouth gin
1/2 ounce (15ml) Campari
1/2 ounce (15ml) passion fruit syrup
1/2 ounce (15ml) lemon juice

Shake with ice and strain into a cocktail glass.

Nuclear Daiquiri

(Created By Gregor De Gruyther, London)

3/4 ounce (22ml) Wray & Nephew Overproof Rum
3/4 ounce (22ml) green Chartreuse
1/3 ounce (10ml) falernum
3/4 ounce (22ml) lime juice

Shake with ice and strain into a cocktail glass.

Nugent

1 1/2 ounce (45ml) light rum
1 ounce (30ml) lemon juice
1/2 ounce (15ml) simple syrup
1/2 ounce (15ml) egg white

Shake vigorously and strain into a cocktail glass.

Nymph

¾ ounce (22ml) Canadian Club
¾ ounce (22ml) apricot brandy
¾ ounce (22ml) Lillet Blanc
1 dash Angostura bitters

Stir with ice and strain into a cocktail glass.

Promotional recipe wheel, circa 1930s

O

Ocean Shore Cocktail

1 ounce (30ml) sloe gin
³/4 ounce (22ml) gin
¹/4 ounce (7ml) raspberry syrup
³/4 ounce (22ml) lime juice
¹/2 ounce (15ml) egg white

Shake vigorously with ice and strain into a cocktail glass.

If you're into 'tangy,'
give this a try.

Adapted from *The World's
Drinks & How To Mix Them* by
William Boothby (1908)

Odd McIntyre

3/4 ounce (22ml) brandy
3/4 ounce (22ml) Cointreau
3/4 ounce (22ml) Lillet Blanc
3/4 ounce (22ml) lemon juice

Shake with ice and strain into a cocktail glass.

Adapted from *"Cocktail Bill" Boothby's World Drinks and How to Mix Them* by William Boothby (1930)

Of Thee I Sing Baby

(Created by William Gaxton, actor)

1 1/2 ounce (45ml) Jamaican dark rum
1/2 ounce (15ml) Cointreau
1 teaspoon (5ml) grenadine
3/4 ounce (22ml) lemon juice

Shake with ice and strain into a cocktail glass.
Garnish with a cherry and a mint leaf.

Adapted from *Bottoms Up* by Ted Saucier (1951)

Oh Gosh

*(Created by Tony Conigliaro, London,
http://drinkfactory.blogspot.com)*

1 ounce (30ml) white rum
1 ounce (30ml) triple sec
3/4 ounce (22ml) lime juice

Shake with ice and strain into a cocktail glass.
Garnish with a lemon twist.

OH! OH! Mac

See Odd McIntyre

Old Chum's Reviver

2 ounces (60ml) brandy
1 ounce (30ml) lemon juice
3/4 ounce (22ml) strawberry syrup
Soda water

Shake with ice (except soda water) and strain into an ice-filled highball glass. Top with soda water and garnish with a lemon slice.

Adapted from *American & Other Iced Drinks* by Charlie Paul (1902)

Old Fashioned

2 ounces (60ml) bourbon
1 teaspoon (5ml) simple syrup
2 dashes Angostura bitters

Mix syrup with a small amount of bourbon and bitters in the bottom of an Old Fashioned glass. Add one ice cube, more whisky and keep stirring. Gradually add more ice and bourbon while stirring. Garnish with an orange twist.

The Old Fashioned is a true classic. If you use sugar syrup rather than a sugar cube, you avoid any undissolved sugar.

Adapted from *Modern American Drinks* by
George Kappeler (1895)

FEATURED DRINK

Old Fashioned

Old Pal

FEATURED DRINK

1 ounce (30ml) bourbon
3/4 ounce (22ml) dry vermouth
3/4 ounce (22ml) Campari

Stir with ice and strain into a cocktail glass.
Garnish with a lemon twist.

Adapted from *"Cocktail Bill" Boothby's World Drinks and How to Mix Them* by William Boothby (1930)

Old Vermont

1¹/₂ ounce (45ml) gin
¹/₄ ounce (7ml) lemon juice
¹/₄ ounce (7ml) orange juice
2 teaspoons (10ml) maple syrup
1 dash Angostura bitters

Shake with ice and strain into a small cocktail glass.

Adapted from *"Cocktail Bill" Boothby's World Drinks and How to Mix Them* by William Boothby (1934)

Olympic

(Created by Frank Meier)

³/₄ ounce (22ml) brandy
³/₄ ounce (22ml) orange curaçao
³/₄ ounce (22ml) orange juice

Shake well and strain into a cocktail glass.

Adapted from *The Artistry Of Mixing Drinks* by Frank Meier (1936)

One Way

(Created by Jack Stagg)

³/₄ ounce (22ml) gin
³/₄ ounce (22ml) Swedish Punsch
³/₄ ounce (22ml) peach brandy
³/₄ ounce (22ml) lemon juice

Shake with ice and strain into a cocktail glass.

Adapted from *Café Royal Cocktail Book* by W. J. Tarling (1937)

Opal

1¹/₂ ounce (45ml) gin
¹/₂ ounce (15ml) triple sec
1 ounce (30ml) orange juice
2 dashes orange flower water

Shake with ice and strain into a cocktail glass.

Opalescent Cocktail

1¹/₂ ounce (45ml) gin
³/₄ ounce (22ml) lemon juice
2 teaspoons (10ml) grenadine
¹/₂ ounce (15ml) egg white

Shake vigorously with ice and strain into a cocktail glass.

Open House

1¹/₂ ounce (45ml) light rum
¹/₃ ounce (10ml) orange juice
¹/₃ ounce (10ml) pineapple juice
1 teaspoon (5ml) apricot brandy

Shake with ice and strain into a cocktail glass.

Opera

1¹/₂ ounce (45ml) gin
¹/₂ ounce (15ml) Dubonnet rouge
¹/₂ ounce (15ml) maraschino liqueur

Stir with ice and strain into a cocktail glass.
Garnish with an orange twist.

Orange Blossom

1 1/4 ounce (37ml) gin
1 1/4 ounce (37ml) orange juice

Shake with ice and strain into a cocktail glass.

Orchid

(Created by Eddie Clarke)

1 1/2 ounce (45ml) gin
3/4 ounce (22ml) crème de noyaux
3/4 ounce (22ml) lemon juice
1 teaspoon (5ml) crème de violette

Shake with ice and strain into a sugar-rimmed
cocktail glass.

Adapted from *Shaking In The 60's* by Eddie Clarke (1963)

Oriental

1 ounce (30ml) rye
1/2 ounce (15ml) sweet vermouth
1/2 ounce (15ml) orange curaçao
1/2 ounce (15ml) lime juice

Shake with ice and strain into a cocktail glass.

Ott's Special

(Created by Jack Powell)

1¹/₂ ounce (45ml) gin
¹/₂ ounce (15ml) Strega
¹/₂ ounce (15ml) dry vermouth

Stir with ice and strain into a
cocktail glass.

Adapted from *Café Royal Cocktail
Book* by W. J. Tarling (1937)

Ox Blood

(Created by R. Emmerich)

³/₄ ounce (22ml) gin
³/₄ ounce (22ml) cherry brandy
³/₄ ounce (22ml) sweet vermouth
1 teaspoon (5ml) orange curaçao
2 dashes orange bitters

Stir with ice and strain into a cocktail glass.

Adapted from *Café Royal Cocktail Book* by W. J. Tarling (1937)

P–Q

Packard Twins

(As mixed at the Hotel Barclay)

1 1/2 ounce (45ml) rye
3/4 ounce (22ml) sherry
2 dashes orange bitters
2 dashes Angostura bitters
2 dashes maraschino liqueur

Stir with ice and strain into a cocktail glass.

Adapted from *Angostura Recipes* (1934)

Paddlin' Madeline Home

(Created by William Gaxton, actor)

1 1/2 ounce (45ml) applejack
1 teaspoon (5ml) triple sec
1 teaspoon (5ml) grenadine
1/2 ounce (15ml) lemon juice
1/2 ounce (15ml) egg white

Shake vigorously with ice and
strain into a cocktail glass.

Adapted from *Bottoms Up*
by Ted Saucier (1951)

Paddy Cocktail

1¼ ounce (37ml) Irish whiskey
1¼ ounce (37ml) sweet vermouth
1 dash Angostura bitters

Stir with ice and strain into a cocktail glass.

Palace St. Moritz Special

(Created by Gustav Doebeli, Palace Hotel, St. Moritz)

1 ounce (30ml) gin
1 ounce (30ml) orange curaçao
½ ounce (15ml) lemon juice
½ ounce (15ml) orange juice
1 dash absinthe

Shake with ice and strain into a cocktail glass.

Adapted from *Bottoms Up* by Ted Saucier (1951)

Pall Mall

(Recipe from "Guido," Café De Paris, Monte Carlo)

¾ ounce (22ml) gin
¾ ounce (22ml) sweet vermouth
¾ ounce (22ml) dry vermouth
1 teaspoon (5ml) white crème de menthe
1 dash orange bitters

Stir with ice and strain into a cocktail glass.

Adapted from *ABC of Mixing Cocktails* by Harry McElhone (1922)

Palm Breeze

(Created by A.C. Davidge)

1¹/₂ ounce (45ml) Jamaican dark rum
1 ounce (30ml) yellow Chartreuse
¹/₂ ounce (15ml) white crème de cacao
¹/₂ ounce (15ml) lime juice
1 dash grenadine

Shake with ice and strain into a cocktail glass.

Adapted from *United Kingdom Bartenders' Guild Guide To Drinks* (1953)

Palm Tree

1¹/₂ ounce (45ml) gin
³/₄ ounce (22ml) dry vermouth
³/₄ ounce (22ml) apricot brandy
1 dash Angostura bitters

Shake with ice and strain into a cocktail glass.

Adapted from *My 35 Years Behind Bars* by Johnny Brooks (1954)

Paloma

2 ounces (60ml) reposado tequila
¹/₂ ounce (15ml) lime juice
Salt
Grapefruit soda

Build over ice in a salt-rimmed highball glass.

FEATURED DRINK

FEATURED DRINK

Papa Doble

1½ ounce (45ml) light rum
1 teaspoon (5ml)
maraschino liqueur
½ ounce (15ml) lime juice
¼ ounce (7ml) grapefruit
juice

Shake (or blend) with ice and
strain into a cocktail glass.

Drink this in honor of
Ernest Hemingway.

Paradise

1½ ounce (45ml) gin
¾ ounce (22ml) apricot brandy
½ ounce (15ml) orange juice
¼ ounce (7ml) lemon juice

Shake with ice and strain into a cocktail glass.

Adapted from *The Savoy Cocktail Book* by Harry Craddock (1930)

Parisian

1½ ounce (45ml) gin
⅔ ounce (20ml) dry vermouth
⅔ ounce (20ml) crème de cassis

Stir with ice and strain into a cocktail glass.

Park Row Cocktail

³/₄ ounce (22ml) rye
³/₄ ounce (22ml) absinthe
³/₄ ounce (22ml) marc

Shake with ice and strain into a cocktail glass.

Adapted from *Barflies & Cocktails* by Harry McElhone (1927)

Parkside Fizz

(Created by Jim Meehan, for PDT in New York)

2 ounces (60ml) citrus vodka
³/₄ ounce (22ml) lemon juice
¹/₂ ounce (30ml) orgeat
6-8 mint leaves
1 ounce (30ml) soda water

Muddle the mint and orgeat in a mixing glass.
Add all (except soda water) and shake with ice.
Strain into an ice-filled Old Fashioned glass. Top with
soda water and garnish with a mint sprig.

Jim recommends using Hangar One Buddha's Hand
for the vodka in this drink.

Adapted from *The Essential Bartender's Guide*
by Robert Hess (2008)

FEATURED DRINK

Passion Fruit Batida

1³/₄ ounce (50ml) cachaça
¹/₂ ounce (15ml) simple syrup
¹/₂ ounce (15ml) condensed milk
Passion fruit

Cut the passion fruit in half and squeeze the pulp into a blender. Add the remaining ingredients and blend with ice. Pour into a coupe.

Passionate Pineapple

2 ounces (60ml) applejack
¹/₂ ounce (15ml) lemon juice
¹/₂ ounce (15ml) pineapple juice
3 dashes Angostura bitters

Shake with ice and strain into a cocktail glass.
Garnish with a lemon twist.

Adapted from *1700 Cocktails For The Man Behind The Bar*
by R. de Fleury (1934)

Pat's Special

³/₄ ounce (22ml) gin
³/₄ ounce (22ml) sherry
³/₄ ounce (22ml) Dubonnet rouge
¹/₂ ounce (15ml) crème de cassis
¹/₄ ounce (7ml) apricot brandy

Shake with ice and strain into a cocktail glass.
Garnish with a cherry and an orange twist.

Paul's Own

(Created by B. Paul, Grosvenor House, London)

3/4 ounce (22ml) gin
3/4 ounce (22ml) dry vermouth
2/3 ounce (20ml) Cointreau
2/3 ounce (20ml) orange curaçao
3 dashes Fernet Branca

Shake well with ice and strain into a cocktail glass.

Adapted from *Bottoms Up* by Ted Saucier (1951)

Peach and Orange Alexander

(Created by Johan Svensson, Drinksfusion, London)

1 ounce (30ml) gin
1/2 ounce (15ml) dark crème de cacao
1 ounce (30ml) cream
1/2 ounce (15ml) crème de peche
1/2 ounce (15ml) orange juice
1 dash simple syrup

Shake with ice and strain into a cocktail glass.
Garnish with grated chocolate and grated orange zest.

FEATURED DRINK

Peach Blow Fizz

1 1/2 ounce (45ml) gin
1/2 ounce (15ml) lemon juice
2 teaspoons (10ml) simple syrup
1/2 peach
Soda water

Cut peach into quarters and muddle in base of shaker. Add remaining ingredients (except soda water) and shake with ice. Strain into an ice-filled highball glass and top with soda water.

Adapted from *Old Waldorf Bar Days* by Albert Stevens Crockett (1931)

FEATURED DRINK

Peacock Alley

1¹/₂ ounce (45ml) light rum
³/₄ ounce (22ml) lime juice
¹/₂ ounce (15ml) maple syrup

Shake with ice and strain into a cocktail glass.

Pegu Club Cocktail

1¹/₂ ounce (45ml) gin
³/₄ ounce (22ml) orange curaçao
¹/₂ ounce (15ml) lime juice
1 dash orange bitters
1 dash Angostura bitters

Shake with ice and strain into a cocktail glass.

Adapted from *ABC of Mixing Cocktails* by Harry McElhone (1922)

Pendennis Cocktail

2 ounces (60ml) gin
1 ounce (30ml) apricot brandy
3/4 ounce (22ml) lime juice
2 dashes Peychaud's bitters

Shake with ice and strain into a cocktail glass.

Penthouse

3/4 ounce (22ml) light rum
3/4 ounce (22ml) Grand Marnier
3/4 ounce (22ml) Dubonnet rouge
1 dash Angostura bitters

Stir with ice and strain into a cocktail glass.
Garnish with a cherry.

Pepper Delirious

(Created by Ryan Magarian)

2 ounces (60ml) gin
3/4 ounce (22ml) lemon juice
3/4 ounce (22ml) simple syrup
2 thin yellow bell pepper rings
2/3 cup loosely packed mint

Muddle everything together in a mixing glass without ice.
Shake with ice and strain into a cocktail glass. Garnish
with a mint sprig and a thin ring of yellow pepper.

Ryan recommends using Aviation gin to make this drink.

Adapted from *The Essential Bartender's Guide*
by Robert Hess (2008)

Perfect Cocktail

2 ounces (60ml) gin
1/4 ounce (7ml) sweet vermouth
1/4 ounce (7ml) dry vermouth
1 dash Angostura bitters

Stir with ice and strain into a cocktail glass. Garnish with a lemon twist.

Perfect Lady

(Created by Sidney Cox, Grosvenor House, London)

1 1/2 ounce (45ml) gin
3/4 ounce (22ml) peach brandy
3/4 ounce (22ml) lemon juice
1 teaspoon (5ml) egg white

Shake vigorously with ice and strain into a cocktail glass.

Adapted from *Café Royal Cocktail Book* by W. J. Tarling (1937)

Petruchio Cocktail

(Created by Jamie Boudreau, Seattle, www.SpiritsandCocktails.com)

1 ounce (30ml) gin
1 ounce (30ml) Aperol
1/2 ounce (15ml) lemon juice
1/2 ounce (15ml) egg white
1 dash simple syrup
2 dashes orange bitters

Shake vigorously with ice and strain into a cocktail glass.

Picador

FEATURED DRINK

1 1/2 ounce (45ml) tequila blanco
3/4 ounce (22ml) Cointreau
3/4 ounce (22ml) lime juice

Shake with ice and strain into a cocktail glass.

Adapted from *Café Royal Cocktail Book* by W. J. Tarling (1937)

Picon Biere

FEATURED DRINK

1 1/2 ounce (45ml) Amer Picon
12 ounces (360ml) beer (Pilsner or wheat beer)

Build in a pilsner glass.

Picon Cocktail

1 1/4 ounce (37ml) Amer Picon
1 1/4 ounce (37ml) sweet vermouth

Stir with ice and strain into a cocktail glass.

Picon Punch

FEATURED DRINK

2 ounces (60ml) Amer Picon
1 ounce (30ml) brandy
1 teaspoon (5ml) grenadine
Soda water

Build over ice in a Collins glass floating the brandy on top.

Pilgrim Cocktail

1¹/₂ ounce (45ml) gold rum
¹/₂ ounce (15ml) Cointreau
¹/₂ ounce (15ml) lemon juice

Shake with ice and strain into a cocktail glass.

Pimm's Cup

FEATURED DRINK

**2¹/₂ ounces (75ml) Pimm's
No. 1 Cup
7-Up or ginger ale**

Build over ice in a highball glass and garnish with some or all of the following: cucumber rind, orange slice, lemon slice, mint sprig, strawberry.

Remember that Pimm's No. 1 Cup is gin based.

Piña Colada

1 ounce (30ml) light rum
1 ounce (30ml) dark rum
2 ounces (60ml) pineapple juice
1 ounce (30ml) coconut cream

Blend with crushed ice and pour into a hurricane glass. Garnish with a cherry and a pineapple spear.

Piña Colada

Piña Partida

(Created by Junior Merino)

1¹/₂ ounce (45ml) silver tequila
2 chunks pineapple
2 slices cucumber
3 lemon wedges
¹/₃ ounce (10ml) simple syrup
¹/₂ ounce (15ml) lemon/lime soda

Muddle the pineapple, cucumber, lemon and simple syrup. Add the tequila and shake with ice. Strain into an ice-filled highball glass and top with lemon/lime soda. Garnish with a slice of cucumber.

In keeping with the name of the drink, Junior recommends using Partida Blanco for the tequila as well as agave syrup instead of simple syrup.

Adapted from *The Essential Bartender's Guide* by Robert Hess (2008)

Pineapple & Cardamom Martini

1¹/₂ ounce (45ml) vodka
¹/₂ ounce (15ml) pineapple juice
2 pineapple wedges
5 cardamom seeds
1 teaspoon (5ml) simple syrup

Hit the cardamom with a muddler in the bottom of a shaker to crack the seeds. Add pineapple wedges, simple syrup and muddle. Add remaining ingredients and shake with ice. Strain into a cocktail glass and garnish with a pineapple leaf.

Ping Pong Cocktail

(Recipe from James E. Bennett, Broken Heart Cafe,
St. Louis, Missouri)

3/4 ounce (22ml) sloe gin
3/4 ounce (22ml) crème de violette
1 ounce (30ml) lemon juice

Shake with ice and strain into a cocktail glass.

Adapted from *Hoffman House Bartender's Guide*
by C. S. Mahoney (1905)

Pink Diamond Martini

(Created by Johan Svensson, Drinksfusion, London)

1 1/4 ounce (37ml) gin
3/4 ounce (22ml) sweet vermouth
1/2 ounce (15ml) triple sec
3/4 ounce (22ml) pink grapefruit juice
1/4 ounce (7ml) simple syrup
1 dash Campari

Shake with ice and strain into a cocktail glass.
Garnish with a grapefruit twist.

FEATURED DRINK

Pink Gin

2 1/2 ounces (75ml) Plymouth gin
6 dashes Angostura bitters

Stir with ice and strain into a cocktail glass.

Pink Lady

1¹/₂ ounce (45ml) gin
¹/₂ ounce (15ml) applejack
³/₄ ounce (22ml) lemon juice
1 teaspoon (5ml) grenadine
¹/₂ ounce (15ml) egg white

Shake vigorously with ice and
strain into a cocktail glass.

Adapted from
The Bartender's Book
by Jack Townsend
& Tom Moore McBride (1951)

Pino Pepe

(Recipe from Trader Vic's, Oakland, California)

2 ounces (60ml) light rum
¹/₄ ounce (7ml) maraschino liqueur
2 ounces (60ml) pineapple juice
¹/₂ ounce (15ml) lime juice
1 teaspoon (5ml) simple syrup

Blend with crushed ice and pour into a hurricane glass.
Garnish with a pineapple spear and a cherry.

Adapted from *Bottoms Up* by Ted Saucier (1951)

Pisco Punch

2 ounces (60ml) pisco
3/4 ounce (22ml) lemon juice
1/2 ounce (15ml) simple syrup
1 ounce (30ml) distilled water
1/4 ounce (7ml) pineapple juice
1 pineapple wedge

Shake with ice and strain into an ice-filled highball glass.
Garnish with a pineapple spear.

Pisco Sour

2 ounces (60ml) pisco
1 ounce (30ml) lemon juice
1/2 ounce (15ml) simple syrup
1/2 ounce (15ml) egg white
3 dashes Angostura bitters

Shake vigorously with ice
(except Angostura bitters)
and strain into a coupe
or a sour glass.
Dash Angostura bitters
on top of drink.

This is both a great
drink and the national
drink of Peru.

Planter's Punch

3 ounces (90ml) Jamaican dark rum
1 ounce (30ml) lime juice
1/2 ounce (15ml) lemon juice
1/2 ounce (15ml) grenadine
12 dashes simple syrup
Soda water

Build over ice in a highball glass. Garnish with a lime
wedge and a lemon slice.

Adapted from *Bartender's Guide* by Trader Vic (1947)

Point and a Half Cooler

(Created by Gabriel Szaszko, 2007,
http://cocktailnerd.com)

1 1/2 ounce (45ml) gin
1/2 ounce (15ml) Punt e Mes vermouth
1/2 ounce (15ml) lemon juice
1 teaspoon (5ml) simple syrup
Soda water

Shake with ice (except soda water) and strain into an
ice-filled highball glass. Top with soda water and
garnish with a lemon twist.

Polish Cooler

(Created by Tomek Roehr, Alkoteka, Poland)

1½ ounce (45ml Żubrówka vodka
¾ ounce (22ml) elderberry syrup
¾ ounce (22ml) apple juice
Soda water

Build over ice in a highball glass. Stir well before serving
and garnish with an apple slice.

FEATURED DRINK

Polish Martini

(Created by Dick Bradsell, London)

¾ ounce (22ml) Żubrówka vodka
¾ ounce (22ml) Krupnik
¾ ounce (22ml) vodka
¾ ounce (22ml) apple juice

Stir with ice and strain into a cocktail glass.
Garnish with a lemon twist.

FEATURED DRINK

Polmos Cooler

1½ ounce (45ml) Żubrówka vodka
1 teaspoon (5ml) crème de peche
½ ounce (15ml) passion fruit syrup
5 ounces (150ml) apple juice
½ passion fruit

Squeeze the pulp from the passion fruit into a shaker with
other ingredients. Shake with ice and strain into a crushed
ice-filled sling glass. Garnish with a lemon twist.

Pomegranate Margarita

1¹/₂ ounce (45ml) reposado tequila
¹/₂ ounce (15ml) Cointreau
³/₄ ounce (22ml) lime juice
³/₄ ounce (22ml) pomegranate juice
1 dash grenadine

Shake with ice and strain into a cocktail glass.

Pompadour

(Created by Frank Meier)

1¹/₂ ounce (45ml) rhum agricole
1¹/₂ ounce (45ml) Pineau des Charentes
¹/₂ ounce (15ml) lemon juice

Shake with ice and strain into a cocktail glass.

Adapted from *The Artistry Of Mixing Drinks*
by Frank Meier (1936)

Pont des Arts

(Created by Adam Elmegirab, Evo-lution,
Aberdeen, Scotland, 2008)

1/2 ounce (15ml) cognac
1/2 ounce (15ml) elderflower liqueur
Vanilla sugar cube*
2 dashes orange bitters
Sparkling wine

Dash bitters onto the sugar cube and place in the bottom
of a flute. Add the spirits and top with sparkling wine.
Garnish with a lemon zest.

*Adam Elmegirab writes: "Supposedly you can buy vanilla
sugar cubes, but I've never come across them. The way I
make my vanilla sugar cubes is really very simple. First
make vanilla sugar by adding a couple of scored vanilla
pods to a bag of caster (superfine) sugar and adding some
sugar cubes to the mixture. Store in a preserving jar for a
week or so. To separate what is now vanilla cubes from the
vanilla sugar, simply pour the contents of the jar through a
colander. The sugar will pass through but not the cubes.
You now have both vanilla sugar and vanilla sugar cubes!"

Pool

(Created by Jack Bamford)

3/4 ounce (22ml) Dubonnet rouge
3/4 ounce (22ml) Lillet Blanc
3/4 ounce (22ml) brandy
1 dash absinthe

Stir with ice (except absinthe) and strain into a cocktail
glass. Dash absinthe on top.

Adapted from *Café Royal Cocktail Book* by W. J. Tarling (1937)

Port Cobbler

See Cobbler

Porto Flip

1 1/2 ounce (45ml) port
1/2 ounce (15ml) brandy
1 egg yolk

Shake vigorously with ice and strain into a cocktail glass.
Garnish with ground nutmeg.

Pousse-Café

1/4 ounce (7ml) grenadine
1/4 ounce (7ml) yellow Chartreuse
1/4 ounce (7ml) crème de cassis
1/4 ounce (7ml) white crème de cacao
1/4 ounce (7ml) green Chartreuse
1/4 ounce (7ml) brandy

Layer in order above in a shot glass.

Prairie Oyster

1 egg yolk
1 teaspoon (5ml) Worcestershire sauce
1 teaspoon (5ml) tomato ketchup
1/2 teaspoon (2.5ml) malt vinegar
2 dashes Tabasco

Place ingredients in a coupe floating the egg yolk on top.
Garnish with black pepper. Swallow in one gulp.

Adapted from *American & Other Drinks* by Leo Engel (1878)

Presbyterian

1½ ounce (45ml) bourbon
Ginger ale
7-Up

Build over ice in a highball glass with equal quantities of ginger ale and 7-Up.

Presidente

¾ ounce (22ml) gold rum
¾ ounce (22ml) orange curaçao
¾ ounce (22ml) dry vermouth

Shake with ice and strain into a cocktail glass. Garnish with a cherry and an orange twist.

Adapted from *Bar La Florida Cocktails* (Havana, Cuba, 1935)

FEATURED DRINK

Presidente Vincent

1 1/2 ounce (45ml) dark rum
3/4 ounce (22ml) dry vermouth
3/4 ounce (22ml) lime juice
1/2 teaspoon (2.5ml) simple syrup

Shake with ice and strain into a cocktail glass.

Primrose

1 1/2 ounce (45ml) sherry
3/4 ounce (22ml) port
1 dash parfait amour
3/4 ounce (22ml) orange juice
1/2 teaspoon (2.5ml) simple syrup
1 scoop ice cream

Shake with ice (except ice cream) and strain into an
ice-filled highball glass. Top with ice cream. Garnish with
mint sprig, a raspberry and a strawberry.

Adapted from *The Flowing Bowl* by William Schmidt (1891)

Princeton Cocktail

1 1/2 ounce (45ml) gin
3/4 ounce (22ml) port
3 dashes orange bitters

Stir gin and bitters with ice and strain into a cocktail glass.
Slowly pour port down the side of the glass, allowing it
to sink to the bottom.

Adapted from *Modern American Drinks* by George Kappeler (1895)

Professor Langnickel

(Created by Mario Kappes, Le Lion • Bar de Paris, Hamburg, Germany)

1 ounce (30ml) kirsch eau de vie
3/4 ounce (22ml) wild black cherry liqueur
3/4 ounce (22ml) Pedro Ximenez sherry

Stir with ice and strain into a cocktail glass.
Garnish with a lemon twist.

Prodigal

(Created by Gabriel Szaszko, 2008, http://cocktailnerd.com)

2 ounces (60ml) sweet vermouth
1/2 ounce (15ml) absinthe
1/2 ounce (15ml) cinnamon syrup

Build over ice in order above in an Old Fashioned glass.
Garnish with a lemon twist.

Provençal Express

(Created by Alexander Day, New York)

1 ounce (30ml) rye
1 ounce (30ml) Lustau East India Sherry
1 ounce (30ml) Amaro Nonino
1 dash Regan's orange bitters

Stir with ice and strain into a cocktail glass.

Prunier

(Recipe from Maison Prunier, London)

3/4 ounce (22ml) Scotch whisky
3/4 ounce (22ml) orange curaçao
3/4 ounce (22ml) sweet vermouth

Stir with ice and strain into a cocktail glass.

Adapted from *Bottoms Up* by Ted Saucier (1951)

P.S. I Love You

3/4 ounce (22ml) Baileys Irish Cream
3/4 ounce (22ml) amaretto
1/2 ounce (15ml) gold rum
1/2 ounce (15ml) coffee liqueur
3/4 ounce (22ml) cream

Shake with ice and strain into a cocktail glass.
Garnish with grated chocolate.

Psittacosis

3/4 ounce (22ml) applejack
3/4 ounce (22ml) dry vermouth
3/4 ounce (22ml) lime juice
1/3 ounce (10ml) grenadine

Shake with ice and strain into a cocktail glass.

Adapted from *My New Cocktail Book* by G.F. Steele (1934)

Puff

2 ounces (60ml) liquor of choice
(bourbon, brandy, etc.)
2 ounces (60ml) milk
Soda water

Build in a highball glass. Stir before serving.

Puritan

1³/₄ ounce (50ml) gin
¹/₂ ounce (15ml) dry vermouth
¹/₄ ounce (7ml) yellow Chartreuse
1 dash orange bitters

Stir with ice in a cocktail glass and serve.

Purple Hooter

1¹/₂ ounce (45ml) vodka
³/₄ ounce (22ml) Chambord
³/₄ ounce (22ml) lime juice
1 teaspoon (5ml) simple syrup

Shake with ice and strain into an ice-filled
Old Fashioned glass.

Purple Kiss

1¹/₄ ounce (37ml) gin
³/₄ ounce (22ml) crème de noyeaux
1 dash cherry brandy
³/₄ ounce (22ml) lemon juice

Shake with ice and strain into a cocktail glass.

Quichua

1¹/₂ ounce (45ml) gin
1¹/₂ ounce (45ml) pisco
1 teaspoon (5ml) simple syrup
1 dash maraschino liqueur
2 dashes orange bitters

Stir and strain into a cocktail glass.
Garnish with a lime slice.

Adapted from *El Libro Del Buen Cocktail*
by Eduardo Eloy Otero (1943)

Queen Anne

(Created by W. J. Tarling)

1¹/₂ ounce (45ml) bourbon
³/₄ ounce (22ml) dry vermouth
³/₄ ounce (22ml) pineapple juice
2 dashes peach bitters

Shake with ice and
strain into a cocktail glass.

Adapted from
Café Royal Cocktail Book
by W. J. Tarling (1937)

Queen's Park Hotel Super Cocktail

1 1/2 ounce (45ml) dark rum
1/2 ounce (15ml) sweet vermouth
1/2 ounce (15ml) lime juice
2 dashes grenadine
4 dashes Angostura bitters

Shake with ice and strain into a cocktail glass.

Adapted from *Trinidad and Other Cocktails*
from the Queen's Park Hotel (1932)

Queen's Park Swizzle

3 ounces (90ml) Demerara rum
1 ounce (30ml) lime juice
1/3 ounce (10ml) simple syrup
6 mint leaves
3 dashes Angostura bitters

Build over crushed ice in a highball glass and swizzle with
a barspoon. Garnish with the empty lime shell
and a mint sprig.

FEATURED DRINK

Quick F.U.

1/3 ounce (10ml) coffee liqueur
1/3 ounce (10ml) Midori
1/3 ounce (10ml) Baileys Irish Cream

Layer in a shot glass in the order above.

Quiet Storm

(Created by Jason Fendick, London)

1 1/2 ounce (45ml) vodka
2 1/2 ounces (75ml) lychee juice
1 1/2 ounce (45ml) guava juice
3/4 ounce (22ml) pineapple juice
2 teaspoons (10ml) coconut cream
1 teaspoon (5ml) lime juice

Shake with ice and strain into an ice-filled highball glass.
Garnish with a half strawberry.

R

R&R

(Created by Jim Meehan, New York)

1 1/2 ounce (45ml) bourbon
2 1/2 ounce (75ml) iced tea
1/4 ounce (7ml) simple syrup
3 raspberries
3 drops rose water

Shake with ice and double strain into an ice-filled highball glass. Garnish with a raspberry with a dried rose inside it.

R.A.C. Cocktail

(Recipe by Fred Faecks, 1914. Robert Vermeire writes, "R.A.C. means Royal Automobile Club. This is the largest club in London, with 16,000 members.")

1 1/2 ounce (45ml) gin
3/4 ounce (22ml) sweet vermouth
3/4 ounce (22ml) dry vermouth
1/2 teaspoon (2.5ml) grenadine
1 dash orange bitters

Stir with ice and strain into a cocktail glass.
Garnish with an orange twist.

Adapted from *Cocktails: How To Mix Them*
by Robert Vermeire (1922)

Radiator

2 ounces (60ml) rye
2/3 ounce (20ml) orange curaçao
2 dashes Angostura bitters
6 cloves

Stir with ice and strain into a cocktail glass.

Adapted from *My 35 Years Behind Bars* by Johnny Brooks (1954)

FEATURED DRINK

Ramos Gin Fizz

(Created by Henry C. Ramos, circa 1888)

2 ounces (60ml) gin
1 ounce (30ml) cream
1/2 ounce (15ml) lime juice
1/2 ounce (15ml) lemon juice
1/2 ounce (15ml) egg white
1/2 ounce (15ml) simple syrup
3 drops orange flower water
Soda water

Shake vigorously with ice (except soda water) for at least one minute. Strain into a small highball glass (without ice) and add a small splash of soda water.

If your arms aren't tired, you haven't shaken enough.

Raspberry & Hibiscus Bellini

(Created by Tony Conigliaro, London,
http://drinkfactory.blogspot.com)

2 ounces (60ml) raspberry and hibiscus purée*
4 ounces (120ml) prosecco

Pour purée into a flute and top with prosecco.

*To make purée, warm 3 ounces (90ml) raspberry purée
with 1/3 ounce (1 gram) hibiscus powder (ground dried
hibiscus powder) for 10 minutes, taking care not to boil.
Use a hand blender to combine and leave to cool.

Raspberry Collins

1 1/2 ounce (45ml) gin or vodka
1 ounce (30ml) lemon juice
3/4 ounce (22ml) simple syrup
6 raspberries
Soda water

Shake with ice (except soda water) and strain into an
ice-filled highball glass. Top with soda water and garnish
with a lemon slice and a raspberry.

Raspberry Martini

1 1/2 ounce (45ml) gin or vodka
3/4 ounce (22ml) Chambord
6 raspberries

Shake with ice and strain into a cocktail glass.
Garnish with a raspberry.

Raspberry Mule

1½ ounce (45ml) vodka
1 ounce (30ml) lime juice
¾ ounce (22ml) simple syrup
6 raspberries
Ginger beer

Shake with ice (except ginger
beer) and strain into an
ice-filled highball glass. Top
with ginger beer and
garnish with a lime wedge.

Red Hook

2 ounces (60ml) rye
½ ounce (15ml) Punt y Mes
¼ ounce (7ml) maraschino liqueur

Stir with ice and strain into a cocktail glass.

Red Lion

(Created by A. Tarling, 1933)

¾ ounce (22ml) gin
¾ ounce (22ml) Grand Marnier
⅓ ounce (10ml) orange juice
⅓ ounce (10ml) lemon juice

Shake with ice and strain into a sugar-rimmed
cocktail glass.

Freshly squeezed juice really brings this drink alive.

Adapted from *Café Royal Cocktail Book* by W. J. Tarling (1937)

Red Snapper

1½ ounce (45ml) gin
3 ounces (90ml) tomato juice
1 teaspoon (5ml) lemon juice
½ teaspoon (2.5ml) Worcestershire sauce
3 dashes Tabasco
½ teaspoon (2.5ml) horseradish (optional)

Softly shake with ice and strain into an ice-filled highball glass. Add salt and black pepper to taste.
Garnish with a lemon slice and a celery stick.

Reform

1 ¾ ounce (50ml) sherry
¾ ounce (22ml) dry vermouth
1 dash orange bitters

Stir with ice and strain into a cocktail glass.
Garnish with a cherry.

Regal Blush

(Created by Eddie Clarke)

¾ ounce (22ml) gin
¾ ounce (22ml) advocaat
¾ ounce (22ml) crème de framboise
1 dash grenadine

Shake with ice and strain into a cocktail glass.

Adapted from *Shake Again With Eddie* by Eddie Clarke (1951)

Regent Star

(Created by C. Chiswell)

1¹/2 ounce (45ml) gin
¹/3 ounce (10ml) orange curaçao
1 teaspoon (5ml) dry vermouth
1 teaspoon (5ml) passion fruit juice

Shake with ice and strain into a cocktail glass.

Adapted from *Café Royal Cocktail Book* by W. J. Tarling (1937)

FEATURED DRINK

Remember the Maine

2 ounces (60ml) bourbon
¹/4 ounce (7ml) cherry brandy
¹/4 ounce (7ml) sweet vermouth
¹/2 teaspoon (2.5ml) absinthe
2 dashes Angostura bitters

Stir with ice and strain into a
cocktail glass.
Garnish with a lemon twist.

Adapted from
The Gentleman's Companion
by Charles H. Baker (1939)

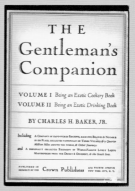

THE
Gentleman's
Companion

VOLUME I *Being an Exotic Cookery Book*
VOLUME II *Being an Exotic Drinking Book*

BY CHARLES H. BAKER, JR.

Including A COMPANY OF HAND-PICKED RECEIPTS, FROM FIVE BELOVED & NOTABLE
IN ITS PLACE, COLLECTED FAITHFULLY OF THESE VINTAGES & IN QUANTITY
Million Miles AROUND THE WORLD, & *Other Journeys*
and A PERSONALLY COLLECTED REGIMENT OF WORLD-FAMOUS LIVELY LIQUID
MASTERPIECES FROM THE ORIENT & OCCIDENT, & the South Seas.

PUBLISHED IN
HONESTY BY THE Crown Publishers 419 FOURTH AVENUE
NEW YORK CITY, N. Y.

Remsen Cooler

2 ounces (60ml) Scotch whisky
¹/2 ounce (15ml) simple syrup
Soda water

Build over ice in a highball glass and garnish with
two lemon twists and two orange twists.

Rendezvous

1 1/2 ounce (45ml) gin
1/2 ounce (15ml) kirsch
1/4 ounce (7ml) Campari

Stir with ice and strain into a cocktail glass.
Garnish with a lemon twist.

Resolute

1 ounce (30ml) gin
3/4 ounce (22ml) apricot brandy
3/4 ounce (22ml) lemon juice

Shake with ice and strain into a cocktail glass.

Reverie

(Created by Phil Dormont)

1 1/2 ounce (45ml) gin
3/4 ounce (22ml) apricot brandy
1/2 ounce (15ml) lemon juice
1/2 teaspoon (2.5ml) kirsch

Shake with ice and strain into a cocktail glass.

Adapted from *Bottoms Up* by Ted Saucier (1951)

Revolución

(Created by Adam Elmegirab, Evo-lution,
Aberdeen, Scotland, 2008)

2 ounces (60ml) light rum
1 ounce (30ml) lemon juice
2 teaspoons (10ml) orgeat
1 teaspoon (5ml) vanilla syrup
1 dash orange bitters

Shake with ice and strain into a coupe.

Richard's Famous Cocktail

(First Prize, Police Gazette Bartenders Contest, 1907,
Fred H. Kramer, Richard's Hotel, Portland, Oregon)

1 1/2 ounce (45ml) bourbon
1 1/2 ounce (45ml) white grape juice
1 dash orange bitters

Stir with ice in an Old Fashioned glass and garnish with a
cherry and an orange twist.

Adapted from *Hoffman House Bartender's Guide*
by C. S. Mahoney (1905)

Ritz of London

1 1/2 ounce (45ml) gin
3/4 ounce (22ml) dry vermouth
3/4 ounce (22ml) lemon juice
1 teaspoon (5ml) simple syrup
1 dash orange bitters

Shake with ice and strain into a cocktail glass.

Adapted from *Bottoms Up* by Ted Saucier (1951)

Ritz of Paris

1/2 ounce (15ml) cognac
1/4 ounce (7ml) Cointreau
1/2 ounce (15ml) orange juice
Champagne

Shake with ice (except champagne) and strain into a coupe. Top with champagne.

Adapted from *Bottoms Up* by Ted Saucier (1951)

Rob Roy

2 ounces (60ml) Scotch whisky
1 ounce (30ml) sweet
vermouth
1 dash Angostura bitters or orange bitters

Stir with ice and strain into a cocktail glass.
Garnish with a cherry.

Rock & Rye Cooler

1 1/2 ounce (45ml) vodka
1 ounce (30ml) rock & rye
1/2 ounce (15ml) lime juice
7-Up

Build over ice in a highball glass and garnish with a lime wedge.

Rob Roy

Rocky Mountain Cooler

2 ounces (60ml) applejack
1/2 ounce (15ml) lemon juice
1/2 ounce (15ml) egg white
1 teaspoon (5ml) simple syrup
Cider

Shake vigorously with ice (except cider) and strain into
an ice-filled highball glass. Top with cider and
dust with nutmeg.

Rolls Royce

11/2 ounce (45ml) gin
1/2 ounce (15ml) dry vermouth
1/2 ounce (15ml) sweet vermouth
2 dashes Bénédictine

Stir with ice and strain into a cocktail glass.

Rose

11/2 ounce (45ml) kirsch
3/4 ounce (22ml) dry vermouth
1/3 ounce (10ml) cherry brandy

Stir with ice and strain into a cocktail glass.
Garnish with a cherry.

Rose Marie

1¼ ounce (37ml) gin
½ ounce (15ml) dry vermouth
¼ ounce (7ml) Campari
¼ ounce (7ml) Armagnac
¼ ounce (7ml) cherry brandy

Shake with ice and strain into a cocktail glass.

Rose Petal Martini

(Created by Dick Bradsell, London)

¾ ounce (22ml) gin
¾ ounce (22ml) Lanique rose petal vodka liqueur
¾ ounce (22ml) lychee juice
2 dashes Peychaud's bitters

Stir with ice and strain into a cocktail glass.
Garnish with an edible flower.

Rossi

⅔ ounce (20ml) gin
⅔ ounce (20ml) Dubonnet rouge
⅔ ounce (20ml) sweet vermouth
⅔ ounce (20ml) orange curaçao

Stir with ice and strain into a cocktail glass.
Garnish with an orange twist.

Rossini

1¹/₂ ounce (45ml) strawberry purée
Champagne

Build in a flute and stir.

Royal Bermuda Yacht Club

**2 ounces (60ml)
Barbados rum
2 teaspoons (10ml)
falernum
1 teaspoon (5ml)
Cointreau
³/₄ ounce (22ml)
lime juice**

Shake with ice
and strain into a
cocktail glass.

A dash of orange
bitters can be a nice ad-
dition.

FEATURED DRINK

Royal Fizz

**1¹/₂ ounce (45ml) gin
1 ounce (30ml) lemon juice
³/₄ ounce (22ml) simple syrup
1 whole egg
Soda water**

Shake vigorously with ice (except soda water) and strain
into an ice-filled highball glass. Top with soda water.

Royal Jubilee

(Created by Harry Craddock)

1 1/2 ounce (45ml) calvados
3/4 ounce (22ml) Cointreau
3/4 ounce (22ml) lemon juice

Shake with ice and strain into a cocktail glass.

Adapted from *Café Royal Cocktail Book* by W. J. Tarling (1937)

Royal Romance

(Created by J. Perosino)

1 1/4 ounce (37ml) gin
1/2 ounce (15ml) Grand Marnier
1/2 ounce (15ml) passion fruit juice
1 dash grenadine

Shake with ice and strain into a cocktail glass.

Adapted from *An Anthology of Cocktails* by Booth's Gin (1930s)

Royal Smile

1 1/2 ounce (45ml) gin
3/4 ounce (22ml) Calvados
1/2 ounce (15ml) lemon juice
1/4 ounce (7ml) grenadine

Shake with ice and strain into a cocktail glass.

Royal Standard

1 1/4 ounce (37ml) gin
1 1/4 ounce (37ml) brandy
3/4 ounce (22ml) lemon juice
1 teaspoon (5ml) simple syrup

Shake and strain into a cocktail glass.

Adapted from *Cocktails and Mixed Drinks*
by Charles A. Tuck (1967)

Ruby

1 1/2 ounce (45ml) gin
3/4 ounce (22ml) applejack
1/2 teaspoon (2.5ml) grenadine

Shake with ice and strain into a cocktail glass.

Rude Cosmopolitan

1 1/2 ounce (45ml) tequila blanco
1/2 ounce (15ml) Cointreau
3/4 ounce (22ml) cranberry juice
1/3 ounce (10ml) lime juice
1 dash orange bitters (optional)

Shake with ice and strain into a cocktail glass.
Garnish with a flamed orange zest.

Rum Cow

1¹/₂ ounce (45ml) dark rum
1 teaspoon (5ml) simple syrup
1 dash Angostura bitters
Milk

Build over ice in a highball glass.

Rum Hound

(Created by Jim Schwenck)

1¹/₂ ounce (45ml) Jamaica
dark rum
1¹/₂ ounce (45ml) Cointreau
³/₄ ounce (22ml) lemon juice

Shake with ice and strain into
a cocktail glass.

Adapted from *The Home
Bartender's Guide & Song Book*
by Charlie Roe &
Jim Schwenck (1930)

Rum Runner

1¹/₄ ounce (37ml) golden rum
1¹/₄ ounce (37ml) light rum
2 ounces (60ml) pineapple juice
¹/₂ ounce (15ml) simple syrup
³/₄ ounce (22ml) lime juice
1 dash Angostura bitters

Shake with ice and strain into an ice-filled highball glass.
Garnish with a pineapple spear and a lime wedge.

Russian Bride

(Created by Miranda Dickson, "Vodka Princess")

1 1/2 ounce (45ml) vanilla vodka
3/4 ounce (22ml) coffee liqueur
1 teaspoon (5ml) white crème de cacao
1 ounce (30ml) milk
1 ounce (30ml) cream

Shake with ice and strain into an ice-filled
Old Fashioned glass. Dust with chocolate powder.

Russian Spring Punch

(Created by Dick Bradsell, London)

1 1/2 ounce (45ml) vodka
1/2 ounce (15ml) crème de cassis
3/4 ounce (22ml) lemon juice
2 teaspoons (10ml) simple syrup
Champagne

Build in a highball glass over ice, adding champagne last.
Garnish with a lemon slice and a raspberry.

FEATURED DRINK

Rusty Nail

1 1/2 ounce (45ml) Scotch whisky
3/4 ounce (22ml) Drambuie

Build over ice in an Old Fashioned glass and
stir before serving.

Rusty Nail

Rye & Ginger

2 ounces (60ml) rye
5 ounces (150ml) ginger ale

Build over ice in a highball glass.

Rye Witch

(Created by Jim Meehan, New York)

2 ounces (60ml) rye
1/2 ounce (15ml) Strega
1/2 ounce (15ml) Lustau Palo Cortado Península sherry
1 sugar cube
1 dash of Regan's orange bitters
1 dash of Fee Brothers orange bitters

Add the orange bitters and sugar cube to a mixing glass
and crush the cube into a paste with a muddler. Add the
remaining ingredients, ice and stir. Strain into a chilled rocks
glass. Twist an orange peel over the surface and discard.

S

Sakepolitan

1 1/2 ounce (45ml) sake
3/4 ounce (22ml) Cointreau
1/2 ounce (15ml) cranberry juice
1/2 ounce (15ml) lime juice

Shake with ice and strain into a cocktail glass.
Garnish with a flamed orange peel.

Salty Dog

1 1/2 ounce (45ml) vodka or gin
Grapefruit juice

Build over ice in an ice-filled highball glass
with a salt rim.

San Juan Sling

3/4 ounce (22ml) light rum
3/4 ounce (22ml) cherry liqueur
3/4 ounce (22ml) Bénédictine
1/2 ounce (15ml) lime juice
Soda water

Shake with ice (except soda water) and strain into
an ice-filled highball glass. Top with soda water.
Garnish with a lime wedge.

San Marco Cocktail

3/4 ounce (22ml) gin
3/4 ounce (22ml) dry vermouth
3/4 ounce (22ml) cherry brandy

Stir with ice and strain into a cocktail glass.
Garnish with a cherry.

Sangaree

2 ounces (60ml) liquor of choice
(rum, whisky, brandy)
1/2 ounce (15ml) port
1 teaspoon (5ml) simple syrup

Pour ingredients (except port) into an ice-filled
Old Fashioned glass. Float port on top. Dust with nutmeg.

Sangrita

1/2 ounce (15ml) tomato juice
1/2 ounce (15ml) orange juice
1 teaspoon (5ml) lime juice
1 teaspoon (5ml) grenadine
1 pinch salt
1 pinch pepper
6 drops Tabasco

Shake with ice and strain into a shot glass.
Serve with tequila.

Santa Barbara

1 1/2 ounce (45ml) bourbon
1/4 ounce (7ml) apricot brandy
3/4 ounce (22ml) grapefruit juice
1 teaspoon (5ml) simple syrup

Shake with ice and strain into a cocktail glass.

Santiago

1 1/2 ounce (45ml) light rum
3/4 ounce (22ml) lime juice
1 teaspoon (5ml) simple syrup
1 dash grenadine

Shake with ice and strain into a cocktail glass.

Santina's Pousse Cafe

1/3 ounce (10ml) cognac
1/3 ounce (10ml) maraschino liqueur
1/3 ounce (10ml) orange curaçao

Layer in order above in a shot glass.

Saratoga Cocktail

3/4 ounce (22ml) brandy
3/4 ounce (22ml) bourbon
3/4 ounce (22ml) sweet vermouth
2 dashes Angostura bitters

Stir with ice and strain into a cocktail glass.
Garnish with a lemon twist.

Adapted from *The Bar-Tender's Guide* by Jerry Thomas (1887)

Saratoga Fizz

1 1/2 ounce (45ml) bourbon
1/2 ounce (15ml) lemon juice
1/4 ounce (7ml) lime juice
3/4 ounce (22ml) simple syrup
1/2 ounce (15ml) egg white

Shake with ice and strain into an ice-filled highball glass.
Garnish with a lemon slice.

Satan's Whiskers

1/2 ounce (15ml) gin
1/2 ounce (15ml) dry vermouth
1/2 ounce (15ml) sweet vermouth
1/4 ounce (7ml) Grand Marnier
1/2 ounce (15ml) orange juice
2 dashes orange bitters

Shake with ice and strain into a cocktail glass.

Savoy

1³/₄ ounce (50ml) gin
¹/₂ ounce (15ml) dry vermouth
¹/₄ ounce (7ml) Dubonnet rouge

Stir with ice and strain into a cocktail glass.
Garnish with an orange twist.

Sazerac

2 ounces (60ml) rye or cognac
¹/₄ ounce (7ml) absinthe
1 teaspoon (5ml) simple syrup
2 dashes Peychaud's bitters

Fill an Old Fashioned glass with crushed ice and add
absinthe. In a separate mixing glass stir remaining
ingredients over ice. Empty the Old Fashioned glass,
leaving a coat of absinthe inside and strain the drink
into the glass. Garnish with a lemon twist.

FEATURED DRINK

Scandina

(Created by John W. H. Evans)

³/₄ ounce (22ml) Swedish Punsch
³/₄ ounce (22ml) Cointreau
³/₄ ounce (22ml) white crème de cacao

Shake with ice and strain into a cocktail glass.

Adapted from *Barflies & Cocktails* by Harry McElhone (1927)

Sazerac

Scarlett O'Hara

1½ ounce (45ml) Southern Comfort
1 ounce (30ml) cranberry juice
½ ounce (15ml) lime juice

Shake and strain into a cocktail glass.

Scoff-Law Cocktail

(Created by "Jock" of Harry's New York Bar, Paris)

2 ounces (60ml) rye
1 ounce (30ml) dry vermouth
1/2 ounce (15ml) lemon juice
1/4 ounce (7ml) grenadine
1 dash orange bitters

Shake with ice and strain into a cocktail glass.

"Jock" created this drink in 1924 immediately after
Webster's Dictionary added the word *scofflaw* (one who
willingly, knowingly and repeatedly ignores the law).
According to McElhone, the drink became exceedingly
popular among American prohibition dodgers in Paris.

Adapted from *Barflies & Cocktails* by Harry McElhone (1927)

Scorpion

1 ounce (30ml) golden rum
1 ounce (30ml) brandy
1 1/4 ounce (37ml) orange juice
2/3 ounce (20ml) lime juice
1/2 ounce (15ml) orgeat

Shake with ice and strain into an ice-filled
Old Fashioned glass.

Screaming Orgasm

$1/2$ ounce (15ml) vodka
$1/2$ ounce (15ml) amaretto
$1/2$ ounce (15ml) Baileys Irish Cream
$1/2$ ounce (15ml) coffee liqueur

Build over crushed ice in an Old Fashioned glass.

Screwdriver

$11/2$ ounce (45ml) vodka
Orange juice

Build over ice in a highball glass. Garnish with
an orange slice.

Seabreeze

$11/2$ ounce (45ml) vodka
Cranberry juice
Grapefruit juice

Build over ice in a highball glass, using cranberry and
grapefruit juice to taste. Garnish with a lime wedge.

Seelbach Cocktail

1 ounce (30ml) bourbon
1/2 ounce (15ml) triple sec
7 dashes Peychaud's bitters
7 dashes Angostura bitters
Champagne

Add bitters to a flute, coat inside and pour out most of bitters. Shake bourbon and triple sec over ice and strain into the flute. Top with champagne.

FEATURED DRINK

Seigniory Club Special

(Created by Larry Denis)

1 1/2 ounce (45ml) rye
1 ounce (30ml) grapefruit juice
1/2 teaspoon (2.5ml) dark rum
1 teaspoon (5ml) maple syrup
1/2 ounce (15ml) egg white

Shake vigorously with ice and strain into a cocktail glass.

Adapted from *Bottoms Up* by Ted Saucier (1951)

September Morn

1 1/2 ounce (45ml) light rum
3/4 ounce (22ml) lime juice
1/3 ounce (10ml) grenadine
1/2 ounce (15ml) egg white

Shake with ice and strain into a cocktail glass.

Adapted from *Recipes for Mixed Drinks* by Hugo R. Ensslin (1916)

Seventh Heaven

1¼ (37ml) ounce gin
1 ounce (30ml) Dubonnet rouge
¼ ounce (7ml) maraschino liqueur
1 dash Angostura bitters

Stir with ice and strain into a cocktail glass.
Garnish with an orange twist.

"75" Cocktail

1½ ounce (45ml) Calvados
1 ounce (30ml) gin
1 teaspoon (5ml) grenadine
2 dashes absinthe

Shake with ice and strain into a cocktail glass.

Adapted from *ABC of Mixing Cocktails* by Harry McElhone (1922)

Sex On The Beach No. 1

1 ounce (30ml) vodka
½ ounce (15ml) peach schnapps
Cranberry juice
Pineapple juice

Shake with ice and strain into an ice-filled highball glass.

Sex On The Beach No. 2

1 ounce (30ml) vodka
½ ounce (15ml) Midori
½ ounce (15ml) Chambord
Cranberry juice
Pineapple juice

Shake with ice and strain into an ice-filled highball glass.

S

Seelbach Cocktail

Shakerato

(Created by Jim Meehan, New York)

2 ounces (60ml) aged rum
1/2 ounce (15ml) Pedro Ximinez sherry
1/2 ounce (15ml) coffee liqueur
1 ounce (30ml) espresso

Shake with ice and strain into a wine glass.
Garnish with three coffee beans.

Shandy

Beer
7-Up

Add 7-Up to a highball glass and top with beer.

Shandy Gaff

Beer
Ginger Ale

Add ginger ale to a highball glass and top with beer.

Sherry Cobbler

See Cobbler

Sherry Cocktail

2 ounces (60ml) sherry
1/2 ounce (15ml) dry vermouth
2 dashes orange bitters

Stir with ice and strain into a cocktail glass.
Garnish with a lemon twist.

Sherry Flip

See Flip

Sherry Lady

(Created by Frank Korhumel)

1 ounce (30ml) gin
1 ounce (30ml) dry sherry
1/2 ounce (15ml) Cointreau
1/2 ounce (15ml) lemon juice

Shake with ice and strain into a cocktail glass. Garnish
with a lemon twist.

Adapted from *The Book of Approved Cocktails*
by the United Kingdom Bartenders' Guild (1934)

Shirley Temple

Ginger ale
1 teaspoon (5ml) grenadine

Build over ice in a highball glass. Garnish with
an orange slice.

Sicilian Sour

(Created by Tony Conigliaro, London,
http://drinkfactory.blogspot.com)

1 1/2 ounce (45ml) amaretto
1/4 ounce (7ml) apricot liqueur
1 ounce (30ml) lemon juice
1/2 ounce (15ml) egg white
1/4 ounce (7ml) simple syrup
Dash Angostura bitters

Shake vigorously with ice (except bitters) and strain into
a sour glass. Garnish with a dash of Angostura
and a lemon wheel.

FEATURED DRINK

Sidecar

1 1/2 ounce (45ml) cognac
1 ounce (30ml) triple sec
1/2 ounce (15ml) lemon juice

Shake with ice and strain into a
sugar-rimmed (optional) cocktail glass.

Cointreau instead of triple sec makes this drink even better.

Adapted from *Cocktails: How To Mix Them*
by Robert Vermeire (1922)

Sidecar

Silk Stockings

FEATURED DRINK

1 ounce (30ml) tequila blanco
3/4 ounce (22ml) white crème de cacao
3/4 ounce (22ml) milk
3/4 ounce (22ml) cream
1/4 ounce (7ml) raspberry liqueur

Shake vigorously and strain into a cocktail glass.

Silver Bullet

1 1/2 ounce (45ml) gin
3/4 ounce (22ml) kümmel
3/4 ounce (22ml) lemon juice

Shake with ice and strain into a cocktail glass.

Silver Cocktail

1 1/4 ounce (37ml) gin
1 1/4 ounce (37ml) dry vermouth
1/4 ounce (7ml) maraschino liqueur
1 dash simple syrup
2 dashes orange bitters

Stir with ice and strain into a cocktail glass.
Garnish with a lemon twist.

FEATURED DRINK

Silver Fizz

1 1/2 ounce (45ml) gin
1 ounce (30ml) lemon juice
3/4 ounce (22ml) simple syrup
1/2 ounce (15ml) egg white
Soda water

Shake vigorously with ice (except soda water) and strain
into an ice-filled highball glass. Top with soda water
and garnish with a lemon slice.

Silver Flower Sour

*(Created by Keith Waldbauer, Seattle, 2008,
http://movingatthespeedoflife.blogspot.com)*

1¹/₂ ounce (45ml) rye
¹/₂ ounce (15ml) lemon juice
¹/₂ ounce (15ml) egg white
1 dash elderflower syrup
1 dash orange bitters

Shake vigorously with ice and strain into a cocktail glass.

FEATURED DRINK

Singapore Sling

1¹/₂ ounce (45ml) gin
¹/₂ ounce (15ml) Cherry
Heering
¹/₂ ounce (15ml) triple sec
¹/₄ ounce (7ml) Bénédictine
2 ounces (60ml) pineapple juice
³/₄ ounce (22ml) lime juice
1 dash Angostura bitters
Soda water

Shake with ice (except soda
water) and strain into an
ice-filled highball glass.
Top with soda water and
garnish with a lime wedge
and a cherry.

FEATURED DRINK

Six O'Clock Cocktail

1/2 ounce (15ml) gin
1/2 ounce (15ml) cherry brandy
1/2 ounce (15ml) Campari
1/2 ounce (15ml) Dubonnet rouge
1/2 ounce (15ml) dry vermouth
1/2 ounce (15ml) sweet vermouth

Shake with ice and strain into a cocktail glass.

Adapted from *The Cocktail Hour* by Louis P. De Gouy (1951)

Sleepy Time Gal

1 1/2 ounce (45ml) gin
3/4 ounce (22ml) grape juice
3/4 ounce (22ml) orange juice
3/4 ounce (22ml) lime juice
1 teaspoon (5ml) grenadine

Shake with ice and strain into an ice-filled
Old Fashioned glass.

Adapted from *How To Mix Drinks* by Bill Edwards (1936)

Slippery Nipple

1/2 ounce (15ml) white sambuca
1/2 ounce (15ml) Baileys Irish Cream

Layer in order above in a shot glass.

Sloe Comfortable Screw

3/4 ounce (22ml) vodka
3/4 ounce (22ml) sloe gin
3/4 ounce (22ml) Southern Comfort
4 ounces (120ml) orange juice

Shake with ice and strain into an ice-filled highball glass.
Garnish with an orange slice.

Sloe Gin Fizz

2 ounces (60ml) sloe gin
1 ounce (30ml) lemon juice
1/2 ounce (15ml) simple syrup
Soda water

Shake with ice (except soda water) and strain into an
ice-filled highball glass. Top with soda water and
garnish with lemon slice.

FEATURED DRINK

Sloe Sour

(Created by Tomek Roehr, Alkoteka, Poland)

2 ounces (60ml) Polish vodka
1/2 ounce (15ml) lemon juice
2 teaspoons (10ml) sloe berry juice
1 teaspoon (5ml) simple syrup
1/2 ounce (15ml) egg white
2 dashes The Bitter Truth aromatic bitters

Shake vigorously with ice and strain into a coupe.
Garnish with a lemon twist.

S

Smart Alec

1 ounce (30ml) cognac
3/4 ounce (22ml) Cointreau
3/4 ounce (22ml) yellow Chartreuse
2 dashes orange bitters

Stir with ice and strain into a cocktail glass.

Smiling Ivy

(Created by S. Cox)

3/4 ounce (22ml) Jamaican dark rum
3/4 ounce (22ml) crème de peche
3/4 ounce (22ml) pineapple juice
1 teaspoon (5ml) lemon juice
1 teaspoon (5ml) egg white

Shake vigorously with ice and strain into a cocktail glass.

Adapted from *United Kingdom Bartenders' Guild Guide To Drinks* (1953)

Smiling Through

(Created by A. Gordon)

3/4 ounce (22ml) Jamaican dark rum
3/4 ounce (22ml) Grand Marnier
3/4 ounce (22ml) maraschino liqueur
1 teaspoon (5ml) lemon juice
1 teaspoon (5ml) grenadine

Shake with ice and strain into a cocktail glass.

Adapted from *United Kingdom Bartenders' Guild Guide To Drinks* (1953)

Smokey Martini

2¹/2 ounces (75ml) gin
¹/2 ounce (15ml) Talisker whisky

Stir with ice and strain into a cocktail glass.

Smuggler

*(Created by Tony Conigliaro, London,
http://drinkfactory.blogspot.com)*

2 ounces (60ml) cider brandy
¹/4 ounce (7ml) Bénédictine
1 ounce (30ml) lemon juice
¹/2 ounce (15ml) simple syrup
Apple juice

Build over ice in a highball glass and stir before
serving. Garnish with a lemon slice.

Snapshot

1¹/2 ounce (45ml) gin
¹/2 ounce (15ml) Cointreau
¹/2 ounce (15ml) orange juice
1 dash Angostura bitters

Shake with ice and strain into a cocktail glass.

Adapted from *My 35 Years Behind Bars* by Johnny Brooks (1954)

Snowball

1½ ounce (45ml) Advocaat
½ ounce (15ml) Rose's lime juice (optional)
7-Up

Build over ice in a highball glass.

Songbird

(Created by Calum Lawrie, Edinburgh)

¾ ounce (22ml) gin
1¼ ounce (37ml) pomegranate liqueur
1¼ ounce (37ml) lychee juice
1 teaspoon (5ml) lemon
1 teaspoon (5ml) simple syrup

Shake with ice and strain into a cocktail glass.

Sonza's (Wilson)

Sonny Rollins Collins

(Created by Gregor De Gruyther, London)

3/4 ounce (22ml) sloe gin
3/4 ounce (22ml) Plymouth Gin
3/4 ounce (22ml) lemon juice
2 teaspoons (10ml) simple syrup
Rosé champagne

Build over ice in a highball glass adding champagne last.
Stir before serving, and garnish with a blackberry.

Sonza's (Wilson)

1 1/4 ounce (37ml) gin
1 ounce (30ml) cherry brandy
1/4 ounce (7ml) lemon juice
1/4 ounce (7ml) grenadine

Shake with ice and strain into a cocktail glass.

South Side

1 1/2 ounce (45ml) gin
1 ounce (30ml) lemon juice
1/2 ounce (15ml) simple syrup
6 mint leaves

Shake with ice and strain into a cocktail glass.
Garnish with a mint leaf.

South Side Fizz

1½ ounce (45ml) gin
1 ounce (30ml) lemon juice
½ ounce (15ml) simple syrup
6 mint leaves
Soda water

Shake with ice (except soda water) and strain into an
ice-filled highball glass. Top with soda water and
garnish with a lemon slice and a mint sprig.

Southern Cross

1 ounce (30ml) gold rum
1 ounce (30ml) brandy
¼ ounce (7ml) orange curaçao
¾ ounce (22ml) lime juice
½ ounce (15ml) simple syrup
Soda water

Shake with ice (except soda water) and strain into an
ice-filled highball glass. Top with soda water and stir.

Spanish Delight

2 ounces (60ml) sweet vermouth
4 dashes Angostura bitters

Extract the zest of four lemon twists, squeezing the oil
into a cocktail glass and discarding the twists. Shake the
vermouth and bitters and strain into the cocktail glass.
Garnish with a fresh lemon twist.

Adapted from *Cocktails: How To Mix Them*
by Robert Vermeire (1922)

Spanish Margarita

(Created by Toby Maloney, The Violet Hour, Chicago, 2007)

2 ounces (60ml) tequila blanco
1/2 ounce (15ml) Licor 43
1/2 ounce (7ml) orange cucacao
3/4 ounce (22ml) lime juice
1/4 ounce (7ml) simple syrup
5 drops Tabasco green pepper sauce

Shake with ice (except Tabasco) and strain into an ice-filled Old Fashioned glass. Garnish with a lime wheel and add five drops of Tabasco.

Speedway

2 ounces (60ml) Jamaica dark rum
1/2 ounce (15ml) maraschino liqueur
2 teaspoons (10ml) lime juice
1 dash orange curaçao
1 dash Angostura bitters

Shake with ice and strain into a cocktail glass.

Adapted from *My 35 Years Behind Bars* by Johnny Brooks (1954)

Speyside Martini

(Created by Calum Lawrie, Edinburgh)

1 1/2 ounce (45ml) Scotch whisky
1/2 ounce (10ml) apricot brandy
1/3 ounce (10ml) grapefruit juice
1 teaspoon (5ml) simple syrup
10 mixed grapes

Muddle grapes with syrup in the bottom of a shaker. Add remaining ingredients. Shake with ice and strain into a cocktail glass. Garnish with a mint sprig.

Splificator

**2¹/₂ ounces (75ml) bourbon
Soda water**

Pour bourbon over ice in an Old Fashioned glass and
add soda water to taste.

Adapted from *The Mixicologist* by C.F. Lawlor (1895)

Spritzer

**4 ounces (120ml) white wine
Soda water**

Build over ice in a wine glass.
Garnish with a lemon twist (optional).

Squashed Frog

**¹/₃ ounce (10ml) grenadine
¹/₃ ounce (10ml) Midori
¹/₃ ounce (10ml) advocaat**

Layer in the order above in a shot glass.

St. Germain

**2 ounces (60ml) green Chartreuse
¹/₂ ounce (15ml) lemon juice
¹/₃ ounce (10ml) grapefruit juice
¹/₂ ounce (15ml) egg white**

Shake vigorously and strain into a cocktail glass.

St. Moritz

2 ounces (60ml) rye
1/2 ounce (15ml) dry vermouth
1/4 ounce (7ml) green Chartreuse
1 dash orange bitters

Stir with ice and strain into a cocktail glass.

Star Cocktail

1 1/4 ounce (37ml) applejack
1 1/4 ounce (37ml) sweet vermouth
3 dashes Peychaud's bitters
1 dash simple syrup

Stir with ice and strain into a cocktail glass. Garnish with a lemon twist.

Adapted from *Modern American Drinks* by George Kappeler (1895)

Stella Maris Cocktail

(Created by Stephan Berg, The Bitter Truth, Germany)

1 ounce (30ml) rye
1 ounce (30ml) cognac
1 1/4 ounce (37ml) LBV port
2 dashes dark crème de cacao
3 dashes The Bitter Truth orange bitters

Shake with ice and strain into a cocktail glass. Garnish with a flamed orange zest.

Stifferino

(Created by W. C. Weaver and dedicated to Dr. Voronoff)

3/4 ounce (22ml) Fernet Branca
3/4 ounce (22ml) dry vermouth
3/4 ounce (22ml) sweet vermouth
1 teaspoon (5ml) brandy

Shake with ice and strain into a cocktail glass.

Adapted from *Barflies & Cocktails* by Harry McElhone (1927)

Stinger

2 1/2 ounces (75ml) brandy
1/4 ounce (7ml) white crème de menthe

Shake with ice and strain into an Old Fashioned glass
filled with crushed ice.

Stolipolitain

1 1/4 ounce (37ml) Stolichnaya Razberi
1/2 ounce (15ml) crème de framboise
1/2 ounce (15ml) Cointreau
3/4 ounce (22ml) cranberry juice
1 dash orange bitters
1/2 teaspoon (2.5ml) lime juice

Shake with ice and strain into a cocktail glass.
Garnish with a lemon twist.

Stone Fence

2 ounces (60ml) brandy
(or scotch, applejack, rum, rye or bourbon)
Cider

Build over ice in a highball glass.

Stork Club

1¹⁄₂ ounce (45ml) gin
¹⁄₂ ounce (15ml) Cointreau
1 ounce (30ml) orange juice
¹⁄₄ ounce (7ml) lime juice
1 dash Angostura bitters

Shake with ice and strain into
a cocktail glass. Garnish with
an orange twist.

The Stork Club Bar Book

Lucius Beebe

Strait's Sling

1¹⁄₂ ounce (45ml) gin
¹⁄₂ ounce (15ml) cherry brandy
¹⁄₂ ounce (15ml) Bénédictine
1 ounce (30ml) lemon juice
2 dashes orange bitters
2 dashes Angostura bitters
Soda water

Shake with ice (except soda water) and strain into an ice-
filled highball glass. Top with soda water. Garnish with
a cherry and a lemon slice.

Strawberry Balsamic 'Tini

13/4 ounce (50ml) vodka
3/4 ounce (22ml) crème de fraise
1/4 ounce (7ml) balsamic vinegar
4 strawberries

Muddle strawberries in the base of a shaker. Add
remaining ingredients and shake with ice. Strain into a
cocktail glass and garnish with a half strawberry on rim.

Strawberry Fizz

11/2 ounce (45ml) gin
1 ounce (30ml) lemon juice
3/4 ounce (22ml) cream
1/2 ounce (15ml) crème de fraise
4 strawberries
Soda water

Muddle strawberries in the base of a shaker. Add remaining
ingredients (except soda water) and shake with ice. Strain
into an ice-filled highball glass. Top with soda water and
garnish with a half strawberry on rim.

Strawberry Frozen Daiquiri

2 ounces (60ml) light rum
1/4 ounce (7ml) crème de fraise
1 ounce (30ml) lime juice
4 strawberries

Blend with crushed ice and pour into a coupe. Garnish
with a half strawberry on rim.

Strawberry Frozen Margarita

2 ounces (60ml) tequila blanco
1/2 ounce (15ml) triple sec
1/4 ounce (7ml) crème de fraise
1 ounce (30ml) lime juice
4 strawberries

Blend with crushed ice and pour into a coupe. Garnish with a half strawberry on rim.

Suffering Bastard/Suffering Bar Steward

(Created at The Shepheard Hotel, Cairo)

1 ounce (30ml) gin
1 ounce (30ml) bourbon
1/2 ounce (15ml) lime juice
1 dash Angostura bitters
Ginger ale

Shake with ice (except ginger ale) and strain into an ice-filled highball glass. Top with ginger ale and garnish with a mint sprig, an orange slice and a cucumber peel.

Adapted from *Bottom's Up* by Ted Saucier (1951)

Sumatra Kula

1 1/2 ounce (45ml) light rum
1/2 ounce (15ml) lime juice
1/2 ounce (15ml) orange juice
1/2 ounce (15ml) grapefruit juice
1 1/2 teaspoons (7.5ml) honey

Blend ingredients with crushed ice and pour into a hurricane glass. Top with more crushed ice and garnish with a mint sprig.

Summer Presse

(Created by Johan Svensson, Drinksfusion, London)

1 ounce (30ml) gin
1/2 ounce (15ml) calvados liqueur
3/4 ounce (22ml) lime juice
3/4 ounce (22ml) elderflower syrup
3 raspberries
3 gooseberries
4 mint leaves
3 dashes absinthe
Soda

Muddle berries and mint in base of a shaker. Add remaining
ingredients (except soda) and shake. Strain into an
ice-filled highball glass, top with soda and garnish
with berries and a mint sprig.

Sunset at Gowanus

(Created by Alexander Day, New York)

2 ounces (60ml) golden rum
3/4 ounce (22ml) lime juice
1/4 ounce (7ml) applejack
1/4 ounce (7ml) yellow Chartreuse
1/2 ounce (15ml) maple syrup

Shake with ice and strain into a cocktail glass.

Sweet & Vicious

(Created by Alexander Day, New York)

2 ounces (60ml) rye
1/2 ounce (15ml) dry vermouth
1/2 ounce (15ml) Amaro Nonino
1 teaspoon (5ml) maple syrup
2 slices Fuji apple

Lightly muddle apple in the base of a mixing glass.
Add remaining ingredients, ice and stir. Strain into a
cocktail glass. Garnish with a thin slice of Fuji apple.

Sweet Grilled Lemon Margarita

(Created by Tony Conigliaro, London,
http://drinkfactory.blogspot.com)

1 1/2 ounce (45ml) tequila blanco
1 ounce (30ml) triple sec
3/4 ounce (22ml) grilled lemon juice (cut lemons in
half, grill until caramelized, then juice)
1 dash orange bitters

Shake with ice and strain into a sugar-rimmed
cocktail glass.

Swizzle

3 ounces (90ml) gold rum
3/4 ounce (22ml) lime juice
1/2 ounce (15ml) falernum
1 dash Angostura bitters

Build over crushed ice in a highball glass and
swizzle with a barspoon.

Syncopation Cocktail

(Created by Harry Cahill)

1 ounce (30ml) brandy
1 ounce (30ml) Calvados
1/2 ounce (15ml) triple sec
1/2 ounce (15ml) lemon juice
1 dash Angostura bitters

Shake with ice and strain into a cocktail glass.

Adapted from *Barflies & Cocktails* by Harry McElhone (1927)

T

T.N.T.

1 1/2 ounce (45ml) gin
3/4 ounce (22ml) absinthe
3/4 ounce (22ml) dry vermouth
2 dashes orange bitters

Stir with ice and strain into a cocktail glass.

Tahitian Honey Bee

1 1/2 ounce (45ml) light rum
3/4 ounce (22ml) lemon juice
2 teaspoons (10ml) honey

Shake with ice and strain into a cocktail glass.

Tailspin

1 ounce (30ml) gin
3/4 ounce (22ml) sweet vermouth
3/4 ounce (22ml) green Chartreuse
1 dash orange bitters

Shake with ice and strain into a cocktail glass.
Garnish with a lemon twist.

While there are a number of different recipes for this drink, this is the one we recommend.

Talent Scout

(Created by Arthur Godfrey, radio and early television star)

2 ounces (60ml) bourbon
1/2 teaspoon (2.5ml) Grand Marnier
1 dash Angostura bitters

Shake with ice and strain into an ice-filled
Old Fashioned glass.

Adapted from *Bottoms Up* by Ted Saucier (1951)

Tango

1 ounce (30ml) gin
1/2 ounce (15ml) sweet vermouth
1/2 ounce (15ml) dry vermouth
1/4 ounce (7ml) orange curaçao
1/2 ounce (15ml) orange juice

Shake over ice and strain into a cocktail glass.

Tarintini

3/4 ounce (22ml) citrus vodka
3/4 ounce (22ml) Aperol
3/4 ounce (22ml) pink grapefruit juice
2 teaspoons (10ml) crème de peche
4 raspberries

Shake over ice and strain into a cocktail glass.
Garnish with an orange twist.

Tatanka

1¹/2 ounce (45ml) Żubrówka vodka
Apple juice

Build over ice in a highball glass. Garnish with a lemon slice.

The grassy notes of this vodka shine in this cocktail.

Telephone Fizz

1¹/2 ounce (45ml) brandy
³/4 ounce (22ml) maraschino liqueur
1 whole egg
1 teaspoon (5ml) simple syrup
Soda water

Shake vigorously with ice (except soda water) and strain into a goblet glass. Top with soda water.

Adapted from *Hoffman House Bartender's Guide*
by C. S. Mahoney (1905)

Tenacity Flux

(Created by George Sinclair, London, 2008)

1¹/2 ounce (45ml) cachaça
1¹/2 ounce (45ml) pineapple juice
¹/2 ounce (15ml) raspberry purée
¹/2 ounce (15ml) lime juice
2 teaspoons (10ml) passion fruit syrup
¹/2 passion fruit

Squeeze passion fruit into shaker, add remaining ingredients and shake with ice. Strain into an ice-filled highball glass and garnish with a mint sprig.

Tennessee Iced Tea

1 ounce (30ml) Jack Daniels
1/2 ounce (15ml) light rum
1/2 ounce (15ml) vodka
1/2 ounce (15ml) triple sec
3/4 ounce (22ml) lemon juice
1 teaspoon (5ml) simple syrup
Cola

Shake with ice (except cola) and strain into an
ice-filled highball glass. Top with cola and garnish with
a lemon slice.

Tequila Dream (or Jarabe Tapatio)

1 1/2 ounce (45ml) tequila
3/4 ounce (22ml) lime juice
1/3 ounce (10ml) grenadine
1/2 ounce (15ml) egg white

Shake and strain into a cocktail glass.
Garnish with a maraschino cherry.

Adapted from *The Food & Drink of Mexico*
by George C. Booth (1964)

Tequila Slammer

1 ounce (30ml) tequila blanco
1 ounce (30ml) 7-Up, ginger ale or champagne

Pour into an Old Fashioned glass. Cover the top of
the glass with your palm, slam the glass onto a hard
surface, quickly drink.

Tequila Sunrise

1 1/2 ounce (45ml) tequila
blanco
1/2 ounce (15ml) grenadine
Orange juice

Build over ice, add the grenadine
last to create the "sunrise" effect.

Tequini

2 ounces (60ml) tequila blanco
1/4 ounce (7ml) dry vermouth

Stir with ice and strain into a cocktail glass. Garnish with a
lemon twist.

Tex Collins

1 1/2 ounce (45ml) gin
1 1/2 ounce (45ml) grapefruit juice
1/2 ounce (15ml) honey
Soda water

Shake with ice (except soda water) and strain into an
ice-filled highball glass. Top with soda water and garnish
with a grapefruit slice.

Texas Iced Tea

1 ounce (30ml) tequila
1/2 ounce (15ml) light rum
1/2 ounce (15ml) gin
1/2 ounce (15ml) vodka
1/2 ounce (15ml) triple sec
1 ounce (30ml) lemon juice
1 teaspoon (5ml) simple syrup
Cola

Shake with ice (except cola) and strain into an ice-filled highball glass. Top with cola and garnish with
a lemon slice.

Third Degree

1 1/2 ounce (45ml) gin
3/4 ounce (22ml) dry vermouth
1 teaspoon (5ml) anisette

Stir over ice and strain into a cocktail glass.

Third Rail Cocktail

3/4 ounce (22ml) light rum
3/4 ounce (22ml) applejack
3/4 ounce (22ml) brandy
2 dashes absinthe

Stir over ice and strain into a cocktail glass.

Adapted from *The Savoy Cocktail Book*
by Harry Craddock (1930)

Thistle Cocktail

1½ ounce (45ml) Scotch whisky
1 ounce (30ml) sweet vermouth
1 dash Angostura bitters

Stir over ice and strain into a cocktail glass.

Adapted from *The Savoy Cocktail Book* by Harry Craddock (1930)

Thornbush

(Created by Jim Meehan, New York)

2½ ounces (75ml) Irish whiskey
1 ounce (30ml) sweet vermouth
¼ ounce (7ml) Caol Ila whisky
2 dashes Angostura bitters
Absinthe rinse

Rinse a coupe with absinthe. Stir remaining
ingredients with ice and strain into the rinsed coupe.
Garnish with a lemon twist.

Ti Punch

2 ounces (60ml) rhum agricole
½ teaspoon (2.5ml) simple syrup
Lime

Pour simple syrup into an Old Fashioned glass.
Cut a slice from the side of a lime, squeeze over syrup
and drop in glass. Add rhum, ice and stir.

FEATURED DRINK

Tiger Lillet

(Created by J. Jones for the 1952 World Cocktail Championship)

1 ounce (30ml) Lillet Blanc
1 ounce (30ml) Van der Hum
1/2 ounce (15ml) dry vermouth
1/2 ounce (15ml) maraschino liqueur

Shake with ice and strain into a cocktail glass.
Garnish with an orange twist.

Adapted from *United Kingdom Bartenders' Guild
Guide To Drinks* (1953)

Tiger Lily

(Created by Robert Bushnell)

1 ounce (30ml) dark rum
1/2 ounce (15ml) orange curaçao
1/2 ounce (15ml) brandy
1/2 ounce (15ml) lemon juice
1/2 ounce (7ml) orange juice

Shake with ice and strain into an ice-filled
Old Fashioned glass. Garnish with a lemon twist.

Adapted from *Bottoms Up* by Ted Saucier (1951)

Tiger Special

(Created at Princeton Club, New York)

2 ounces (60ml) light rum
1/2 ounce (15ml) Cointreau
1/2 ounce (15ml) lime juice

Shake with ice and strain into a cocktail glass.

Adapted from *Bottoms Up* by Ted Saucier (1951)

Tiger's Milk

2 ounces (60ml) applejack
1 teaspoon (5ml) simple syrup
1/2 ounce (15ml) egg white
1 drop each of vanilla, clove, orange and
cinnamon extract
Sweet cider
Milk

Beat egg white with sugar and extracts. Add applejack,
shake with ice and strain into a highball glass. Add milk
and cider in equal quantities. Dust with grated nutmeg.

Tipperary

1 ounce (30ml) Irish whiskey
3/4 ounce (22ml) green Chartreuse
3/4 ounce (22ml) sweet vermouth

Stir with ice and strain into a cocktail glass.

Tokyo Iced Tea

1/2 ounce (15ml) light rum
1/2 ounce (15ml) gin
1/2 ounce (15ml) vodka
1/2 ounce (15ml) tequila
1/2 ounce (15ml) triple sec
1/2 ounce (15ml) Midori
1 ounce (30ml) lime juice
7-Up

Shake with ice (except 7-Up) and strain into an ice-filled
highball glass. Top with 7-Up and garnish
with a lemon slice.

Tom & Jerry

FEATURED DRINK

1½ ounce (45ml) añejo rum
½ ounce (15ml) brandy
1 egg yolk
1 egg white
Small pinch allspice
Small pinch ground cloves
Small pinch ground cinnamon
Small pinch nutmeg

Beat egg yolk and sugar together, then add rum and brandy. Separately, beat egg white with spices (except nutmeg) until stiff. Slowly fold egg white mixture into yolk mixture. Pour into a mug and top with hot water. Sprinkle nutmeg on top.

Adapted from *How To Mix Drinks* by Jerry Thomas (1862)

Tom Collins

FEATURED DRINK

1½ ounce (45ml) gin
1 ounce (30ml) lemon juice
¾ ounce (22ml) simple syrup
Soda water

Shake over ice (except soda water) in a highball glass. Top with soda water and garnish with a lemon slice.

Adapted from *The Bar-Tender's Guide* by Jerry Thomas (1876)

Tomate

2 ounces (60ml) pastis
1/4 ounce (7ml) grenadine
Water

Build over ice in a highball glass and stir.

Tommy's Margarita

(Created by Julio Bermejo, San Francisco)

1½ ounce (45ml) tequila blanco or reposado
3/4 ounce (22ml) lime juice
2 teaspoons (10ml) agave syrup

Shake with ice and strain into either a cocktail glass or an ice-filled Old Fashioned glass.

It's worth seeking out agave syrup to make this perfectly balanced margarita. Why use a pre-made mix when this drink is so easy to make?

Too Too

1 ounce (30ml) brandy
1 ounce (30ml) dark rum
1 teaspoon (5ml) simple syrup
1 teaspoon (5ml) raspberry syrup
1 whole egg

Shake vigorously with ice and strain into an ice-filled Old Fashioned glass.

Adapted from *American & Other Iced Drinks*
by Charlie Paul (1902)

Top Cat

(Created by Gregor De Gruyther, London)

1¼ ounce (37ml) Talisker whisky
¾ ounce (22ml) sweet vermouth
¾ ounce (22ml) lime juice
⅓ ounce (10ml) simple syrup
2 sprigs mint
Ginger ale

Lightly press mint with simple syrup in the bottom of a
highball glass. Add other ingredients and stir with ice,
finishing with ginger ale.

FEATURED DRINK

Toreador

1½ ounce (45ml) tequila blanco
¾ ounce (22ml) apricot brandy
¾ ounce (22ml) lime juice

Shake with ice and strain into a cocktail glass.

Adapted from *Café Royal Cocktail Book* by W. J. Tarling (1937)

Tornado Cocktail

1 ounce (30ml) gin
1 ounce (30ml) apricot brandy
1 ounce (30ml) Southern Comfort
¼ ounce (7ml) orange juice

Shake with ice (except Southern Comfort) and strain into
an Old Fashioned glass filled with crushed ice.
Float the Southern Comfort on top.

Adapted from *Cocktail and Wine Digest* by Oscar Haimo (1943)

Transvaal

1 1/4 ounce (37ml) gin
1 1/4 ounce (37ml) Dubonnet rouge
2 dashes orange bitters

Stir with ice and strain into a cocktail glass.

Tre

(Created by Asa Nevestveit, Sweden)

1 1/2 ounce (45ml) light rum
1/4 ounce (7ml) Chambord
3/4 ounce (22ml) apple juice
1/4 ounce (7ml) simple syrup

Stir over ice and strain into a cocktail glass.
Garnish with a lemon twist.

FEATURED DRINK

Treacle

(Created by Dick Bradsell, London)

1 1/2 ounce (45ml) dark rum
1/2 ounce (15ml) apple juice
1 teaspoon (5ml) simple syrup
2 dashes Angostura bitters

Stir syrup and bitters with small amount of rum in the
bottom of an Old Fashioned glass. Add one ice cube, more
rum and keep stirring. Gradually add more ice and rum
while stirring, and crown with apple juice.
Garnish with a lemon twist.

FEATURED DRINK

Trident

(Created by Robert Hess, 2002)

1 ounce (30ml) dry sherry
1 ounce (30ml) Cynar
1 ounce (30ml) aquavit
2 dashes peach bitters

Stir with ice and strain into a
cocktail glass.
Garnish with a lemon twist.

Adapted from *The Essential
Bartender's Guide*
by Robert Hess (2008)

Trilby Cocktail

1³/₄ ounce (50ml) Scotch whisky
³/₄ ounce (22ml) sweet vermouth
2 dashes orange bitters

Stir with ice and strain into a cocktail glass.

Trini Daddy

2 ounces (60ml) gin
2 ounces (60ml) grapefruit juice
1 teaspoon (5ml) honey

Shake with ice and strain into an ice-filled
Old Fashioned glass. Garnish with a cherry.

Adapted from *Trinidad and Other Cocktails*
from the Queen's Park Hotel, Trinidad (1932)

Trinity

1 ounce (30ml) gin
3/4 ounce (22ml) dry vermouth
3/4 ounce (22ml) sweet vermouth

Stir with ice and strain into a cocktail glass.

Tropical Cocktail

3/4 ounce (22ml) dry vermouth
3/4 ounce (22ml) maraschino liqueur
3/4 ounce (22ml) white crème de cacao
1 dash Angostura bitters

Stir with ice and strain into a cocktail glass.

Turf Cocktail

1 1/4 ounce (37ml) Plymouth gin
1 1/4 ounce (37ml) dry vermouth
2 dashes orange bitters
2 dashes maraschino liqueur
2 dashes absinthe

Stir with ice and strain into a cocktail glass. Garnish with a lemon twist.

This is one of the early dry martini type of cocktails that marry gin and dry vermouth.

Adapted from *Bartender's Manual* by Harry Johnson (1900)

FEATURED DRINK

Turrita de Palmero

(Created by Federico Cuco of 788 Foodbar, Buenos Aires; Palermo is actually one of the wealthiest districts in Buenos Aires and the girls down there are famous for being as swank as pretty. When Federico created this drink, it was very common to see these girls wearing micro skirts and sucking lollipops as the "official look" of the fanciful girl. Turrita—diminutive for the more aggressive Turra!—is the local slang for those beautiful/nasty girls.)

2 ounces (60ml) cranberry vodka
1/2 ounce (15ml) lemon juice
1/2 ounce (15ml) simple syrup
1/4 ounce (7ml) Starka vodka

Shake with ice (except Starka) and strain into a cocktail glass. Garnish with a strawberry lollipop and float Starka.

Tuscan Mule

1 1/2 ounce (45ml) Tuaca
1/2 ounce (15ml) lime juice
Ginger beer

Build over ice in a highball glass. Garnish with a lime wedge.

Tuxedo

1 1/2 ounce (45ml) gin
1 1/2 ounce (45ml) dry vermouth
2 dashes orange bitters
1 dash absinthe
1 dash maraschino liqueur

Stir with ice, strain into a cocktail glass and garnish with a cherry and a lemon twist.

Twelve Five Cocktail

(Created by Jamie Boudreau, Seattle,
www.SpiritsandCocktails.com)

1½ ounce (45ml) scotch
¾ ounce (22ml) Punt e Mes vermouth
¼ ounce (7ml) absinthe
¼ ounce (7ml) Bénédictine

Stir with ice and strain into a cocktail glass.
Garnish with a lemon twist.

Twentieth Century Cocktail

(Created by C. A. Tuck)

1½ ounce (45ml) gin
½ ounce (15ml) Lillet Blanc
½ ounce (15ml) white crème de cacao
½ ounce (15ml) lemon juice

Shake and strain into
a cocktail glass.

What might seem like an
odd combination of lemon
and cocoa actually results
in a delicious cocktail.

Adapted from
Café Royal Cocktail Book
by W. J. Tarling (1937)

T

21st Century

(Created by Jim Meehan, New York)

1 1/2 ounce (45ml) tequila blanco
3/4 ounce (22ml) white crème de cacao
3/4 ounce (22ml) lemon juice
Pernod rinse

Rinse a coupe with Pernod. Shake remaining
ingredients with ice and strain into the rinsed coupe.

Twinkle

(Created by Tony Conigliaro, London,
http://drinkfactory.blogspot.com)

1 ounce (30ml) vodka
2 teaspoons (10ml) elderflower syrup
Champagne

Shake vodka and elderflower syrup with ice and double
strain into a flute. Top with champagne and
garnish with a lemon twist.

U–V

Ulysses

¾ ounce (22ml) brandy
¾ ounce (22ml) dry vermouth
¾ ounce (22ml) cherry brandy

Stir over ice and strain into a cocktail glass.
Garnish with an orange twist.

Uncle Vanya

(Adapted from a popular drink served at TGI Friday's)

1¼ ounce (37ml) vodka
½ ounce (15ml) crème de mûre
1 ounce (30ml) lemon juice
½ ounce (15ml) simple syrup

Shake with ice and strain into an ice-filled
Old Fashioned glass. Garnish with a lemon slice.

Union League Club Special

1½ ounce (45ml) bourbon
½ ounce (15ml) Jamaican dark rum
½ ounce (15ml) orange curaçao
½ ounce (15ml) lemon juice
½ ounce (15ml) orange juice
½ teaspoon (2.5ml) simple syrup

Shake well and strain into an ice-filled Old Fashioned glass.

Unisphere

1¹⁄₂ ounce (45ml) gold rum
¹⁄₄ ounce (7ml) Bénédictine
¹⁄₄ ounce (7ml) anisette
¹⁄₂ ounce (15ml) lime juice
¹⁄₄ ounce (7ml) grenadine

Shake with ice and strain into a cocktail glass.

Up to Date

1¹⁄₄ ounce (37ml) bourbon
1 ounce (30ml) sherry
¹⁄₄ ounce (7ml) Grand Marnier
2 dashes Angostura bitters

Stir with ice and strain into a cocktail glass.

Upstarter

1¹⁄₂ ounce (45ml) Galliano
1 ounce (30ml) vodka
¹⁄₄ ounce (7ml) peach brandy

Shake with ice and strain into a cocktail glass.

Vanderbilt

1¹/₂ ounce (45ml) brandy
³/₄ ounce (22ml) cherry brandy
2 dashes Angostura bitters

Stir with ice and strain into a cocktail glass.

Velvet Glove

1¹/₂ ounce (45ml) Lillet Blanc
³/₄ ounce (22ml) brandy
³/₄ ounce (22ml) dark crème de cacao

Stir with ice and strain into a cocktail glass.

Vendome

1 ounce (30ml) Dubonnet rouge
1 ounce (30ml) gin
¹/₂ ounce (15ml) dry vermouth

Stir with ice and strain into a cocktail glass.

Vermouth Cassis

2 ounces (60ml) dry vermouth
¹/₂ ounce (15ml) crème de cassis
Soda water (optional)

Build over ice in an Old Fashioned glass. Add soda water (optional). Stir before serving. Garnish with a lemon twist.

Vesper Martini

(As ordered by James Bond in Casino Royale
by Ian Fleming, 1953)

2 ounces (60ml) gin
2/3 ounce (20ml) vodka
1/3 ounce (10ml) Lillet Blanc

Shake with ice and strain into a cocktail glass. Garnish
with a lemon twist.

Vieux Carre

1 ounce (30ml) rye
1 ounce (30ml) cognac
1 ounce (30ml) sweet vermouth
1 teaspoon (5ml) Bénédictine
2 dashes Peychaud's bitters
2 dashes Angostura bitters

Stir ingredients with ice in an Old Fashioned glass.

Adapted from *Famous New Orleans Drinks and How To Mix 'Em*
by Stanley Clisby Arthur (1937)

Vieux Mot

(Created by Don Lee, PDT, New York, 2007)

11/2 ounce (45ml) Plymouth Gin
1/2 ounce (15ml) St-Germain elderflower liqueur
3/4 ounce (22ml) lemon juice
1/2 ounce (15ml) simple syrup

Shake with ice and strain into a cocktail glass.

Violet Fizz

1 1/2 ounce (45ml) gin
1/2 ounce (15ml) crème
de violette
1 ounce (30ml) lemon juice
1/4 ounce (7ml) simple syrup
Soda water

Shake with ice (except soda water)
and strain into an ice-filled highball
glass. Top with soda water and
garnish with a lemon slice.

Virgin Mary

6 ounces (180ml) tomato juice
1 teaspoon (5ml) lemon juice
1/2 teaspoon (2.5ml) Worcestershire sauce
3 dashes Tabasco
1/2 teaspoon (2.5ml) horseradish (optional)

Softly shake with ice and strain into an ice-filled
highball glass. Add salt and black pepper to taste.
Garnish with a lemon slice and a celery stick.

Vodka & Tonic

2 ounces (60ml) vodka
Tonic water

Build over ice in a highball glass. Squeeze in juice from a
lime wedge. Garnish with lime wedge.

Vodka Espresso

(Created by Dick Bradsell, London)

1 ounce (30ml) vodka
1/2 ounce (15ml) coffee liqueur
1 ounce (30ml) espresso
1/4 ounce (7ml) simple syrup

Shake vigorously with ice and strain into a cocktail glass.
Garnish with three coffee beans.

Vodka Gimlet

2 ounces (60ml) vodka
3/4 ounce (22ml) Rose's lime juice

Shake with ice and strain into a cocktail glass.

Vodkatini

2 1/2 ounces (75ml) vodka
1/4 ounce (7ml) dry vermouth

Stir (or shake if you have to) with ice and strain into a
cocktail glass. Garnish with a lemon twist or an olive.

Volstead

(Created at Harry's New York Bar, Paris)

3/4 ounce (22ml) rye
3/4 ounce (22ml) Swedish Punsch
1/2 ounce (15ml) orange juice
1/2 ounce (15ml) raspberry syrup or grenadine
1/4 ounce (7ml) anisette

Shake with ice and strain into a cocktail glass.

Voodoo Doll

(Created by Daniel Estremadoyro, Argentina)

1 1/2 ounce (45ml) tequila blanco
1/2 ounce (15ml) limoncello
2 ounces (60ml) pineapple juice
1/2 ounce (15ml) egg white
3 drops Branca Menta
1 dash simple syrup

Shake vigorously with ice and strain into an ice-filled
Old Fashioned glass. Garnish with a mint sprig.

FEATURED DRINK

Vowel Cocktail

(Created by Bill Henly)

1 ounce (30ml) Scotch whisky
1 ounce (30ml) sweet vermouth
1/2 ounce (15ml) kümmel
1/2 ounce (15ml) orange juice
1 dash Angostura bitters

Shake with ice and strain into a cocktail glass.

Adapted from *Barflies & Cocktails* by Harry McElhone (1927)

Voyager

(Created by Robert Hess, 2006)

2 ounces (60ml) rum
1/2 ounce (15ml) lime juice
1/2 ounce (15ml) Bénédictine
1/2 ounce (15ml) falernum
2 dashes Angostura bitters

Shake with ice and strain into an ice-filled
Old Fashioned glass. Garnish with a lime wedge.

Adapted from *The Essential Bartender's Guide*
by Robert Hess (2008)

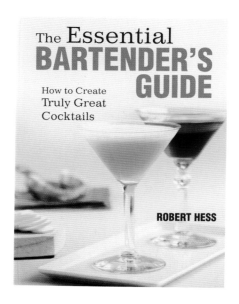

W

Wagner Cocktail

3/4 ounce (22ml) sloe gin
3/4 ounce (22ml) sweet vermouth
3/4 ounce (22ml) cherry brandy
1 dash orange bitters

Shake with ice and strain into a cocktail glass.

Waldorf

1 1/2 ounce (45ml) Swedish Punsch
1/2 ounce (15ml) gin
1/2 ounce (15ml) lemon juice

Shake with ice and strain into a cocktail glass.

Waldorf Fizz

1 1/2 ounce (45ml) gin
1/2 ounce (15ml) orange juice
1/2 ounce (15ml) lemon juice
1 whole egg
1 teaspoon (5ml) simple syrup
Soda water

Shake vigorously with ice (except soda water) and strain
into an ice-filled highball glass. Top with soda water
and garnish with a lemon slice.

Ward Eight

2 ounces (60ml) rye
³/4 ounce (22ml) lemon juice
³/4 ounce (22ml) orange juice
1 teaspoon (5ml) grenadine

Shake with ice and strain into
a cocktail glass.

This drink originated in Boston at
the Locke-Ober restaurant.

Adapted from
Cocktails: How To Mix Them
by Robert Vermeire (1922)

Watermelon & Basil Martini

2 ounces (60ml) gin
¹/2 ounce (15ml) simple syrup
4 chunks of watermelon
6 basil leaves

Muddle melon in the base of a shaker. Add remaining
ingredients, shake and strain into a cocktail glass.
Garnish with a watermelon wedge on rim.

Watermelon Cassis

2 ounces (60ml) gin
1/2 ounce (15ml) crème de cassis
1/2 ounce (15ml) lemon juice
Soda water
4 watermelon chunks

Muddle melon in the base of shaker. Add the remaining ingredients (except soda water), shake and strain into an ice-filled highball glass. Top with soda water and garnish with a watermelon wedge.

Watermelon Martini

2 ounces (60ml) vodka
1/2 ounce (15ml) simple syrup
4 chunks of watermelon

Muddle melon in the base of shaker. Add remaining ingredients, shake and strain into a cocktail glass. Garnish with a watermelon wedge on rim.

Wells Cocktail

2 ounces (60ml) cognac
1/4 ounce (7ml) white
crème de menthe
1/4 ounce (7ml) crème de cassis
1/4 ounce (7ml) Fernet Branca

Shake with ice and strain into a cocktail glass.

Adapted from *Louis' Mixed Drinks* by Louis Muckensturm (1906)

West Indies

2 ounces (60ml) Jamaican dark rum
1/2 ounce (15ml) lime juice
1 teaspoon (5ml) simple syrup
1 dash maraschino liqueur
2 wedges of pineapple

Blend ingredients with crushed ice and pour into a coupe.

Adapted from *The Bartender's Book* by Jack Townsend & Tom
Moore McBride (1951)

West Indies Yellow Bird

1 1/2 ounce (45ml) light rum
1 ounce (30ml) Galliano
1/4 ounce (7ml) crème de bananes
2 ounces (60ml) pineapple juice
2 ounces (60ml) orange juice

Shake with ice and strain into a highball glass.
Garnish with an orange slice and a cherry.

Wink, The

*(Created by Tony Conigliaro, London,
http://drinkfactory.blogspot.com)*

2 ounces (60ml) gin
1/4 ounce (7ml) triple sec
1/4 ounce (7ml) absinthe
1 teaspoon (5ml) simple syrup
2 dashes Peychaud's bitters

Fill an Old Fashioned glass with crushed ice and add
absinthe. Shake remaining ingredients with ice.
Empty the Old Fashioned glass, leaving a coat of absinthe
inside and strain drink into glass. Garnish with a wink.

Whiskey Cooler

1 1/2 ounce (45ml) whiskey
1 ounce (30ml) lemon juice
1/2 ounce (15ml) simple syrup
Ginger ale

Build over ice in a highball glass. Garnish with a lemon slice.

Whiskey Flip

See Flip

Whiskey Rickey

1 1/2 ounce (45ml) whiskey
3/4 ounce (22ml) lime juice
Soda water

Build over ice in a highball glass.
Garnish with a lime wedge.

Whiskey Sangaree

See Sangaree

Whiskey Scaffa

1 ounce (30ml) whiskey
1 ounce (30ml) maraschino liqueur
1 dash Angostura bitters

Stir with ice and strain into a cocktail glass.

Whiskey Skin

2 ounces (60ml) whiskey
1 teaspoon (5ml) simple syrup
Hot water

Build in a toddy glass. Stir and garnish with a lemon twist.

Whiskey Smash

1½ ounce (45ml) whiskey
1 teaspoon (5ml) simple syrup
6 mint leaves

Gently muddle mint leaves with syrup at the bottom of an
Old Fashioned glass. Add whiskey and fill with crushed ice.
Stir before serving. Garnish with a mint sprig.

FEATURED DRINK

Whiskey Sour

1½ ounce (45ml) whiskey
3/4 ounce (22ml)
lemon juice
½ ounce (15ml) simple syrup
½ ounce (15ml)
egg white

Shake and strain into an ice-filled Old Fashioned glass.
Garnish with a lemon slice or an orange slice.

The addition of the egg white adds a great frothy
head to this drink.

Whiskey Sour

Whisky Mac

1¹/₂ ounce (45ml) Scotch whisky
1 ounce (30ml) ginger wine

Build over ice in an Old Fashioned glass.

FEATURED DRINK

White Lady No. 1

1¹/₂ ounce (45ml) gin
1 ounce (30ml)
Cointreau
1 ounce (30ml) lemon juice

Shake well and strain into a cocktail glass.

Adapted from *The Savoy Cocktail Book*
by Harry Craddock (1930)

White Lady No. 2

1 1/2 ounce (45ml) Cointreau
1/3 ounce (10ml) white crème de menthe
1/3 ounce (10ml) brandy

Shake well and strain into a cocktail glass.

Adapted from *ABC of Mixing Cocktails*
by Harry McElhone (1922)

White Lion

2 ounces (60ml) gold rum
1 ounce (30ml) lime juice
1/2 ounce (15ml) raspberry syrup
1/4 ounce (7ml) orange curaçao

Build over crushed ice in an Old Fashioned glass. Garnish
with two raspberries and a mint sprig.

Adapted from *Bartender's Manual* by Harry Johnson (1882)

White Russian

1 ounce (30ml) vodka
1 ounce (30ml) coffee liqueur
1 ounce (30ml) cream

Shake with ice and strain into an ice-filled
Old Fashioned glass.

Whiz Bang

1½ ounce (45ml) whiskey
¾ ounce (22ml) dry vermouth
2 dashes absinthe
2 dashes orange bitters
2 dashes grenadine

Stir with ice and strain into a cocktail glass.
Garnish with a lemon twist.

Adapted from *Cocktails: How To Mix Them*
by Robert Vermeire (1922)

Wibble

(Created by Dick Bradsell, London)

¾ ounce (22ml) gin
¾ ounce (22ml) sloe gin
¾ ounce (22ml) grapefruit juice
⅓ ounce (10ml) crème de mûre
⅓ ounce (10ml) lemon juice
1 teaspoon (5ml) simple syrup

Shake with ice and strain into
a cocktail glass. Garnish with
a lemon twist.

Crème de Mûre (blackberry
liqueur) can be difficult to
find in the U.S., but it's worth
the effort. Dick Bradsell uses
it in a few amazing cocktails.

Widow's Kiss

3/4 ounce (22ml) parfait amour
3/4 ounce (22ml) yellow Chartreuse
3/4 ounce (22ml) Bénédictine
1/2 ounce (15ml) egg white

Shake vigorously with ice and strain into a cocktail glass.
Garnish with a strawberry slice on top of the drink.

Wildflower

(Created by George Sinclair, London, 2008)

1 1/4 ounce (37ml) rye
1/2 ounce (15ml) crème d'abricot
2 teaspoons (10ml) Demerara simple syrup
6 raspberries

Shake with ice and double strain into a cocktail glass.
Garnish with a lemon twist.

Winchell

1 ounce (30ml) cognac
1 ounce (30ml) gin
1/4 ounce (7ml) lemon juice
1/4 ounce (7ml) Cointreau

Shake with ice and strain into a small cocktail glass.

Windy City

(Created by Nate Cross)

1 1/2 ounce (45ml) gin
3/4 ounce (22ml) triple sec
1/4 ounce (7ml) lemon juice
1/4 ounce (7ml) orange juice

Shake with ice and strain into a cocktail glass.

Adapted from *Bottoms Up* by Ted Saucier (1951)

Winter Old Fashioned

2 ounces (60ml) Scotch whisky
1/2 ounce (15ml) apple juice
1 teaspoon (5ml) honey
2 dashes Angostura bitters

Dissolve honey with a small amount of scotch in the
bottom of an Old Fashioned glass. Add one ice cube, more
scotch and keep stirring. Gradually add more ice and
scotch while stirring and crown with apple juice.
Garnish with a lemon twist and an apple wedge.

Wise Old Sage

(Created by Tad Carducci, Tippling Bros.)

1¹/2 ounce (45ml) rhum agricole
¹/2 ounce (15ml) Clement Creole Shrubb
2¹/2 ounces (75ml) grapefruit juice
¹/2 ounce (15ml) agave syrup
6 sage leaves
2 dashes Regan's orange bitters

Muddle sage and agave syrup in a shaker. Add remaining ingredients (except bitters) and shake with ice. Strain into a cocktail glass and add bitters. Garnish with finely diced pineapple which has been macerated overnight with chopped sage leaves.

Witch Doctor

(Created by Jamie Boudreau, Seattle,
www.SpiritsandCocktails.com)

3 ounces (90ml) Sauvignon Blanc
1¹/2 ounce (45ml) light rum
1¹/2 ounce (45ml) pineapple juice
¹/2 ounce (15ml) lime juice
3/4 ounce (22ml) simple syrup
4 sage leaves

Shake with ice and double strain into an ice-filled highball glass. Garnish with a sage leaf skewered into a pineapple wedge.

Wonder Bar

³/4 ounce (22ml) gin
³/4 ounce (22ml) Cointreau
³/4 ounce (22ml) pineapple juice

Shake with ice and strain into a small cocktail glass.

Woo Woo

2 ounces (60ml) vodka
¹/2 ounce (15ml) peach schnapps
Cranberry juice

Build over ice in a highball glass.
Garnish with a lime wedge.

X.Y.Z. Cocktail

1½ ounce (45ml) light rum
¾ ounce (22ml) Cointreau
¾ ounce (22ml) lemon juice

Shake with ice and strain into a cocktail glass.

Yale Cocktail

2 ounces (60ml) gin
3 dashes Peychaud's bitters
1 dash Angostura bitters
Soda water

Shake with ice (except soda water) and strain into a
flute. Top with soda water. Garnish with a lemon twist.

Adapted from *Modern American Drinks*
by George Kappeler (1895)

Yellow Bird

1½ ounce (45ml) light rum
½ ounce (15ml) Galliano
½ ounce (15ml) triple sec
1 ounce (30ml) lemon juice

Shake with ice and strain into a cocktail glass.

FEATURED DRINK

Yellow Carvel

(Created by Blair "Trader Tiki" Reynolds, Portland, 2008,
http://www.tradertiki.com)

1½ ounce (45ml) Drambuie
½ ounce (45ml) grapefruit juice
1 ounce (30ml) simple syrup
2 dashes Angostura bitters
Pinch salt
Soda

Shake with ice (except soda) and strain into an ice-filled
highball glass. Top with soda and garnish with
a grapefruit twist.

Yellow Parrot

1 ounce (30ml) yellow Chartreuse
1 ounce (30ml) anisette
1 ounce (30ml) apricot brandy

Stir with ice and strain into a cocktail glass.

Yokohama

1 ounce (30ml) gin
½ ounce (15ml) vodka
½ ounce (15ml) grenadine
1 ounce (30ml) orange juice
1 dash absinthe

Shake with ice and strain into a cocktail glass.

Adapted from *ABC of Mixing Cocktails* by Harry McElhone (1922)

York Cocktail

1 1/2 ounce (45ml) bourbon
1 1/2 ounce (45ml) sweet vermouth
3 dashes orange bitters

Stir with ice and strain into a cocktail glass.
Garnish with a lemon twist.

Adapted from *Modern American Drinks*
by George Kappeler (1895)

Zaza

1 3/4 ounce (50ml) gin
3/4 ounce (22ml) Dubonnet rouge
1 dash Angostura bitters (optional)

Stir over ice and strain into a cocktail glass.

FEATURED DRINK

Zazarac

3/4 ounce (22ml) rye
1/2 ounce (15ml) anisette
1/2 ounce (15ml) light rum
1/2 ounce (15ml) pastis
1/2 teaspoon (2.5ml) simple syrup
1 dash orange bitters
1 dash Angostura bitters

Shake with ice and strain into a cocktail glass.
Garnish with a lemon twist.

Adapted from *Bartender's Guide* by Trader Vic (1947)

Zim-Zala-Bim

(Created by Jamie Boudreau, Seattle, 2008,
www.SpiritsandCocktails.com)

2 ounces (60ml) reposado tequila
2 teaspoons (10ml) elderflower liqueur
2 teaspoons (10ml) Regan's orange bitters
1 teaspoon (5ml) extra fine sugar

Dissolve sugar in ingredients in a mixing glass. Stir with ice
and strain into a cocktail glass.

Zipper

2 ounces (60ml) brandy
2/3 ounce (20ml) Grand Marnier
2/3 ounce (20ml) dry vermouth

Stir with ice and strain into a cocktail glass.

Adapted from *My 35 Years Behind Bars* by Johnny Brooks (1954)

Zombie

(Donn Beach formula)

²/₃ ounce (20ml) Jamaican dark rum
²/₃ ounce (20ml) añejo rum
²/₃ ounce (20ml) gold rum
²/₃ ounce (20ml) overproof rum
²/₃ ounce (20ml) light rum
¹/₂ ounce (15ml) maraschino liqueur
¹/₂ ounce (15ml) falernum
¹/₂ ounce (15ml) simple syrup
³/₄ ounce (22ml) lime juice
³/₄ ounce (22ml) grapefruit juice
3 dashes grenadine
1 dash absinthe
2 dashes Angostura bitters

Shake with ice and strain into an ice-filled highball glass. Garnish with an orange slice, cherry, mint sprig and a pineapple spear.

Zoom

1¹/₂ ounce (45ml) spirit (brandy, rum, gin or whiskey)
¹/₂ ounce (15ml) cream
1 teaspoon (5ml) honey

Shake vigorously with ice and strain into an ice-filled Old Fashioned glass.

The **BIG** Bartender's Book

Photography Credits

istockphoto:
David Cannings-Bushnell (page 2); Joe Biafore (page 6); Michael Bryc (page 16); David Palmer (pages 18, 19); Ashley Kirk (page 20); Christian Lazzari (page 23); Viola R. Joyner (page 30); In Communicado (page 34); Floor Klaassen (pages 93, 272); Ivan Mateev (page 113); Mark Hayes (page 172); Lepas 2004 (page 201); Phillip Pellat (page 205); Felinda (page 219); Suzifoo (page 252); David Smith (page 277); Joske038 (page 288 [bottom]), John Clines (page 289); Shorrocks (page 291); Mistikas (page 298 [bottom]); Pannonia (page 334); Apomares (page 344); Entienou (page 396); Elnur (page 416); Abbie Images (page 436)

Rick Stutz (pages 3, 108, 127, 161, 197, 217, 224, 226, 233, 236, 275, 300, 304, 315, 327, 330, 348, 373, 379, 441)

Greg Boehm (pages 12, 41, 44, 50, 51 [bottom], 57, 65, 78, 90, 105, 110, 115, 151, 153, 165, 168, 182, 187, 208, 241, 260, 263, 288 [top], 307, 337, 342, 354, 357, 362, 384, 389, 401, 407, 413, 419, 424, 432)

J. Longo (pages 24, 71, 87, 143, 144, 157, 166, 173, 192, 212, 241, 245, 249, 269, 273, 298, 306, 314, 318, 350, 360, 391, 422, 425, 430)

F. William Lagaret (pages 29, 36, 220, 234, 294)

Alan Carr (pages 51 [top], 70)

Amy K. Sims (pages 68, 82, 102, 123, 131, 135, 141, 147, 175, 255, 280, 310, 322, 326, 331, 368, 377, 410, 429)

Bibliography

Abeal, Jose and Valentin Garcia. *Sloppy Joe's Cocktails Manual: Season 1934* (pamphlet). Havana, Cuba: Diaz y Paredes, 1934.

Amis, Kingsley. *On Drink*. London: Jonathan Cape, Ltd., 1972.

An Anthology Of Cocktails. London: Booth's Distilleries, Ltd., 1934.

Arthur, Stanley Clisby. *Famous New Orleans Drinks*. New Orleans: Roger's Printing Company, 1937.

Bacchus & Cordon Bleu (school: Paris, France). *New Guide For The Hotel, Bar, Restaurant, Butler and Chef: being a handbook for the management of Hotel and American bars, and the manufacture of the principal new and fashionable drinks; hotel and restaurant cookery, as now practiced, with the newest entrees and dishes.* London: W. Nicholson & Sons, 1885.

Baker, Charles H. *Gentleman's Companion*. New York: Derrydale Press, 1939.

Baker, Charles H. *South American Gentleman's Companion*. New York: Crown Publishers, 1951.

Bauwens, Emile. *Livre De Cocktails*. Brussels, Belgium: Un Coup de Des, 1949.

Bergengren, Erik. *Benjamins Cocktailsbok*. Stockholm: Albert Bonniers Förlag, 1931.

Bergeron, Victor Jules. *Trader Vic's Bartender's Guide*. Garden City, NY: Doubleday & Co., 1947.

Bergeron, Victor Jules. *Trader Vic's Book Of Food & Drink*. Garden City, NY: Doubleday & Co., 1946.

Berry, Jeff. *Sippin' Safari*. San Jose, CA: SLG Publishing, 2007.

Birmingham, Frederick A. *Esquire Drink Book*. New York: Harper & Brothers, 1969.

Booth, George C. *The Food & Drink Of Mexico*. Los Angeles: Ward Ritchie Press, 1964.

Boothby, William. *Cocktail Boothby's American Bar-Tender*. Sacramento, CA: H. S. Crocker Co., 1891.

Boothby, William. *World's Drinks & How To Mix Them*. San Francisco: Boothby's World Drinks Co., 1908, 1930, 1934.

Brooks, Johnny. *My 35 Years Behind Bars*. New York: Exposition Press, 1954.

Byron, O. H. *Modern Bartender's Guide*. New York: Excelsior, 1884.

Byron, O. H. *Modern Bartender's Guide, 2nd edition*. New York: Excelsior, 1891.

Castellon, Fernando. *Larousse Cocktails*. London: Octopus Publishing, 2005.

Clarke, Eddie. *King Cocktail: Shake Again With Eddie*. London: Eddie's Club, 1957.

Clarke, Eddie. *Shaking In The 60's*. London: Cocktail Books, Ltd., 1963.

Cotton, Leo. *Old Mr. Boston Official Bartender's Guide*. Boston: Ben Burk, 1935.

Craddock, Harry. *Savoy Cocktail Book*. London: Constable & Co, Ltd., 1930.

Crockett, Albert Stevens. *Old Waldorf Bar Book*. New York: Dodd, Mead & Co., 1934.

Crockett, Albert Stevens. *Old Waldorf Bar Days*. New York: Aventine Press, 1931.

De Fleury, R. *1700 Cocktails For The Man Behind The Bar*. London: Heinemann, 1934.

De Gouy, Louis P. *Cocktail Hour*. New York: Greenburg Publishers, 1951.

Degroff, Dale. *Craft Of The Cocktail*. New York: Clarkson Potter, 2002.

Duffy, Patrick Gavin. *Official Mixer's Manual*. New York: Long & Smith, 1934.

Edwards, Bill. *How To Mix Drinks*. Philadelphia: David McKay Co., 1936.

Embury, David A. *The Fine Art Of Mixing Drinks*. Garden City, NY: Doubleday & Co., 1948.

Engel, Leo. *American & Other Drinks*. London: Tinsley Brothers, 1878.

Ensslin, R. Hugo. *Recipes for Mixed Drinks*. New York: privately printed, 1916.

Fouquet, Louis. *Bariana*. Paris: Duvoye, 1902.

Gaige, Crosby. *Cocktail Guide & Ladies' Companion*. New York: M. Barrows & Co., 1941.

Gaige, Crosby. *Standard Cocktail Guide*. New York: M. Barrows & Co., Inc., 1944.

Gale, Hyman and Gerald F. Marco. *How And When*. Chicago: privately printed, 1937.

Gibson, Joseph W. *Scientific Bar-Keeping*. New York: E.N. Cook & Co., 1884.

Grohusko, Jack. *Jack's Manual*. New York: privately printed,

1910.

Haigh, Ted. *Vintage Cocktails & Spirits*. Gloucester, MA: Rockport Publishers, 2004.

Haimo, Oscar. *Cocktail & Wine Digest*. New York: privately printed, 1943.

Haney, Jesse. *Haney's Steward & Barkeeper's Manual*. New York: Haney & Co., 1869.

Hess, Robert. *Essential Bartender's Guide*. New York: Mud Puddle Books, 2008.

Hotel Lincoln Cock-tail Book. Havana: Hotel Lincoln, 1937.

How To Properly Mix Drinks. Los Angeles: Federal Printing Co., 1934.

Johnson, B. A. and S. P. Johnson. *Wild West Bartenders' Bible*. Austin, TX: Texas Monthly Press, 1986.

Johnson, Harry. *Bartender's Manual*. New York: privately printed, 1882, 1888, 1900.

Jones, Stan. *Jones' Complete Barguide*. Los Angeles: Barguide Enterprises, 1977.

Kappa. *Bartender's Guide to the Best Mixed Drinks*. Tokyo: Kasuga Boeki K.K., 1952.

Kappeler, George J. *Modern American Drinks*. Ohio: Saalfield Publishing, 1895.

Lawlor, C. F. *The Mixicologist*. Ohio: Burrows Brothers, 1895.

Mahoney, Charles S. *Hoffman House Bartender's Guide*. New York: Richard K. Fox, 1905.

McElhone, Harry. *ABC Of Mixing Cocktails*. London: Odhams Press, 1922.

McElhone, Harry. *Barflies & Cocktails*. Paris: Lecram Press, 1927.

Meier, Frank. *Artistry Of Mixing Drinks*. Paris: Fryam Press, 1936.

Montague, Harry. *Up-to-Date Bartenders' Guide*. Baltimore: I & M Ottenheimer, 1914.

Muckensturm, Louis. *Louis' Mixed Drinks*. Boston: H.M. Caldwell Co., 1906.

Newman, Frank P. *American Bar*. Paris: Société Française D'Imprimerie et de Librairie, 1904.

Paul, Charlie. *Recipes Of American & Other Iced Drinks*. London: Farrow & Jackson, 1902.

Pequena Historia Del Bar Boadas Graficas Vila. Barcelona: Boadas Bar, 1993.

Phillips, A. Lyman. *Bachelor's Cupboard*. Boston: John W. Luce &

Co., 1906.

Proskauer, Julian J. *What'll You Have?* New York: A.L. Burt, 1933.

Regan, Gary. *Joy of Mixology*. New York: Clarkson Potter, 2003.

Ribalaigua, Constantino. *Bar La Florida Cocktails*. Havana: Obispo y Monserrate, 1935.

R I P. *Cocktails de Paris*. Paris: Editions Demangel, 1929.

Roe, Charlie and Jim Schwenck. *Home Bartender's Guide & Song Book*. New York: Experimenter Publications, 1930.

Saucier, Ted. *Bottoms Up*. New York: Greystone Press, 1951.

Schmidt, William. *The Flowing Bowl: What and When to Drink*. New York: Charles L. Webster & Co, 1891.

Schraemli, Harry. *Amateur Mixen*. Basel: Verlag für WIT AG, 1956.

Stafford, John Boyle. *One Hundred Ways*. New York: privately printed, 1932.

Steele, G. F. *My New Cocktail Book*. New York: G.F. Steele, 1934.

Straub, Jacques. *Drinks*. Chicago: The Hotel Monthly Press, 1914.

Tarling, W. J. *Café Royal Cocktail Book*. London: Pall Mall, Ltd., 1937.

Thomas, Jerry. *Bar-Tender's Guide*. New York: Dick & Fitzgerald, 1876, 1887.

Thomas, Jerry. *How To Mix Drinks*. New York: Dick & Fitzgerald, 1862.

Townsend, Jack and Tom Moore McBride. *The Bartender's Book*. New York: Viking Press, 1951.

Toye, Nina and A. H. Adair. *Drinks - Long & Short*. London: William Heinemann, Ltd., 1925.

Trinidad & Other Cocktails. Port of Spain, Trinidad: Queen's Park Hotel, 1932.

Tuck, Charles A. *Cocktails & Mixed Drinks*. London: Kaye & Ward, Ltd., 1967.

United Kingdom Bartenders' Guild. *The U.K.B.G. Guide To Drinks*. London: United Kingdom Bartenders' Guild, 1953.

United Kingdom Bartenders' Guild. *UKBG Book Of Approved Cocktails*. London: United Kingdom Bartenders' Guild, 1934.

Vermeire, Robert. *Cocktails: How To Mix Them*. London: Herbert Jenkins, Ltd., 1922.

Wondrich, David. *Esquire Drinks*. New York: Hearst Books, 2002.

Wondrich, David. *Imbibe*. New York: Penguin Group, 2007.

General Index

Index of Recipes by Main Alcoholic Ingredients